The Observer
and the Observed

The Observer and the Observed

*Valuable Personhood
and a Theory of Everything*

(Is there an anything out there
that corresponds to what's in here?)

CHRIS STEED

RESOURCE *Publications* · Eugene, Oregon

THE OBSERVER AND THE OBSERVED
Valuable Personhood and a Theory of Everything

Copyright © 2024 Chris Steed. All rights reserved. Except for brief quotations in critical publications or reviews, no part of this book may be reproduced in any manner without prior written permission from the publisher. Write: Permissions, Wipf and Stock Publishers, 199 W. 8th Ave., Suite 3, Eugene, OR 97401.

Resource Publications
An Imprint of Wipf and Stock Publishers
199 W. 8th Ave., Suite 3
Eugene, OR 97401

www.wipfandstock.com

PAPERBACK ISBN: 978-1-6667-3662-5
HARDCOVER ISBN: 978-1-6667-9522-6
EBOOK ISBN: 978-1-6667-9523-3

VERSION NUMBER 110124

To Lynda

"It is as impossible to conceive that pure incogitative Matter should produce a thinking intelligent Being as that nothing should of itself produce Matter" —John Locke, Essay Concerning Human Understanding[1]

"If you can look into the seeds of time and say which grain will grow and which will not, speak then to me" (Shakespeare Macbeth)[2]

Contents

Preface | ix
   Endnotes | xxv

Chapter One
Albert and the lion | 1

Chapter Two
The Conscious Observer and A Participant Cosmos | 11

Chapter Three
Being Seen: The Inter-Personal Gaze | 29

Chapter Four
Valuable Personhood and The Innermost Gaze | 43

Chapter Five
The 'I' in The Eye: Identity snd Personhood | 57

Part Two: Ways of Seeing

Chapter Six
All by Itself: The Limits to Scientific Naturalism | 79

Chapter Seven
Field Theory and A Conscious Cosmos | 91

Chapter Eight
The Topography of Reality | 111

Chapter Nine
Wifi Universe | 131

Chapter Ten
An Impersonal Universe and A Theory of Correspondence | 143

Chapter Eleven
In Conversation: The Analogy of Being | 155

Chapter Twelve
The Seeing God | 169

Critique: Difficulties with This Proposal | 189

Postscript—Concluding Unscientific Postscript | 207

Endnotes | 213

Index | 241

Preface

THE WONDERFULLY EVOCATIVE FILM 'a theory of everything' depicts the brilliant physicist Stephen Hawking developing approaches to the cosmos. His accounts of black holes and of time became part of the staple diet of contemporary physics; sparked off as the narrative shows by a quest to find a single equation that can constitute a theory of everything that lives, moves and has its being. What makes the film an absorbing story is the drama of personal life and love against the backcloth of motorneurone disease. On the one hand is the scientific quest; on the other is a very human story of loss, persevering love and difficulty generating narrative drive and points of identification. As observed at one moment in the film, the quest to find what lies at the heart of ultimate reality is due to the best two descriptions not aligning. General Relativity, theorised by Albert Einstein, does not map on to quantum mechanics. One way of phrasing this is that the physics of the very large and the physics of the very small are incompatible partners. They seem to play by different rules.

But there has to be more—far more—to a theory of everything than squaring this mathematical circle. What about the private dramas we play out in the brief history of our personal time? How do they cohere with a material reality that equations attempt to describe? They are every much as real as the 'hard' objects we see and encounter around us. Where do they fit in? How can an account of reality that seeks to be in any way totalising not take account of any notion that we cannot thrive without being worthwhile people living worthwhile lives? Is this really a theory of everything?

I walk amidst soft grandeur of trees. The way in which my thoughts blend in with the landscape shows that my inner being is integrally related to what is around me. A theory of everything that can encompass the very people who endeavour to find it surely needs to point to how what gives our lives significance and meaning folds into the fabric of everyday reality- how the 'soft' stuff can possibly relate to the 'hard' stuff. In so doing, it might need to accomplish at least two objectives:

i) It must give an account of how humans derive a realm of value, love, meaning and Spirit from the unpromising materials of quarks and leptons: the building blocks of material reality being entirely neutral regarding what makes our existence worthwhile:

ii) It must give an explanation of how the human self-consciousness of its own personhood and value derives from the fabric of the cosmos and is, so to speak, 'switched on' from it

There are many moves available in such a project. We might say that physical reality is all there is: that physics describes everything ultimately: even our lives and loves. Those who espouse the view that 'nature' by itself is responsible for our consciousness and our self-consciousness are holding to a perspective that goes by several names- scientism, naturalism, materialism or physicalism.

We might say that we will be agnostic in relation to the ontological nature of ultimate reality but in practice pursue science and philosophy as if nature is all—a stance of 'methodological naturalism.'

We might say that the cosmos is impersonal cosmic energy as in Dao or is conscious (panpsychism).

Or we might infer that there is a deeper and greater reality underpinning the cosmos: a universe that welcomes us and both instigates and responds to our personhood. This is our quest. It leads us to the personal: to a Subject that holds our subjectivity and to the Observer who sees and acts.

SETTING THE SCENE

Wanted: a worldview in which scientifically embedded reality and consciousness, including that of our own value, would not be fragmented from each other.

Life is a continuous interplay between the subjective reality of what it feels like to be alive, to be downcast or rise with jubilation—what it feels like to be us—and the objective reality of a universe seemingly blind and deaf to our hopes and fears, the elements of the human subject at the heart of consciousness. The inference the book is going to make is that there is a locus of consciousness or meaning in matter or behind the material world; hence our need for meaning corresponds to something outside itself. There really is a 'you' inside rather than being illusory. As Dennet argues, *"a brain was always going to do what it was caused to do by current, local, mechanical circumstances*".[3] On this reading, free will is therefore a problem.[4]

The question being addressed here is what account can be given of how these two dimensions are integrated into a totality; how the realm of physical reality folds back into the overall scheme of things is the focus of our exploration. The proposal is that we live in an 'I-thou' Universe. Our experience as a subject is not answered by Object any more than an AI entity can fully understand us. Human personhood points to an Ultimate Personhood beyond our own who is the ground of all being—both physis and psyche. The moral order and physical order are thus coordinated. The very ground of our being and personhood, that wants to see itself as valuable, comports with the cosmos.

Ian McGillChrist argued that whatever fundamental reality might exist, we live out our lives in a subjective reality defined by what we attend to. Our attention constructs our reality and becomes the beating heart with which we love the world.[5] However, the question arises. Is there anything within the fabric of reality that attends to us, responsive to our personhood to which we respond?

What is it about the universe and the fabric of reality that can give any promotion of personhood and the value of human beings? Having considered philosophically the GAP between the limits of scientific explanation and our sense of personhood being valuable, we will explore what options there are for a complete description of reality. A full 'theory of everything' surely requires it beyond the intricacies of mathematical physics. This is the 'stuff of life' we actually live by. As Thomas Nagel argues, all conscious entities have a subjective viewpoint on the world.[6] A scientific approach cannot capture the reality of conscious experience: seemingly objective attempts remove us from what we seek to understand. The importance of an individual perspective is philosophically, amply warranted.

The inexorable rise and rise of artificial intelligence generates new questions about personhood. Whatever the potential for its use in all aspects of human endeavour, including medicine, it seems extremely unlikely that AI could ever engage in fields such as therapy where inter-subjectivity is needed. Person to person exchange seems vital to such I-thou encounters. Unless (as in sci-fi scripts) an emotion chip is programmed in, an AI entity could never be anything other than neutral to human concerns. In such neutrality, it parallels a cosmos indifferent to us and to which we cannot respond.

Time and again in everyday life and in our dreams and aspirations, we encounter realities that are not accommodated within scientific explanation. Our experiences as human beings are profoundly important to how we function. Whether or not we actually carry it out in practice to others, our inner sense of ourselves tells us that we need to be treated as if we are significant, that we matter. Our little lives count as do the struggles, the relationships and the many-coiled layers of life. Most would find it hard to define what is meant by 'personhood' or 'the self' but we are conscious of ME. Even if we theoretically reduce value to matter/brain states we cannot live as though that were true.

Personhood and its dilemmas are the centre of gravity of everyday life. Scientists may work on aspects of their field and probe the layers and functioning of material reality. But they go home at night to the ambiguities of the human situation; the joy of personhood but also its heartache. They go from manipulating the material world to domestic emotional manipulation or depression where people lose the point of themselves. From peering deeply into the inner constituents of matter or cosmos, they go to highs and lows of the human situation- the cry of the heart and sigh of the soul.

We live in a land of such contrasts, where gentleness and jagged roughness live side by side and where beauty and pain are intertwined. For the world is abrasive to the human spirit and to rub against others is to reel with the discovery of an unexpected sharpness. Amidst the good and the kind, how did the blue and white planet become an arduous place, a world carved out of an inhospitable wilderness, so friendly to human life, so unfriendly to itself? We begin with a cry; we leave with a sigh. The entrance is a door of immense struggle and difficulty to be born, before bells joyfully proclaim the end of the ordeal and a new story. The exit is a lonely soul dying in discomfort, attended by raw, hurting people. Between entrance and the exit comes the land of contrasts, the land of ashes and delight, of joy and mourning, litter and flowers, of grime and colour.

Surely we are image—bearers—that at least is the theist response. It is the source of this endless creativity, the riddle of our humanity, our flair for technology and innovation, our capacity for artistic expression, our introspective consciousness, our morality and conscience. Who shall adequately explain us to ourselves? We are in the image of another. Is that why we fill our lives with images? Our first awakening is the awakening to life. We find ourselves alive, a mystery to ourselves, adrift on open sea. Everywhere extends the house we call self. Mothers, fathers, primitive comfort, primeval security and objects: where boundaries begin and end we learn in our first education.

We have heard that the cosmos renders us not even a speck of dust. But who amongst us can live with such insignificance? Do we not die unless we matter? All that we live by is disintegrating.

For many, aloneness is the stuff from which existence is wrought. Naked and alone we came: we leave one soul at a time. The fear is that we disappear. Over a perilous precipice we teeter, out of sight and out of mind. Loneliness will suck us in. The void claims us. All the lonely people! We have parcelled your connections into two—everyone else and then there's me. I am separate, cut off from connections with meaningful others with no one to share. But we are all connected.

How does the personal realm, where value carries such weight, fold into the fabric of physical reality? Are we obliged to speak constantly of two different realms that are incommensurate?

This is primarily a philosophical rather than scientific enquiry. For the reasons developed, this takes us into theological territory as the form of explanation that gives best fit for a mentality behind physical reality that validates our personhood. As philosopher Alvin Plantinga argues, the claim that science refutes the idea that God acts in the world is wholly mistaken. "*According to theistic belief, God has created the world and created human beings in his image. It is perfectly possible that he did so by employing, guiding and directing the process of genetic variation and natural selection*".[7]

What makes a problem philosophical is itself a large question. Science deals with calculation, with experiment: philosophy with issues such as the one we probe presenting dilemmas for the human spirit that are 'hard' rather than 'easy'; often intractable. Though they have been wrestled with for centuries, philosophical issues can be reframed with fresh perspectives from the 'natural' or human sciences such as neuroscience. As an important facet of the age-old debate about mind and matter, we will look here at the limits to scientific naturalism through a particular lens; that of the value of personhood and why anyone should think it matters that WE matter. It will be for conversation partners to assess whether carefully articulated positions can be debated anew.

The idea of extrapolation from human experience to ultimate truth is not new. In the 18th century, Kant did that by saying that there is in human consciousness a sense of moral obligation that does not make sense without freedom, immortality and belief in God being postulated. One of his spiritual heirs, Schleiermacher argued from moral consciousness to religious consciousness. The starting point of his interpretation of Christianity was the feeling (read, 'intuitive grasp of reality') of absolute dependence. The self-consciousness of this dependence, in all things, not religion only) was at heart a consciousness of God.[8] Our exploration is from human experience towards the cosmos.

Our exploration here is framed in terms of 'the Observer and the Observed'. We will draw together:

- The role that the conscious observer and act of measurement plays in quantum physics where any decision to measure means that you are involved.
- The role that the maternal gaze plays in infant neurobiology that is relational
- The role of mutual exchange in psychotherapy, drawing on two subjectivities and eye contact
- The role that the social gaze in conferring recognition to human subjects

It is not inevitable that where these ideas lead is towards the divine gaze, a Cosmic Observer whose Personal Being provides correspondence, an Analogy of Being and whose seeing of us is constitutive. But it is hard to see on any other terms than such metaphysical idealism that our personhood is validated and our subjectivity held. The cosmos is surely relational.

Somehow we have ended up with a neocortex "*so complex that we have become capable of spoken and written language, self-consciousness and the construction of both private and social selves*". [9] And also to feel that we matter. One life shaped by the struggle for emancipation, that of Mary Robinson former President of Ireland and UN High Commissioner for Human Rights, was entitled 'Everybody Matters'. [10]

At issue are ways of seeing and knowing. A scientific way of looking at the world that is purely naturalistic will not see a 'higher' power or 'deeper' ground of reality (to anticipate reference to the topography of reality in Chapter....). A secular way of looking at things will invoke other forms of the social imaginary beyond a religious vision of the world. [11] Belief in God is now seen as one option among others. Yet a moral or spiritual vision must be rooted in something, unless a flight of fancy.

The proposal is that there is a deep field, beyond the fabric of material reality to which our personhood responds. It is a theory about the mental field behind matter. We infer that there is a supra-personal field behind everything which our personal sense of ME connects with. David Papineau contends that it is almost psychologically impossible to believe that conscious experiences are actually physical processes in someone's brain. [12] Evoking a contemporary technology most of us are very aware of, we live in Wi-Fi-world where a field is set up that allows for connection. That ubiquitous transducer will serve as a metaphor for the way our personhood responds to what is there and allows for the validation of the self. If we can infer that personhood is affirmed within a wider view of reality somehow, there then follows the question of what we could infer about the realm at whatever level that valuable personhood connects with. We cannot discern directly what is in the same way as experimentation and observation leads to a 'scientific method'. But as Einstein remarked, "*try and penetrate with our limited means the secrets of nature and you will find that, behind all the discernible concatenations, there remains something subtle, intangible and inexplicable*". [13] Science provides a framework for understanding material reality but only yields the way we experience that reality. The reality itself lies forever beyond the range of our telescopes.

In contemporary physics, whether or not a conscious observer feels of worth does not seem to add anything to quantum weirdness becoming intelligible and being seen. A sense of worth is rather more to do with the observer being seen and regarded by other human observers. There is profound synchronicity between objects being regarded and us being regarded. Such acts of being seen (and heard) call us to life and meaning in a parallel act by which we notice the external world and call that into being. The reductive standpoint entails that consciousness is illusory or simply a function of matter. If so, then value is also reductive to this and our need for it to be real and external is false.

The essence of naturalism (or scientific materialism) is that there is nothing else ultimately needed. Life and human self-awareness develop step by step from non-living matter without any special action of God. From the laws of physics and chemistry, nature by itself produces everything. Here we enter what we might label 'the topography of reality'. For there is no 'deeper' realm. There is no 'higher' purpose or guiding hand. There is no alternative reality slightly to the left of us (or right—it matters not) or a dimension 'in parallel' with ours that supplies another form of explanation. All the explanation that is necessary is to be found 'within' the system; ultimately knowable through the empirical methods of 'hard' science that will produce 'hard' results. Naturalism becomes a comprehensive worldview because nature is self-sufficient. Nothing external is needed to explain it.

As biologist Edward Wilson put it: "*Every part of existence is considered to be obedient to physical laws requiring no external control.*"[14]

Limits to methodological naturalism mean that it is very hard to explain aspects of our existence we live by. If such materialism is true and everything is reduced to physical objects and forces between them, it is illusory to treat other people -let alone nonhuman creatures—as a nexus of value and significance. Bestowing legal rights on everyone as having equal potential for meaning is a fairy tale.

Especially, any sense that we matter, that our lives count and are worth something. This is a shift from the naturalistic to the 'meaningful' and consciousness perspective yet without that, we wither. It might be that we project our sense of significance collectively and say that 'we matter' in our family, our tribe. But whether it is in ourselves or in a larger unit, implicitly our lives have potential for meaning. This derives not from sentient consciousness per se but personhood.

The problem of consciousness has proved a very tricky question, let alone self-consciousness. The observer in physics is one thing and seems to make some difference to quantum reality. Though a move to the merging of the two realms, i.e. in quantum physics where consciousness affects the material world, and the interior life of personhood, a self-aware observer is another dimension. A self-aware observer who needs to feel of worth presents another dimension beyond that.

Our personhood is of a different order as it goes to the heart of being human; though of course there is a large debate about whether animals can be considered persons. For pondering humans, however, our sense of significance is matched against cosmic and sometimes interpersonal insignificance. It is existential.

At some point, the realm of value, love and meaning by which we live psychologically must fold into the realm of hard matter that surrounds us every day. Maybe such folding-in takes place in our head. Alternatively, there is a deeper layer of reality that connects profoundly and maybe analogically with personhood. Could a subject-object ('I-thou') awareness of personhood be intrinsic to the cosmos? That will take us to huge question about the very nature of reality and what instantiates wholeness.

The conundrum partly (or entirely?) reflects how we see, how we think. Our notions of cosmology and of the general nature of reality must have scope to allow an account of consciousness and of valuable personhood. But that works both ways. Our sense of consciousness must be able to permit a view of 'reality as a whole.' The two accounts taken together should then permit an understanding of how reality and the consciousness of our value are related. We will keep coming back to the question, how can reality as it is, i.e. the material world with no meaning, co-exist with a consciousness that demands meaning? The approach from scientific naturalism is hard put to address this. Its practitioners could usefully look inside to their inner quest to be significant, to be worthwhile, and ask if there is a reality outside themselves that is at issue here, a reality that attunes us to the ultimate nature of things.

It is through taking personhood into account that an integral perception of the world becomes possible, witness the vision of the Swiss philosopher Greber. His contribution to the evolution of human conscious awakening involved development of mutating consciousness on principles that are redolent with moving from magic and animism and animalism to becoming self-aware. Atypically, Eastern religions are thought to be in tune with this vision of the world.[15]

What, however, would it mean to have an holistic view of reality? Our vision here though is one that stresses personhood as the integrating principle; one that encompasses the bigger picture of material reality but also the sense of value, love and meaning by which humankind derives significance.

To contextualise what it is we are searching for, the locus of meaning behind material reality, in physics we infer a field for what lies behind local forces which shapes action and interaction. Can we infer a deeper field that underlies both matter and mind and which generates consciousness as well as endorsement of value, love and meaning sustaining our flickering human consciousness?

The claim in this proposal is that there is a deep field, beyond the fabric of material reality to which our personhood responds and participates in. How else can we give an account of what gives personhood a sense, not just of itself but of significance and worth? The realm of value, meaning, love and spirituality is one that humans need for psychological survival yet which has neither anchorage nor correspondence in purely physical descriptions of reality where all life- including the messy life of humans—is an accidental by-product of the blind forces of nature.

This book explores how these two realms—the 'hard' material world described by laws of physics and the 'soft' world of meaning-making where significance is played out- might conceivably align.

Human significance feels so frail against a seemingly limitless cosmos. Here is one encounter with vastness pitted against private dramas that are very real to its writer:

"One night, when I was sleepless enough to pad downstairs in search of a crossword, I decided to step outside for a few moments to see if the moon was visible above the rooftops. And there she was, bright and gibbous, surrounded by a drift of clear stars. Bathing in that pale light, I realised that I had been a fool to pine after mountains. I had access to abundant awe, three footsteps from my back door. There, stretching across the sky, was Orion, the first constellation I'd learned to identify. There was Mars, slightly red to the naked eye. And there was I, a tiny speck in a vast universe with an inflated sense of my own self-importance." …. *"But there was a yearning still there in me, a persistent, insurgent desire to connect and engage in shifting acts of understanding. The input of my own senses so often told me that there was something more to this life than the mere observable facts."*[16]

This is the situation of one attuned to dissonance; jarring jaggedness, the police-siren grating that shouted that something is wrong. What made sense now? All the old views of life have been plunged into crisis, what the post-pandemic world needs is a symphony that takes in the healing of the blue and white planet in which we dwell; stunning complexity and all the bewildering experience that lay at the heart of invitation to be human. What is our vision of the world? Is there a supreme power guaranteeing a unity in things and a direction to events; a single story making sense of the impotence and vulnerability of existence? Human significance is not just experienced as a cosmic, existential question. Our situation is indeed suspended between the familiar life on the third rock from the sun and the vastness of a cosmos where ten hundred thousand million suns immolate in endless distance. Yet our sense of significance and worth is not only cast in terms of astronomical relativity, but it is also as psychological as it is sociological. It relates to a sense of worthwhileness or its lack that is fundamental to the context within which human personhood thrives. The mismatch between an account of the cosmos defined in physical and natural processes and the dramas of individual and social life is such that it is hard to see how the latter can be encompassed within the former as an objective basis for moral truth.

If we think of reality as constituted of independent fragments, then that is how our mental apparatus will often see things. If our worldview grasps everything coherently and harmoniously in an overall whole, undivided, unbroken, then we will see the world in a similar way.[17]

The way the universe is made is such that it can evoke value; specifically value and worth of human beings and bequeath significance. This is something that either we feel inside or lament its absent (in which case we will not flourish). How can we account for this through our understanding of reality? The content of material reality is both backcloth to all our experiences and in which we participate. It has potential for meaning—meaning as something internal, yet which we want to find. Search for 'the big picture'- the nature of ultimate reality and our place in it—constitutes a vital task for humans who are concerned with meaning-making.[18]

This is a philosophical quest for correspondence. But it is rooted in the very human search for re-assurance and recognition that characterises our lives. Does my sense of value and worth relate to anything 'out there' that affirms me and corresponds to me? We will probe whether an impersonal universe can ever do that and give validation to ourselves and what we hold most dear. If a neutral structure of material reality is all there is, then we as conscious observers, who sigh for significance, have risen far above the source. We are thereby greeted with the laugh of an empty horizon. Not only do we wish for meaning, but we need the meaning to be 'real' i.e. rooted in something out there, external, not only internal. Can the universe outside of us do that?

PREFACE

There is a gap; a vast and yawning gap that both intrigues and elicits sharply differing reactions. This generates the quest that is the subject of this book. Therefore, our quest is a question. It is an exploration of how two sharply different dimensions of reality fit together.

One dimension is the quest for material reality; the fabric of the universe. This is to do with the way that matter and energy are woven together to form chairs and tables, planets and galaxies.

The second dimension is the quest for the first-person perspective; the ME at the heart of interpersonal exchange and my frame of reference for social life. This is to do with the way that I count, I matter, and moreover seem to require a degree of value and worth in order to flourish in a universe with significance and purpose as well as hoping people will be treated humanely.

How these dimensions cohere is perplexing. How does the fabric of material reality come to bear an imprint—an imprint of a personhood that claims to be valuable, that we count for something? On the face of it, material reality is neutral with no interest in the gallery of spectators; observers such as ourselves. It does not care about us and is completely indifferent to our flourishing and our fate.

That is indeed the picture provided by forms of science that investigate what is real and measurable (the one being defined by the other). As the dimensions of the cosmos have exploded into unimaginative scale, human insignificance seems smaller and smaller. Yet there is a huge gap. Our personal lives protest hugely against de-personalisation. The gap is between the objective laws of physics and the subjective experience that yearns for significance.

What we will call 'valuable personhood' is but one of many challenges to a strictly materialist view of the universe that asserts matter is all there is; that reality is defined in terms of physical laws and that all our life experiences are generated by material processes such as are to be found in our brain.

Other challenges have been posed in philosophy through metaphysical idealism; the notion that the primary basis of the universe is Mind, refracted through countless other minds and sentience. Or we could go to the insistence by the great religions and spiritual practices across the centuries that there is a spiritual realm beyond what we can see with our eyes and our hands can touch. Panpsychism represents another challenge, with its insistence that consciousness is a fundamental layer that is ubiquitous. Another form of challenge is the multi-faceted claim to forms of knowing and awareness that go beyond the confines of the body, such as extra-sensory perception or near-death experiences. High on the contemporary agenda though is the unresolvable issue of what consciousness is and how mind and brain could be related in such a way that we are aware of our own emotions and thinking and can share with others the colours of day. The challenge presented in this book is of a particular form of consciousness; the secret knowledge that we are valuable (or at least aspire to be); that we feel it keenly when that is in deficit or are resigned to its absence with wistfulness. Such awareness that we are a valuable human being laden with significance is not a fringe concern. It goes to the heart of our place in the universe; our own humanity and the meaning we attempt to wrap around our lives, at least to get through the day (and the night!).

One of the classics in the field of spirituality and psychology was William James' seminal work on the varieties of religious experience. He asserted that there is something within people that seeks meaning beyond the immediate concerns of life.[19] Harmony with the world beyond, the highest universe, is our true end and destiny but this is developed through prayer or inner communion with the spirit thereof.

The age-old spiritual quest has caught the attention of neuroscientists such as Andrew Newberg, who presents evidence from brain scan studies that prayer and meditation permanently change numerous structures and functions in the brain, values and the way we perceive reality. The benefit is strengthening neural functioning in specific parts of the brain that aid in lowering anxiety and depression, enhancing social awareness and empathy, and improving cognitive functioning. Newberg was a founder of the new interdisciplinary field called neurotheology. Evoking the title of one of his books, along with therapist Mark Waldeman, human beings are born to believe.[20] Newberg examined not only the neural activity of the religious brain, but also the effects of various religious beliefs and practices on human mental and physical health. Using an academic approach into what he calls "objective measures of spirituality," Newberg sought to explain the neuroscientific basis for why religion and spirituality have played such a prominent role in human life. In one account of the interaction between religion and brain science, God is a hallmark of the very way in which we think.[21]

Larry Culliford, in his book about the psychology of spirituality, suggests that belief is a form of attachment.[22] People love whatever they feel bound to. Culliford argues that human beings are bio-psycho-spiritual in nature. This three-fold essence is one and indivisible. The mind-body-spirit scheme seems to have resonance with how people understand God—either the Christian vision of the Trinity or other conceptions of the divine. Health professionals, Culliford argues, pay attention to one or other of those aspects but invariably omit the third component, that of a spiritual dimension.

PREFACE

I began this philosophical exploration on the day in summer of 2022 that the new James Webb telescope began to fulfil its purpose. Developed over many years by an international team, the new means of exploring the cosmos began to pour stunning images into our phones. In its first year, there came an update of the iconic Hubble Space Telescope image "The Pillars of Creation", depicting billowing clouds of dark gas—part of the Eagle Nebula. Webb brought into view the young red stars that are sprinkled throughout the nebulous clouds: "protostars," because they're not yet massive enough and hot enough to burn hydrogen in their cores. Thanks to the observatory's ability to see in the infrared, Webb revealed star-forming regions of galaxies, how galaxies interact, the atmosphere of exoplanets, and the famous 'deep field' captured by Hubble but now magnified with more distant galaxies in the background. [23]

On an inter-galactic level, the dimensions and sheer scale of physical reality are a cascade of cosmic wonder; sights never before glimpsed by human eyes were now sharply visual, readily accessible by anyone with a device. Clearly, the universe is big; of immense scale incomprehensible to human imagination; only faintly discernible to the most advanced scientific instruments like James Webb.

On a quantum level, the world of the most minute and microscopic, the building blocks of material reality have come into view in a new way in the last generation courtesy of another marvel of scientific engineering; the large hadron collider (LHC). It has emerged that we live in a quark and lepton universe assembling in complex patterns of energy.

And then there is us, ME, the individual thrown into life together with myriads of other beings like ourselves in complex patterns of human society.

The scientific philosophy of naturalism asserts that all these layers of reality are generated from the smallest scale. Ultimate reduction to the interaction of quarks and leptons (the building blocks of protons/neutrons and electrons) at the most minute level goes further behind the curtain even than the tiniest particles into the swirl of energy from which they are made. These are the foundations underlying everything from which 'higher' systems emerge. They are self-organising rather than directed but in vastly complex ways, from these building blocks are quarried everything that has ever existed. Chemistry, biology, psychology and human societies eventually emerge.

Is this, however, the universe we actually live in? Naturalistic science would assert that everything we need to fathom the furthest reaches of space and time or the component parts of matter and energy are, in principle, discoverable and quantifiable. That extends not just to 'hard' empirical reality but to the 'soft' questions of purpose and significance; questions of value, questions of love.

The philosopher David Hume wrestled with this, empirical philosopher though he was. Einstein echoes such mystery as we shall see. "*The scientific method can teach us nothing else beyond how facts are related to, and conditioned by, each other.…yet..the knowledge of what is does not open the door directly to what should be. One can have the clearest and most complete knowledge of what is, and yet not be able to deduct from that what should be the goal of our human aspirations*".[24]

The logic of reductionism is atheistic rather than theistic. That is to say, there is no need for a more intelligible and satisfying explanation for our existence and all its quandaries than the reality of what science can reveal through patient testing. It is clearly the case that quantum theory shows how nature is replete with multiple interactions and genuine novelty. Yet though this leaves most people scratching their heads in puzzlement, it does not necessarily require explanation outside science. Sooner or later, theory will catch up. Newtonian laws are applicable for a closed system. An account of special divine action is more compatible with the open and less predictable quantum cosmos.

Much depends of course on definitions and on ways of seeing. As an alternative to being dismissive, scientific colleagues in laboratories and universities could ask the question, 'what is you see that I don't see?' Or they could look inside and ponder the existential questions that permeate the human situation. For there are some big questions that trouble our existence that show the limits of a strictly scientific explanation in terms of causes and physical laws and which present a serious GAP.

There are at least five explanations for the GAP:

- That it is an illusion: the cosmos really is constituted on materialist conceptions and has been generated from matter by natural processes and quantum relations.

- That the cosmos is emergent - emergent properties account for the universe as we know it (despite mental and spiritual aspects of life ultimately being subordinate to the material).[25]

- That at some level the universe thinks and we live in a conscious cosmos—the argument of panpsychism which is receiving increasing attention in philosophical circles. [26]

- That there is a divine, supra-personal entity that guides and directs though not necessarily personal; indeed is more likely to be a cosmic life energy as in Daoism

- That there is a God as represented in the Abrahamic religions.

We will ponder these stances in the course of this exploration, leaving the notion that things just looks 'designed' by dint of teleological laws (a la Aristotle) to fulfil purposes such as promoting life and future states. Any serious thinker pondering such claims must grapple with why there are physical laws at all and why they operate as they do. Fine-tuning their constants has led to the emergence of life and us. Yet our subjectivity and personal being must also be taken into account. It is unlikely that an impersonal cosmos and framing divinity as a life force can do this .

In this volume, we will not be discussing the tricky question of what exactly is going on in the human brain when we experience the feeling of worth. Whether there is dedicated neural circuitry which fires when we are having spiritual experiences has been the subject of considerable research.[27]

Our focus rather is the subject experience of the human person who requires 'I-thou' to respond to. Huge debates have raged and ranged over whether we do have free will and if there are no counterfactuals. [28]It seems incontrovertible though that human freedom can still exist because we live our lives in a macroscopic world, where different rules apply, compared to fundamental particles and forces at work at the subatomic level. The same perspective probably applies to the higher order level of the human person—the 'I-thou' and if there is an ultimate 'thou' that our 'I' responds to.

Scientist materialists are people too. They live with issues of love, purpose and value that are not illusory; every bit as real and baffling as the work on theoretical physics that is their day job! It is part of what makes us human that we look for what is mysterious or the extra dimension that makes our existence special. Linked with these issues are those appertaining to a moral vision. How we treat people is a throbbing question to those who care about right and wrong: whether or not humans practice this. It is one thing to say that people have value and worth. It is quite another to say that societies and inter-personal behaviour reflects this. What can be said with some confidence surely is that humans usually want to be treated with respect and fairness; even when they do not practice it.

Endnotes

1. John Locke (2008) *An Essay concerning Human Understanding* (Oxford World's Classics) IV, x, 10 Oxford: OUP

2. Act 1 Scene 3

3. Dennet, D. (1998) *Brainchildren: Essay on Designing Minds* Cambridge, M.A.: MIT Press p346

4. Dennet, D. (2003) *Freedom Evolves* New York: Viking Press

5. McGilchrist I. (2009) *The Master and his Emissary: The Divided Brain and the Making of the Western World*. Yale University Press: New Haven and London

6. Nagel, T. (2023) *Moral Feelings, Moral Reality and Moral Progress* Oxford: OUP

7. Plantinga, A. (2011) *Where the conflict really lies* Oxford: OUP p129

8. Friedrich Schleiermacher (2016) *The Christian Faith* Sheffield: T&T Clark

9. Cozolino, L. (2022) *The neuroscience of Psychotherapy* New York: W.W.Norton p12

10. Robinson, M. (2012) *Everybody Matters*. London: Hodder and Stoughton

11. Taylor, C. (2007) A Secular Age Cambridge, M.A.: Belknap Press

12. Papineau, D. (2020) 'The problem of consciousness' in U. Kriegel ed. *The Oxford Handbook of Consciousness* Oxford: OUP

13. Kessler, H. (1999) *The diaries of a Cosmopolitan 1918–1937 London:* Weidenfeld & Nicolson p332

14. Wilson, E. (1979) *On Human Nature* New York: Bantam Books p200–201

15. Greber, J. (1985) *The Ever present origin* tr Noel Barstad Athens, Ohio:Ohio University Press

16. 'There I was, a tiny speck in a vast universe' How awe made my life worth living again- Katherine May Guardian 29th March 2023 cf May, K. (2023) Enchantment: Reawakening Wonder in an Exhausted Age London: Faber

17. Bohm, D. (2002) Wholeness and the Implicate Order London: Routledge

18. Caroll, S. (2016) *The Big Picture: on the origins of life, meaning and the universe itself* London: Oneworld

19. James, W. (1982) *The Varieties of Religious Experience: a study in human nature* London: Penguin p2

20. Newberg, A. & Waldeman, M.R. (2020) *How God Changes Your Brain: Breakthrough Findings from a Leading Neuroscientist* New York: Ballantine Books

21. Alper, M. (2009) *"God" Part of the Brain: A Scientific Interpretation of Human Spirituality and God* Sourcebooks

22. Culliford, L. (2011) *The Psychology of Spirituality* London: Jessica Kingsley

23. Dan Falk 'Seven Amazing Accomplishments the James Webb Telescope Achieved in Its First Year' Smithsonian July 5th 2023

24. Einstein, A. (1954) *Ideas and Opinions* New York: Crown Publishers p41–2

25. Clayton, P. (2008) *Adventures in the Spirit: God, World, Divine Action* Minneapolis MN: Fortress Press

26. Strawson,G. (2006) 'Realistic Monism: Why Physicalism Entails Panpsychism and its Place in Nature' in *Consciousness and its place in Nature: Does physicalism entail Panpsychism* ed Anthony Freeman Exeter: Imprint Academy p18

27. Joseph, R. (2002) *Neurotheology* Berkeley, C.A.: University of California Press pp267–84

28. Murphy, N., Brown, W. (2007) *Did my neurons Make Me Do it? Philosophical and Neurobiological Perspectives on Moral Responsibility and Free Will* New York: Oxford University Press p79–80

Chapter One

Albert and the lion

"*My God created laws.....his universe is not ruled by wishful thinking but by immutable laws*" —Albert Einstein [1]

" "*The most beautiful emotion we can experience is the mystical. It is the power of all true art and science. He to whom this emotion is a stranger, who can no longer wonder and stand rapt in awe, is as good as dead*". —Albert Einstein[2]

" "*Nature shows us only the tail of the lion. But I do not doubt that the lion belongs to it even though he cannot at once reveal himself because of his enormous size*". —Albert Einstein [3]

WANTED: A RICHER VISION of the universe. What we see, namely the tail of the lion, reflects a far greater reality.

It was central to Einstein's response to the world he investigated so brilliantly that there is a deep harmony to underlying reality. He sought the big picture; what he called his Weltbild. [4] He would not have aligned with the subsequent post-modernity that was suspicious of anything other than local realities. Seeing the cosmos as the totality of entities interacting gravitationally led him to reject the philosophy of Kant for whom grasping the concept of an objective universe was unreliable. For Einstein, the universe was both real and fully rational. This did not mean he rejected the implication Kant had made that any step from the universe to the Creator was unreliable. Four years before his death, Einstein wrote to his lifelong friend Maurice Solovine to insist that he had not become a theist though he foresaw his cosmology could be interpreted in that way. *"It cannot be helped. . .I add this lest you think that weakened by old age, I have fallen into the hands of priests".*[5]

Matter is the ultimate reality. This is what the human mind with its dramas is reducible to. With a thoroughgoing scientific naturalism, matter is the fundamental substance in nature. All that we see around us is the result of material interactions but so also are mental states. Material substances are the only things that exist in nature. The corollary is that nothing else exists apart from material matter. Any talk of a deeper layer of reality from whence questions of spirit and consciousness are derived refers ultimately to forms of matter. What was matter made of? Matter was regarded as inert and passive, something to be acted upon by external forces.

Yet the world is a comprehensible place, capable of being grasped by thought once further information is known. There is, as Einstein pointed out, a high degree of order which we are in no way entitled to expect. [6] The universe is intelligible, implying amenability to consciousness. It is not something science can explain that reality has created conscious things that can understand it. This is surely why much of his scientific career was dedicated to the formulation of a single grand theory that would weave together relativity with quantum mechanics into a coherent whole. Yet, as McGrath points out, the unity of all things—die Einheitlichkeit—was more of an intuition than something that could be proved. [7] It is a way of seeing, a richer way of grasping reality as all good theory should offer. For Einstein, this was central to the scientific imagination- an intuitive starting point in the quest for truth. The cosmos just had to be unified—even if we could not fathom how!

Progressively, Einstein made statements about the indispensability of metaphysics.[8] This caused consternation amongst those who insisted that there are no absolutes and that everything is relative. [9] In popular culture, the relativisation of values was regarded as part of Einstein's legacy though he would have strongly disputed this. As Jaki notes, *"for all his dismissal of religion and of belief in a personal God, Einstein insisted on the unquestionable superiority of the Judeo-Christian perspective in which unconditional value is attributed to each and every human being".* [10]

Heisenberg suggested that the cosmos should be seen, not as *"different groups of objects but different groups of connections".* [11] The dynamic patterns of the subatomic world, it is claimed, support a cosmos replete with energy rather than symmetrical patterns. Separate systems of local connections were a postulate that Einstein firmly sought to upheld in opposition to the fundamental role of probability espoused by Niels Bohr. This was expressed in Einstein's famous epigram 'God does not play dice'. [12] This was a view of God as underlying an external reality where separate spatial elements joined by local connections is inconsistent with the probability of quantum theory. Expressed in the Einstein-Podolosky-Rosen (EPR) experiment, [13] it is said to be overturned by the Bell experiments in the 1970's demonstrating non-local connection. Such a view of reality, if continued to be borne out by experimental data and theoretical physics need not point, however, to a continuous flux of energy as being the ultimate reality.

Einstein's personal faith has been the subject of much critical examination as it was in his own day. In November 1929, he wrote an article for the New York Times called 'Religion and Science' in which he expressed the critique of religion common to educated freethinkers of the time. But he also emphasised a higher level of 'cosmic religiosity' based on *"the miraculous order that manifests itself in nature as well as in the world of ideas."* Religiosity was, he concluded, *"the strongest and noblest mainspring of scientific research".* [14]

As he developed his ideas and the world grew dark, he became more exercised about the threat to value of life and meaning posed by Nazism in Germany where he worked. This dimension was not revealed by the science in which he had laboured which only showed us a partial view of reality. *"How small a part of nature can be formulated and expressed in an exact formulation",* he wrote in the Preface to Max Planck's 'Where is science going?', *"while all that is subtle has to be excluded".*[15]

The big drawback in current ideas about the nature of reality is that there is nothing that corresponds to our personhood. As can the case in our personal relationships, there is no one out there for me, nothing to impart significance. An 'I-it' relationship, be it the relation of human beings to an impersonal universe blank with meaning, or relation to cosmic energy and dynamic patterns of interaction, fails to provide such correspondence. Humans need SOMEONE to relate to. Evidently, Einstein did not consider his denial of a personal God as a denial of God. [16]

However, it is an astounding proposition that it is only what can be counted that can provide a total picture of reality. For that we enter into the interpretive world of what is often called 'the human sciences'. Science can tell us how many tears we shed, what tears are and how they are secreted. It cannot tell us WHY we cry. We will return to this important distinction. For now, it is important to note that the qualitative features of things are very difficult to ground in what is solely quantitative. Aspects of human behaviour cannot be accommodated within a deterministic frame of reference. It is not something science can explain that reality has created conscious things that can understand it (material reality).

A revolution in physics might come because we have found a way of integrating descriptions of how measurable objects and forces behave that eluded Einstein. That might constitute a totalising theory represented perhaps in a single equation that can explain everything. What it is unlikely to include at the present level of understanding is how our emerging grasp of the physical description of matter and energy in the cosmos can possibly explain what we may call- the 'I' in the eye. The problem of consciousness and how that fits into the fabric of reality is an immense challenge to a view of science that sees a materialist conception of forces and particles as a complete description of what is out there. Our undeniable sense of significance and need to feel that we matter pertains to a different realm surely, totally different to the stuff that physics talks to us about.

The Quantum revolution uncovered a hidden reality. This was a reality beyond what we experience in daily life and is very much behind the scenes. The cosmos as we see it now has features such as black holes, white holes and worm holes that could connect two distant points in time. Quantum theory changed the picture of materialism from the preceding centuries—particles can be linked despite distance and time. Matter is not simply building blocks: the mind plays a part in affecting it.

At the very moment that an act of measurement has taken place for a first particle, the momentum of a 2nd particle is fixed. Collapse of its wave function has mysteriously occurred. It seems that the first particle was transmitting information to the other, even faster than the speed of light. It was this that Einstein saw as voodoo action and argued that quantum theory must be incomplete.

Quantum entanglement may well be a description of how parts are integrated into a whole. It raises the question of how far all entities have interacted with each other at some point. Entanglement implies that the universe is monistic, that on the most fundamental level, everything in the universe is part of a single, unified whole.

Quantum mechanics has to be more than a theory of knowledge. It must surely point to being a theory of nature, of reality. A philosophical monist, physicist David Bohm suggested that *"it seems necessary to give up the idea that the world can correctly be analysed into distinct parts, and to replace it with the assumption that the entire universe is basically a single, indivisible unit"*. [17]

It was a great intellectual feat to show that there is no loophole in Einstein's view of the world when it came to General Relativity. But entanglement implies particles only have a definite reality when we observe. Entanglement is now part of modern technology, for example, quantum computers. Entanglement allows for the possibility that there is a single reality behind everything. There is but a single, indivisible entity consisting of everything that exists. As David Bohm had written, although classical physics depicted that *"the world can be analysed into distinct elements"*............*"quantum physics implies "the indivisible unity of all interacting systems"*.[18]

Here now, it is how the inner, existential and not just quantum world marries up with the external world shaped by physical laws that is the question. For giants of these matters, such as Einstein, Dirac or Hawking, the vast chasm of their own inner world runs in parallel with their discoveries. Kant suggested that the realm of the physical universe and the moral world of meaning, refer to two different and incommensurable realms. But surely there should be some tie up?

What material reality actually is has been hugely disrupted by 20th century physics.

Space-time can be re-framed as an outcome of entanglement. In his General Relativity theory, Einstein's great legacy was that gravity is not a force like other forces. It is embedded in space and time taken together. *"Time and space appear to be aspects of a single four-dimensional reality."*[19]

The observer was central to Einstein's project. Special relativity was rooted in the realisation that two observers moving at different speeds will not agree about the timing of two events or which took place first. With his by now famous example of a witnesses in a railway carriage observing lightning bolts in conjunction with observers on a platform, Einstein probed whether two events (two strokes of lightning) *"which are simultaneous with reference to the railway embankment, are also simultaneous relatively to the train?"* [20] Space and time can be stretched. But space-time distances, conceived integrally, stay independent of an observer. It depends on frames of reference.

As Einstein's mathematics mentor, Herman Minkowski, remarked, *"Henceforth space by itself, and time by itself, are doomed to fade away into mere shadows and only a kind of union of the two will preserve an independent reality"*. [21] Earlier in his career, Einstein had showed that space, time, matter and energy were part of a four-dimensional symmetry that was a larger dimension. However, that symmetry had nothing to say about gravity and acceleration. The key would lie in unification; the unification of space and time and matter and energy. Einstein failed to find a unified field theory partly because he was missing a vital piece of the puzzle—the nuclear force.

Einstein's metaphysic will continue to be the subject of great interest and invocation, given his place in the scientific pantheon. A disproof of the contingency of the universe does not seem possible, subject to something transcendental. The mental road to an extra-cosmic absolute remains open.[22]

Jose Ortega, the Spanish philosopher, made a very pertinent observation regarding the link between the work of science and scientists themselves. Scientists are human beings. Science gets on with its methods and tools that have transformed human existence but bigger questions of that existence are not addressed. [23] One exception is Carlo Rovelli, the Italian theoretical physicist whose *Seven Brief Lessons on Physics*, argued that there is no contradiction between a vision of the universe that makes human life seem small and irrelevant, and our everyday sorrows and joys. Or indeed between "cold science" and our inner, spiritual lives. We are part of nature, and so joy and sorrow are aspects of nature itself—nature is much richer than just sets of atoms. [24]

We are first pointing out the limits to scientific naturalism (the term that will be used mostly in this volume). We will seek to demonstrate that a degree of value is a vital psycho-social need. Then we will lay out pathways by which valuable personhood' leads to a conception of reality in which that personhood is endorsed and valued. Does that take us to a personal God? Consider alternatives. Does an impersonal universe shaped by objective laws of physics have any space for our subjectivity and dilemmas of personhood? 'I ache. . . .I sigh. . .I celebrate. . .I mourn. . . .I pray': these form a rich tapestry of being human; instantly recognisable but so unyielding to scientific explanation.

Even if we accept the proposition that human beings need to be valued at some level in order to flourish, there are some weighty objections to that taking us in the direction of omnipresent being.

It may be, as David Walsh argues, that the contemporary world is preoccupied with the self in that self-discovery narratives are our default discourse. The self in search of itself is not the fleeting awareness of the self but is sustained by the substantive reality of the person. Beyond the self is the person who is its reality. [25] The primacy of the person is what we live by. Persons know one another as persons because they are known in themselves. The reality of the person is irreducible: it cannot be known by anything other than itself. [26] As Walsh goes on to observe ref the project of philosopher Thomas Nagel, *"the challenge of calling forth an alternative worldview to reductionist materialism is more formidable than we are inclined to admit"*. The Person is the horizon to science and also reflection on it. If you do not believe in a personal God, the question: 'What is the purpose of life?' is unaskable and unanswerable.

There is a difference between subjectivity (being a subject, experiencing things) and personhood, finding self or regarding oneself as a thing observed by others. As Graham Ward suggests, subjectivity, though not necessarily tied to a concept of the transcendental ego, is fundamentally concerned with discrete individuals. Personhood, on the other hand, is that sense of self that continually comes from being in relation. [27]

For Thomas Nagel, the widely accepted world view of materialist naturalism is untenable. The mind-body problem cannot be confined to the relation between animal minds and animal bodies. If materialism cannot accommodate consciousness and other mind-related aspects of reality, then we must abandon a purely materialist understanding of nature in general. Since minds are features of biological systems that have developed through evolution, the standard materialist version of evolutionary biology is fundamentally incomplete. The cosmological history that led to the origin of life cannot be a merely materialist history. An adequate conception of nature vis a vis the unification of all known physical interactions would have to explain the appearance in the universe of materially irreducible conscious minds, let alone persons. [28]

Naturalistic philosophy dominates science, though that has not always been the case. Those who are committed to it recognise that there are elements to our existence that are more than quantum level particles and forces. There is mind as well as matter, there is spirituality that seeks to connect with something bigger that is 'beyond' the rushing world of the everyday. There is a religious consciousness that has been a dynamic aspect to human culture for millennia. And there is value.

What is meant by that in this essay is not 'values' (plural) though these are no doubt derivative. By 'value' means the scale of importance and worth humans ascribe to every dimension of life. In particular, it denotes the value that people place upon themselves and each other. Most of us have a need that seemingly is inbuilt to be worthwhile people living worthwhile lives. In its absence, something happens and humans do not flourish. 'I-thou' interactions are essential.

Scientific materialism is a perfectly adequate philosophy for certain types of explanation. But it has no provenance in the things that really matter to our emotional life. It can count the number of tears but cannot tell us why we are crying. Science has little to say about the moral worth of human beings that should be accorded to people because they ARE worthy. It is not a question of moral practice only. Humans need to live in an environment which engenders high worth in all its forms. Without we wither; with it we thrive. Our sense of ourselves; our personhood seems to require it. We will lay this out and note the need for significance- all the more astonishing against the backcloth of cosmic insignificance in a universe of inconceivably vast proportion.

Much has been written about the limitations of naturalist philosophy to explain the spiritual nature of humanity. Our lens here though is from another perspective. It is how we can possibly reconcile the scientific materialism that offers explanations from within nature relating to our personhood.

Some explanation for this could lie in the notion of dualities; two different ways of seeing being true at the same time. Light has been understood in this way; both waves and particles are valid. Dualities sometimes make it hard to maintain a sense of what is real in the world, as there are radically different ways you can describe a single system. Maybe the realm of value, love and meaning is one that is such a duality and we just have to accept it.

As contemporary physicist Ed Witten has argued, when you have dualities, things that are easy to see in one description can be hard to see in the other description. If there is a radically different dual description of the real world the dual description might be one in which everyday life would be hard to describe. [29] He derived value from John Wheeler's view that the physical universe arises from information. [30] Wheeler had envisaged the universe as an eye looking at itself—referring to quantum mechanics when the observer is part of the quantum system. Observing a quantum system irreversibly changes it, creating a distinction between past and future. With the AdS/CFT duality [31]- a conjectured relation between quantum field theory and a higher-dimensional gravity proposed in 1997- it seems that a new spatial dimensions can pop up like a hologram from quantum information.

Witten is noted for theoretical explorations of superstring theory that could conceivably pass muster as a 'theory of everything' about what underpins material reality. Yet here he is being pessimistic that we can ever hope to comprehend consciousness and Mind itself.

"I think consciousness will remain a mystery. Yes, that's what I tend to believe. I tend to think that the workings of the conscious brain will be elucidated to a large extent. Biologists and perhaps physicists will understand much better how the brain works. But why something that we call consciousness goes with those workings, I think that will remain mysterious. I have a much easier time imagining how we understand the Big Bang than I have imagining how we can understand consciousness..." [32]

Chapter Two

The Conscious Observer and A Participant Cosmos

"One of the fundamental characteristics common to all living things is that of being objects endowed with a purpose or project. . .it must be recognised as essential to the very definition of living things". [33]

THE OBSERVER AND THE OBSERVED

Constructing a metaphysic about the nature of reality has to take into account the one making observation. This is not just the role of measurement where it seems we get involved but also subjective experience. A totalising worldview has to include both what is observed and the observer.

According to the laws of fundamental physics that purportedly govern the external world, we are only a collection of particles—'a bag of stuff'. Fully shaped by laws of physics acting out on body and brain, decisions and emotions are just the motion of particles. Our essence, our spirit, our lives and loves, are due to interaction of completely neutral particles and physical forces. Consciousness, freedom and meaning are all products of chemicals. The brain is a natural object that follows the laws of physics. There is no freewill; only predictable outcomes. We could look at ourselves and say that laws of physics operate in this way. But who can live in this way? How is there any basis for saying black lives matter—or any lives come to that?

When mental activity is examined through the philosophy and methods of a naturalistic worldview, neuroscience points to such views as mind-brain identity or central-state materialism. The dual attribute theory speculates that some brain processes have inner mental attributes. These theories of the mind-brain relationship fail to give a satisfactory account of what consciousness actually is. Explanations such as seeing consciousness in terms of a non-physical reality such as epiphenomena (akin to a shadow) fail to show how it could be created by electro-chemical processes. Mystery remains. Are there more complete accounts of reality that can take us further?

A huge challenge has been to explain how the brain produces consciousness. Despite huge attention to it, bringing consciousness into the prospectus of scientific explanation has far proved elusive. Much of this discussion hinges on what one thinks of thinking; of consciousness. [34]We are not just conscious in the sense of the feeling of being inside our head, looking out. We dare to claim a sense of value, of significance. The 'mind-body problem' has been probed for centuries since Descartes and before. René Descartes identified the dilemma that would tie scholars in knots for years to come. As his 'Meditations' demonstrate, Descartes did not think that all he could believe in for definite was his own existence. Yet the mind, he concluded, must be made of some special, immaterial stuff that didn't abide by the laws of nature. Yet many scientists who study consciousness and the brain argue that consciousness is purely the result of illusory physical processes. That would apply to a concept of valuable personhood; perhaps the epitome of self-consciousness. Psychotherapy relies on subjective self-report by patients but properly understood, this constitutes useful evidence.

For Descartes, reality is made up of two different kind of things. Matter is what fills time and space: it is geometric and does not include colours or qualities such as the blue of the sky (what we might term 'qualia'). Mind, or soul, is characterised by thought.

A major question here is that of freedom vs the determinism derived from materialism. The concept of free-will is not uncontested. Connecting it to moral responsibility allows us to go beyond these old debates. Free-will makes it permissible to hold someone morally responsible for their actions. Whether someone is morally justified in a course of action is a question of what we 'ought to do'; not just whether we will do something because we have been so programmed.

The perennial debate about the relationship between mind and matter has re-focussed in our time with the new understanding of the brain through neuroscience. Physics yields very precise understandings of matter, such as can be incorporated from a materialistic view of the universe. Yet there is much that lies outside its scope. David Chalmers labels the first aspect 'easy' but the second 'hard'. [35]It is one thing to explore how cognitive processes work (the 'easy' part); quite another to explain why we have conscious experience in the first place. This became a disputed approach if you are a scientific naturalist (which Chalmers remained) but there does seem to be distinction between qualia (the subjective feeling of 'aboutness' and physical descriptions of cognition). Either consciousness is immaterial or it is a product of our brain. But how does mind make bodies move through mental -physical interaction?

Consciousness is not the same as thinking but how we can come to have a conscious experience of a subjective inner life is fraught with freight of intellectual difficulty. Arise it will because of the very entities asking the question. This needs to be pressed further. Much interest has been shown in non-local consciousness; our ability to know things beyond that which is derived from our physical senses What must be probed is not just consciousness per se but the enduring belief that we count, that we are valuable which is so vital for our psychological flourishing. Is this illusory too? Surely, human entities could be the functional equivalent of self-driving cars or indeed any AI-driven automaton.

It may be beyond our capability to answer but it does feel as if there is a difference. The quest to understand how anything could be conscious is hard enough and has eluded enquiry thus far, despite best efforts. Why should these little grey cells, though marvellously organised actually 'feel' like anything? The doctrine of materialism or physicalism, asserting that only physical entities exist, have so far failed to come up with an understanding of the relationship between mind and brain. But the consciousness problem is not the only challenge in this field. A question that must be posed is how the human mind can arrive at a sense of significance and of the valuable self. A different type of systematic account of nature would be called for that take fully into account, not only consciousness but awareness of valuable personhood corresponding to sighs of significance that stalks human life.

Consciousness studies used to be more of a philosophical pursuit than a serious scientific one. The domain of subjective experience was considered to be too subjective rather than the proper content of objective empirical study using the scientific method. The field has matured into that of neuroscience. [36]

Psychology has studied questions like how the brain processes information, how different sensory inputs are integrated, how memories are formed, and how we can focus our attention. They are "easy" relative to the hard problem in that they are more scientifically tractable. The central issue in seeking to explain consciousness is what is labelled the "hard problem" of consciousness—the problem of subjective experience: Why it *feels* like something to be conscious.1 The philosopher Thomas Nagel famously formulated it as an organism has conscious mental states if and only if there is something that it is like to *be* that organism—something that it is like *for* the organism." [37] Famously this was expressed in terms of 'what it's like to be a bat?

This is the explanatory gap.

Initially research sought to identify the "neural correlates of consciousness" (NCCs) - the vital neural events needed to produce conscious states. Attention is more focussed on developing theories of consciousness (ToCs). The contrast is between an NCC approach that looks for *correlations* between brain activity and consciousness, and ToCs that seek *explanatory links* between neural mechanisms and consciousness.[38]

Seth and Bayne lay out four prominent theoretical approaches to consciousness. [39]

1. Higher-order theories (HOTs): Thoughts become conscious when basic perceptions ("lower-order" representations) become re-represented as higher-order representations at higher levels of the brain, specifically in the prefrontal cortex.

2. Global workspace theories (GWTs): Perceptions, thoughts and emotions become conscious as if the mind were a theatre and conscious thought is the activity in the spotlight on the stage at a given moment.

3. Integrated information theory (IIT): How parts of a brain interact to create a unified experience. Consciousness relates to how much information is integrated among the different parts of the brain. The more information that is connected and integrated, the more conscious the system is thought to be. By implication, not just brains but any complex system with the right level of interconnectedness and integration of information could exhibit consciousness. The *quality* of conscious experience suggests that it is the unique pattern of relationships between the elements of the system is what defines a particular conscious experience.

4. Re-entry and predictive processing theories: Conscious mental states are associated with top-down signalling- the process by which higher-level brain regions send information, expectations, or context to lower-level brain regions. This interaction shapes how the brain perceives and interprets bottom-up information received via its sense organs from the world around it.

Besides the above four categories of theories, Seth and Bayne also acknowledge other well-developed approaches to consciousness—ones that involve attention; learning, and affect:

- *Attention schema theory* (AST):
- *Unlimited associative learning* (UAL
- *Affect-based theories* such as Damasio's "self comes to mind" theory. Consciousness depends on interactions between homeostatic routines and multilevel interoceptive maps, with affect and feeling at the core. Some affect-based theories consider cortical mechanisms to be unnecessary for consciousness. Mechanisms of consciousness lie in the brainstem. [40]

How matter turns into mind has occupied the attention of many thinkers. [41] Possessing simple life is one thing but the mental operations of more advanced life forms endowed with conscious minds is quite another. The step up in information is immense. How the gap between mind and matter could be bridged and physical things generate desire and private dramas, let alone any sense of significance, can seem a total mystery. Although in theory, we could just be amazing robots capable of responding to stimuli and challenges but inside there is no one at home, we *know* differently. We are betrayed by secret knowledge. How the brain gives rise to *being* that lump of pink matter and looking out with a body remains a total mystery.

Questions like these, which straddle the border between science and philosophy, remain perplexing.

In response to the real difficulties in understanding consciousness scientifically, Daniel Dennett argues that consciousness, as we think of it, is an illusion: nothing exists in addition to the pink stuff of the brain, and that it does not actually give rise to something called consciousness. Common sense may tell us there is a subjective world of inner experience—but intuition once told us that the sun orbits the Earth, and that the world was flat. There is no problem in trying to explain how the brain produces the inner subjective world where we live. Consciousness is also a conjuring trick.[42]

This is not the same point, be it said, as arguing that consciousness is generated by the brain. In a materialist philosophy such as held by Daniel Dennett, feelings and perceptions ARE brain states. Our experiences of qualitative phenomena and of our own first-person perspective are purely what is going on the brain; they are not produced by the brain. For many observers and researchers, consciousness of feelings and qualitative aspects of things are very hard to explain through objective language of physical sciences. Consciousness must be a false illusion. That consciousness could be an illusion has been argued for many decades.[43]

This is where emergence theory has gained a considerable amount of traction in the natural sciences but also the philosophy of mind. Consciousness and indeed human identity and capacities are, it is proposed, emergent from the complexity of the natural world. *"Consciousness emerges as an incessant creation of something from nothing, a process continually transcending itself. To be human is to know what it feels like to be evolution happening".* [44]

The philosophical genesis can be traced back at least to John Stuart Mill's discussion of table salt from two toxic substances. [45]'A new qualitative class of phenomena' emerges which 'cannot be reduced to the sum of their difference'. As emergence theory progressed, it was proposed that reality is layered into hierarchical divisions. There are qualitative differences between lower-level substrates and higher layers. At higher levels, there is an increase in the complexity of physical systems from which new properties emerge. A strong version of emergence has the idea of downward causation such that the higher order exerts an influence over its parts. Seemingly, this could provide an analogy for the relationship between ultimate reality (even God) and the cosmos. *"Emergence is the theory that cosmic evolution repeatedly includes unpredictable, irreducible, and novel appearances."*

It is an approach that does not suppose divine intervention or anything external. This seems to offer an account of humanity that is congruous with evolution and the inherent gradualism implied. Many theologians and philosophers of Mind have embraced the idea and expressed an articulation of God in these terms. Nevertheless, it still leaves the immaterial realm of mind and human consciousness as dependent on the material realm. [46] Attempts to give a coherent account of this have been problematic and seem to be an expansive way of describing reality rather than falsifiable theory. There is no straightforward way of arguing that physical processes behave like mental processes. It is an assumption. A correlation of supervenience between mind and brain is purely phenomenological.

Much interest has been shown in recent years about the relentless advance of artificial intelligence and the possibility that we could be on the brink of sentient machines. Some in Silicon Valley think this has already been achieved. The seemingly insoluble barrier was, however, what sentience and indeed consciousness actually is. We know that certain electrochemical processes are involved but how they do this and why remains shrouded in mystery. How do they give rise to you, or to me? Bennet argues for five major breakthroughs in evolutionary development that led to human intelligence—[47]the ability of an organism to steer '(bilateral symmetry'), the ability to learn through experience and over time, the ability to model the world and imagine it to be different to what it is, the ability to mentalise and put ourselves in the place of others and crucially, the language capability. But he does not claim to have solved the 'hard problem' of what has given rise to the first person perspective. Despite the billions of dollars and computer power in Silicon Valley, this still eludes us.

Human consciousness remains a mystery though neuroscientists can detect how it is manifested in the brain. Clearly AI systems lack a brain so traditional methods of measuring brain activity for signs of life are not relevant. That has not prevented neuroscientists having theories about what consciousness in AI systems might look like, whether it is a feature of the software or more to physical hardware. Tests have been suggested for AI consciousness such as asking questions it should only be able to answer if it is itself conscious. Can it grasp the concept of dreaming—or even report dreaming itself? Can it conceive of reincarnation or an afterlife? Creating consciousness in artificial intelligence systems is an ambition but it remains highly contested. [48]

It used to be held though that scientific thought was free of faith or commitments and that we can determine objective reality free of the interference of observers and their consciousness. To say that results depend on the standpoint of the observer might be regular talk in the human sciences but for physical science, it has been a base-line assumption that a given theory must be true and valid for anybody, irrespective of their perspective. Any admission of subjective properties dependent on the observer—the blueness of sky and greenness of grass—means we have ceased to describe reality from the objective terminology of quantitative methodology informed by mathematics.

If there were no conscious beings observing it, the workings of the universe would still continue as before. As Einstein famously remarked, the Moon is still there regardless of whether we see it.

A description about the fundamental nature of reality does, however, require more than the empirical methodology of science. A particular challenge is to do with the interpreter, the observer. It should not matter who or what is observing something or whether there is anyone to see or hear the sound of one hand clapping. A thunderstorm in the desert still happens surely even if it is far from civilisation. The laws of nature generating it cannot be waiting for humans to show up. Publicly validated knowledge rests on the assertion that anyone can go out to measure a particular phenomenon or test a given theory. There does exist an objective reality that can be grasped.

The Copenhagen interpretation demonstrates Heisenberg's uncertainty principle. We cannot know both the speed and position of an electron; thereby putting boundaries on what we can know. Objects that can be measured lie waiting, with their potential, amidst uncertainty. Objects that do the measuring are usually classical devices that ought to yield clear results. This creates a tension as to make a measurement of the quantum world, an unambiguous tool of measurement is needed.

If we are a dedicated philosophical realist, we will be convinced that objects and objective reality are integrally linked. By that is usually meant that all experimental results refer to an underlying reality that is unchanging, despite what is measured. A 'weak' version of objectivity is that all observers can agree on the rules on what will happen when a given experimental step is taken. A stronger version would go further and declare that agreement on the outcomes is identical to something that exists outside of us. The consistently agreed results represent a reality independent of us.

Yet the observer effect is fundamental to quantum physics. It is the very act of measuring the location and speed of a particle so as to determine its position that fixes the frame. Probing whether entities are really particles or waves is not the right question to ask it seems. An implication of this well-verified effect is that we are creating the very thing we wish to observe. An observer always gets answers appropriate to the question that is asked. The thing observed cannot be separated from the observer: they are part of the same system. To put it simply, what you get is what you measure. No phenomena is real until it is measured and observed. An electron, previously in an uncertain state, once measured becomes fixed in an 'up' or 'down' position when measurement has occurred. Uncertain indeterminacy is transformed into classical 'hard' knowledge but or when this occurs cannot be determined. The famous paradox proposed by Einstein in 1935 together with Podolsky and Rosen (EPR) sought to show that Heisenberg's Uncertainty Principle could not be upheld. Physical reality was maintained.

Famously, as Schrodinger theorised, it is not possible to describe a cat in a lethal and sealed box without quantum states that show whether it is alive or dead. The only way to tell is to open the box and make an observation. The wave function collapses into a live or dead cat. Observation determines existence. This requires consciousness as if consciousness interacts physically with entities; wave function is affected by brain function.

This has led on to speculation that the brain is a quantum system. There has been a shift going on about the fundamental nature of the mind. The mind-brain relation does not point to the mind being just physical. Something else may be going on. This effectively rules out the position that consciousness is an illusion or reduceable simply to brain states as Dennet argues. If observation itself has an effect then consciousness must, in itself, be a causal force and therefore exist. We could take the view that the existence of observable reality depends on my consciousness. The probing question is how then we are able to agree on the 'facts' around us such as colour and objects and the colour of objects.

Musser probes these questions from the perspective of a physicist interested in the potential role that quantum physics might play in consciousness. His contention is that solving the hard problem requires contributions from physics but thereby, many problems in physics will be answered. Musser is excited by Integrated Information Theory (ITT) charting how entities might be conscious in a single measure (Phi theory). Some digital circuits might satisfy such criteria. This is controversial. ITT theory predicts consciousness at higher-than-human levels where it would be puzzling to find it existing at all.[49] Yet Musser is surely right that to decode consciousness, it is necessary to put ourselves in the equation. It may be that there is a definite link between this and the mysteries of cosmic reality.

Maybe the very concept of a universe depends upon the presence of consciousness at some level. Did consciousness simply emerge as an effect of evolution? Or was it, in some sense, always "out there" in the world? Some have suggested that reality is permeated with mentality, right down to the most fundamental level. Could this explain why we matter? It can be argued that this is a postulate in inter-personal life and in social exchange. If so, this is completely misaligned with a strict materialist view of the cosmos where we are a product of blind chance configurations, delivered randomly by the pressures of natural selection.

It might be that because complex systems emerge in nature, consciousness emerges much as complex sand patterns form when there is enough quantity for it to be acted on by wind and wave. However, the properties of a higher system are emergent; that this, they derive from lower-level aspects of the system. With consciousness, what can allow us to deduce the qualities of subjective experience from any properties of lower order existence?

A star does not know it is there. Primitive forms of perception have arisen in sentient beings but how do we reckon with the lack of a consciousness that can affix coordinates of time and space for a star? As humans, we transcend a blind, merely existing form of being. We project on to the external world what we are- our own spirit, soul and consciousness. Yet our own internal sense of ourselves means that we infuse nature with spirit and soul yet it turns back on itself. Our knowledge of ourselves is self-referential if there is no ultimate, overarching consciousness.

The literature about consciousness and why it continues to elude us is truly vast. It is not the purpose of this book to add to it or probe possible solutions. What will concern us is the question of validation. Social validation is crucial to our life in society. Most humans seem to need the validation of a group. Endorsement by those around us is also crucial to interpersonal life. Humans seem to thrive on validation by others. These are acts of recognition without which we cannot derive value. Who is the 'I'? who can look out upon the world and claim first person significance? A psychological necessity to be of worth purely reflects movements of subatomic particles—or does it? Why those configurations should be accompanied by inner experience is deeply problematic. This problem is usually posed as one of consciousness and the question of how that is generated by brain wiring.

A RESPONSE FROM NEUROSCIENCE

Our sense of the mind separate from the body might be illusory. Our sense of value could arise from early experience and be entirely explained by emotional history. It is what the human organism does to survive as intelligent mammals in a meaningless world.

Brain science has underlined a recurrent debate in Western psychology and philosophy about how mind and body can possibly relate. In the Greek philosophy of Plato, mind and body were considered to be made of two different entities. Mind or soul was an immaterial substance; body was material and physical in which the soul was imprisoned. The soul existed in the world of pure forms and outlived the body. Augustine continued this approach, arguing for an immortal soul that is the real essence of someone and which survives the body. Twelves hundred years later, Rene Descartes made a string distinction between mind and body, which was like a machine and explained by the law of nature. The soul was the ghost in that machine: it made humans different from animals.

Descartes regarded mind and body as separate realms. The body pertains to matter and substances that have physical form and therefore spatial and open to direct investigation. Mental events were relegated to the realm of the intangible and spiritual. Such mind-body dualism was the foundation of Enlightenment thought. The big gap and mystery lay in how body and consciousness can be linked such that thoughts as this is read can generate physical activity. If such dualism is valid, questions and practice that focus on the body are in a different realm to counselling that emphasise the mind.

Under the spotlight of neuroscience, the same area of the brain is active with visual perception as when we 'see' an object in imagination.[50] There are similar close connections between activity in a brain and mental operations such as memory, decision making and even judgments like forgiveness.

The pioneers of psychology and indeed psychotherapy were working in the dark regarding how the brain is organised. They were aware of neurological disorders and some, including Freud, were specialists in this area. Psychology is essentially the physiology of the brain. However, brain science as obtainable through scans were yet to be invented. The technology was not there.

Much has changed. We now have the means of showing neural imaging networks in the brain. We can see far more clearly the mind-brain patterns of functioning as a whole unit. Cognitive neuroscience has allowed utilisation of neuroimaging techniques, such as Positron Emission Tomography (PET) and functional Magnetic Resonance Imaging (fMRI). These are tools in order to investigate structures and functions of the brain both physiologically but also pathologically when disturbances and dysfunction become apparent. When developmental processes have not proceeded in a healthy way, these show up in brain scans. Neuroscience has much to say about the structural organization of a brain; how it functions over a course of early and lifelong development. It throws much light on social interactions that sculpts individuals' becoming who they are.

It is clearer what happens when different activities are undertaken and which areas of the brain light up as it were. It is also clear what is the brain response to stress and the neurophysiology of trauma. With these powerful tools, the new landscape has acquired a new vocabulary. We speak now of neural pathways—the routes in the brain through different aspects of experience are activated. Visual experience involves paths in the brain which are well-trodden. By sending electrical signals from nerve cell to nerve cell in a vast network of connections, the brain creates thoughts as mundane as 'what is for lunch?' Or 'who am I?', 'Does God exist?'. We speak of neural transmitters—the chemicals involved in synaptic transmission. Some are well known and have entered the popular imagination such as acetylcholine, dopamine, endorphin and serotonin. Neural transmitters are vital in shaping subjective experience and mood as well as brain functions. And then there is neural plasticity—how nerve cells and brain tissue recovers from trauma or injury. Children can do this as damaged brain cells can recover through remaining brain tissue taking over. Adults can also do this but motivation and effort involved with repair and re-direction of neural pathways is high. Embedded too in the popular mind is the language of the firing of synapses that connect brain neurons to neurons in the rest of the body. Inspired by the work of Donald Hebb (1949) and Pavlov's "associative learning rule", it emerged that as connections between two neurons fire together, sending off impulses—the synapses—grow stronger. Learning takes place.

What neuroscience has revealed is that it is the connections between the numbingly numerous cells that make the brain so amazing. The infant is an interactive entity replete with connected systems that communicate with each other through chemical and electrical messages. The growth of the brain represents a seething, dynamic system of responding to environment and whether the parents are responsive to the needs of the baby. Clinical psychology and clinical neuropsychology confirm this picture. To those who have worked with early relational right brain attachment trauma such as Allan Schore, the deeper realms of human emotion and motivation operate at the unconscious level.

These deep-seated influences were thought to be processed in the right and not the left brain. Schore argued for the centrality of the right side of the brain in development not only of the self but in how loving relationships but also psychopathology could arise. Neuroscience has much to say about the structural organization of the brain and how it functions over the course of early and lifelong development. It has uncovered the intricate and vast social interactions that sculpts an individual to become who they are. What it has not done is confirm the idea of two different hemispheres operating on very different terms. This idea of brain structure has been debunked. Left-brained people are thought to be logical and good with math and language, while right-brained people are thought to be more creative and artistic. [51]The areas of the brain work together in complex ways, and we are not, generally, left- or right-brain dominated. The left-brain/right-brain idea is considered a "neuromyth." "It's absolutely true that some brain functions occur in one or the other side of the brain," Anderson says. "*Language* tends to be on the left, attention more on the right. But people don't tend to have a stronger left- or right-sided brain network."[52]

Considerable progress has been made over the past 20 years in relating specific circuits of the brain to emotional functions. Joseph LeDoux, pioneered the study of emotions as biological phenomena, using rats to trace routes of fear. Psychologists and writers have described the churn of rage, lust, envy and shame in the human psyche. Understanding the origin and architecture of human emotions in the brain is another matter altogether though. There is evidence of a neuronal pathway that connects perception with a fear response that bypasses conscious cognitive processes. Seeing something or someone that reminds someone of a past incident triggers a response below the level of consciousness. Studies of fear conditioning show that the amygdala plays a critical role in linking external stimuli to defence responses. [53] Emotion and cognition are separate but interacting mental functions mediated by separate but interacting brain systems. This pathway does not allow for cortical processing and may be responsible for emotional responses that pass understanding.[54]

Neuroscience has also demonstrated that our earliest experiences occur before major brain structures affecting memory are formed. We cannot call them to conscious mind but they still affect us. This parallels the idea of the unconscious.

So could complex neuro-activity such as knowledge of one's own value be attributed to brain science and neuro-impulses? A more nuanced approach is almost certainly needed when it comes to such impulses as hope, worthiness and spirituality. What areas of the brain light up when these human strivings are activated? Maybe we must wait until the deeper puzzle of what gives rise to consciousness is solved. That after all is the prize. The mystery of self-consciousness can follow.

There is a both a caution and a question here. It is to do with the relationship of biology and culture. [55] Can you reduce adult interaction to neurobiology; do mental events translate into images of the brain? Brain circuitry cannot be understood surely without reference to one's environment and the forces that shape our lives. Just because nothing happens without a brain does not mean our psychology is fixed by early events. [56] The dynamic flux of connection with our world shapes us and our self-esteem. We are an island chain, not separate from other islands. A sense of value must be successfully internalised for it to grow within personal life. This is vital for social connection and indeed provides its template.

The emerging field of interpersonal neurobiology (IPNB) suggests complex interrelationship between the mind, the body, the brain (including genetics), the environment, and especially the role of close relationships. [57]

IPNB strongly emphasizes the role of attachment relationships across the whole spectrum of caregiving—ranging from parent-child to teacher-student to professional-therapeutic—in shaping both the brain and the mind.[58] Recent findings in neuroplasticity, memory, and brain differentiation have helped shape an integrative paradigm for psychotherapy. Psychotherapy is thus becoming understood not simply as a transfer of factual information but as interpersonal learning that occurs implicitly and explicitly. *"Theories of psychotherapy must take seriously the role of the therapist as an image-bearer of God who provides clients with opportunities to learn new ways of understanding their behaviour and relating to themselves, others, and God."* [59]

The challenge to theory is how a sense of value can be recruited in situations where attachment styles were considerably in deficit. How does any notion of worth arise when all is against having any legacy of being worthwhile? Client work shows that there is something that can be mobilised which lies latent. It might be a relationship of mutuality; affirmation from a youth club leader, pastoral role model or close colleague. There are no guarantees yet pathways can be developed from positive experiences that go someway to repair what was either lost or never put in place in the first place.

Since the brain is highly complex—with the human brain having 100 billion neurons and each neuron having some 10,000 synaptic connections—it is hardly surprising that the relationship between mind and brain is complex. In a materialist science, matter is everything: the riddle of consciousness is solvable because Mind is a spasm of the brain. However, mind really does matter![60]

What we do here is somewhat different to exploring consciousness. It is to explore how notions of a valuable self might conceivably interact with the fabric of material reality. These are not the same thing. One can be conscious on an instinctual level. There are different levels of conscious awareness that enable living things to react with their environment. To think oneself as being worthwhile and significant depends surely on a level of consciousness that is self-reflective; able, not just to react but to draw a conclusion that one is valuable and ought not to be trashed. (Not that it will stop the mistreatment). This is not just a question of conscious awareness but the 'I' that can look upon itself and dare to claim significance or ponder meaning. Our lives and loves belie any sense that we do not count. Surely, on an existential level we feel it to be otherwise. If the total description of reality is about the swirl of particles- and the first person is only a complex formulation of that -where can there be any basis for these brief human years of ours constituting lives that actually matter?

Kant's philosophical revolution was not that objective reality contains structures that are grasped by the mind so much as the human subject provides the structural categories we use by which objects that appear in consciousness are categorised. Relations are forms through which the human subject grasps reciprocity. Does consciousness only perceive reality though, or does reality depend upon it?

The subject-object dichotomy no longer seems to be a necessary aspect of science. The underlying assumption was a desire to reconstruct the methods of the natural sciences into formally logical, ahistorical procedures of 'pure objectivity or 'pure reason' cut off from any trace of subjectivity. We have traditionally accepted this dichotomy and insisted our science be 'objective.' Science requires is that the predictions be testable, not necessarily objective. Quantum mechanics shows that the separation of objectivity from subjectivity is not meaningful; this is shown clearly in observer-dependent phenomena. In order to understand the behaviour of an electron, one has to use two contradictory pictures: the wave picture and the particle picture. This is complementarity. The Copenhagen Model says that the collapse of the wave function occurs in measuring devices. Reality, according to this view, is created by the act of observation. As renowned physicist John Wheeler argued, the old word 'observer' simply has to be crossed off the books, and we must put in the new word participator. In this way we have come to realize that the universe is a participatory universe. [61] John Wheeler thought much about the observer and the observed in physics and the reality that the act of observation accords. *"Insofar as the active observation has anything to do with what we ascribe reality to. . .then we can say this observer who was brought into existence by the universe has, by his act of observation, a part in bringing that universe itself into being".* [62]

Wheeler was expressing the Copenhagen view of quantum reality in which the act of measurement played a decisive role. As Heisenberg had articulated it, *"everything observed is a selection from a plenitude of possibilities".* [63] Only what is finally observed is real.

The strange quantum world can described in terms of:

1. Superposition
2. Entanglement
3. Complementarity

What kind of reality underlay these phenomena? Is there an objective reality?

The participatory universe resulting from quantum mechanics, more than the mechanistic universe, has a greater chance of reconciliation with religion where knowledge is possible only by participation. The proponent of consciousness-created reality, John von Neumann, suggested that it is only the presence of consciousness that help to solve the "measurement problem." So, in effect, if there are no conscious beings around and only a detector, say a telescope, is operating, reality is still being created by the detector according to the Copenhagen interpretation. Von Neuman's interpretation is similar to the Copenhagen interpretation. But it goes beyond it in saying that everything is quantum mechanical, including ordinary objects. The major difference is that only an apparatus endowed with consciousness is privileged to create reality, not any measuring device.

Are the operations of our minds informed by quantum mechanics? Some writers argue for this. "*Consciousness is relevant to solving. . . ..the quantum factorisation problem.*" [64] As Oxford philosopher Michael Lockwood suggested regarding reality, "*I see the preference for a particular basis as being rooted in the nature of consciousness, rather than in the nature of the physical world in general*". [65]

There are physical correlates of consciousness, namely neurons in the brain. Inside the mind of someone walking through woods, their consciousness is interacting with the outside world. [66] The challenge is that if space-time is absent in a description of the cosmos at quantum level, if our sense of self and personhood relies on these as fundamental preconditions, why do they exist at all? "*Temporal flow has no place within the physicist's worldview, so we must consign it to the mind*". Yet, "*it seems to be of the very essence of consciousness and, as such, as inescapable a feature of our being as is consciousness itself*". [67]

Why do the same laws of physics govern all parts of the universe, usually deemed to be due to everything in the universe is compromised of the same set of particles. Given that quantum physics regards these particles as excitations of a quantum field throughout the universe, the implication is that there is a single quantum field underlying everything. Entities are entangled once they have been in contact with each other.

An intriguing suggestion is that it is our consciousness that determines how the quantum field translates into classical physics. At a quantum level, it is maybe the self that is resolving the old philosophical conundrum posed by the German philosopher Gottfried Wilhelm Leibniz (1646–1716) in the early 18th century. He argued for psychophysical parallelism; a version of dualism in which mental and physical processes are perfectly correlated but not causally connected, akin to two clocks standing side by side. On this view, mental and bodily events are perfectly coordinated. [68]

The physicist, Fröhlich suggested the pumping of biochemical energy could sustain quantum states of many particles oscillating in phase, known as Bose-condensates, at high temperatures. Marshall argued that this could form the basis of quantum computing in the brain as the basis of mental states. The holistic state of the Bose condensates might be the basis of the unity of consciousness. No classical physical system could play the role. Among quantum systems a Bose-Einstein condensate has the right properties. The brain probably contains one and only one system of this kind. Fröhlich suggested that this the substrate of human consciousness. [69]

It may be that it is our consciousness that converts the weird and wonderful quantum world into the reality we see around us. But how can what is observed maintain itself between observations? And is it one single consciousness that does that for each local observer? Something is relative to us, to our determinate quantum state, but there many millions of minds and loci of consciousness. *"What one should normally think of as the state of anything, at a given time, should really be thought of as merely its state relative to the given designated state of oneself; and this goes for the state of the universe as a whole."* [70] The brain could be a quantum system capable of interacting with quantum states. What happens when there are multiple observers, or are we part of a single consciousness?

I write much of this on-board ship. Water dripping from a bottle falls vertically downwards onto the floor of the ship's cabin, it does not fall towards the stern of the ship, which it would if it were to fall vertically towards the spot on the planet that the water was directly above when it started to fall. This was an important insight from Galileo. It showed that there was no absolute spatial frame of reference in the universe. Each observer had an individual frame of spatial reference. Theologians and philosophers alike could usefully move from the safe, known worldview of Newtonian physics and engage with the more problematic matter of quantum theory.[71]

Perhaps the mind is fundamental to assigning order and making sense out of chaos. It is possible that our experience is a construct arising from a physical process in neurons linked to consciousness that shapes how we think and feel. Hofstadter, in 'Godel, Escher, Bach' suggested that the emergence of self and the classical world we see everyday are inextricably linked in self-reinforcing feedback loops. Matter emerges from a local perspective in a universe that exists in a person's consciousness. If consciousness is produced by the brain made of matter this is a circular loop. [72]

Physicists such as Hugh Everett sought to explain how quantum mechanics and everyday experience might be related. His solution did not invoke the collapse of the wave function into a single outcome but rather to theorise that everything does in fact take place. All quantum possibilities are realised. The observer splits into a multitude of observers. A multitude of possible states constantly arise in which every alternative state is realised (the 'many worlds' interpretation of Quantum theory.) [73]

The problem with the role of the conscious observer—irrespective of whether the observer can be self-regarding—is how are fellow observers able to agree on so much? If the disposition of entities depends on our consciousness, how come quantum indeterminacy disappears both for me when I observe the world but also for you when you observe it? The fuzzy world becomes solid and clear. It could be that anyone's consciousness makes something real for everyone with something observed. Yet what defines the self of observers, or indeed their location? Perhaps the reason why we experience reality in a concrete way is because our own eyes and ears are located in defined places. If it is our choice what we observe, how is it that all of us seem to agree about objective reality—such as cars coming towards us on a motorway.

This is where a cosmic Observer might conceivably come in. The tension between objective reality and our own private and localised response to things points towards a bigger view of reality. Solipsism is the belief that there is nothing outside one's own mind. Its debates throw light on one of the most central problems of psychology: the boundaries between the self and the world. Positing an ultimate Observer and Creator allows us to conceive of the overall template within which local observation takes place without distorting the whole field.

If the universe is one entity, why do we experience a multitude of different realities? [74]

Chapter Three

Being Seen
The Inter-Personal Gaze

"I was never seen, never heard, never noticed"
—woman referring to reason for her divorce aged 59.[75]

"It's not about drugs anymore; all anyone wants is respect —that's what it' about". —gang member [76]

From the act of observation in delineating physical reality we turn to the one doing the observing.

This is not just a question of the psychology of perception but the very real dialectic between acts of seeing and being seen: how the external gaze operates in symbiosis with the way we view ourselves. In human interaction as in physics, observation is also crucial. The social or interpersonal gaze is a vital part of our experience. It is a conduit, transmitting the value that is needed for psychological survival. Take that away and we die inside.

One major reason why people experience organisations as de-personalising places to encounter or to work in is because of the recurrent complaint of not being noticed or heard. To be ignored is distressing for humans. It drives anxiety because it plugs into the need to be handled as a valuable self. Not being heard is profoundly devaluing. In the political sphere, it sets up too many avoidable problems. In organisations, employees that are not consulted quickly feel a sense of existential angst precisely because of our reflex against indifference. To affirm we count, that we matter, is crucial for the human self to flourish. To encounter indifference seems to belie this. we become invisible.

Perhaps this is why so many people go in for conspicuous consumption in the West. "I acquire these symbols of material sophistication—you give me more respect.....I acquire status- you give me greater worth." It becomes a symbolic transaction around notions of worth and value. This transaction has its roots in the discontent that arises from the unbearable possibility of being greeted by a yawn. As William James wrote,

"No more fiendish punishment could be devised, were such a thing physically possible, than that one should be turned loose in society and remain absolutely unnoticed by all the members thereof. If no one turned around when we entered, answered when we spoke, or minded what we did, but if every person we met 'cut us dead', and acted as if we were non-existent things, a kind of rage and impotent despair would before long well up in us, from which the cruellest bodily torture would be a relief"- [77]

To be seen (noticed) and heard communicates that I am worth listening to.

Behind a prison manual on the risk of abuse, lurks the dread power of indifference. *"Being desired can seem like a tempting alternative to being ignored all your life. Intimacy itself can be very powerfully attractive if you feel isolated and lonely."* [78] And here are some offenders on an anger management course, trying to give expression through art of how they react against being worthless scum, the kind other people looked down on (or so they've been told). [79]

Such responses are often framed in terms of such social psychology theories as self-verification. [80] People want to be known and understood by others according to beliefs and feelings grounded in how the self is viewed by itself and through consequent self-esteem. It is because self-view plays a key role in making sense of life that people are motivated to maintain them through self-verification.

Issues of value are not just an aspiration; they are key narratives in human functioning. A pivotal point in which human value is either eroded or enhanced is through not being heard, seen or given voice. This is a strategy of persistent lack of sensory response by those without eyes or ears. To be heard rather than ignored; to be seen rather than disregarded are actions that generate strong positive feelings of personal value rather than a denial of our full humanity.

To be shown face or to offer face is a fundamental human need. Is this, for instance, why there has been a shift from a top-down model of international development to a bottom-up model? The issue of welfare dependency offers a parallel concern. Where there is an impersonal system without face that renders people passive, participants are robbed of agency and have no opportunity to do 'facework' and return the gaze.

Practitioners in any field will notice how the plea to be noticed, or not treated as rubbish occurs repeatedly. Here are some disgruntled staff and workers. Why are they disgruntled and fed up? Often their struggle is do with not being heard, treated with indifference or as not having lots to offer. Behind many problems that clients work through lie experiences of devaluation. Statements will often surface such as: "*I wanted a simple acknowledgement that I had been heard, that I was struggling with a feeling I wanted understood but what I got back all the time was something different so I felt all the time that my needs were not actually being heard.*" [81]

Someone leaving the Army with a fine military record will derive a far greater sense of value than someone who left with a dishonourable discharge. This is social esteem, social status yet it digs deep into whether those concerned will feel valuable and worthwhile in themselves. Reputation matters so profoundly to most people. It is threatened by indifference. A soldier leaving the British Army with a serious injury is incredibly frustrated with the lack of attention from either public or the State.

"*We're not getting listened to. It's not being noticed after all we've done, not getting the respect we deserve.*"[82]

Where personal and social worlds intertwine, people are crippled by a devalued self. They may find it an uphill struggle against those who have greater internal resources. Indeed, it is the accumulation of internal resources that marks out someone who has 'voice', the ability to respond to life positively as a person of worth. For many, the capacity to exercise the choice that seems so obvious to others is not there. Internal resources need building up first. Almost always, growth in confidence is related to growth in a sense of a valuable self. Crucial to this strategy is removing blindness so that social participants see with fresh gaze.

Often, teachers and professionals are heard, saying of children, *"it's all about attention-seeking!"* [83] Such a reaction ought not to attract disdain. This is what humans do. Those same professionals would complain strongly in their field if they are not being heard.

Such responses are often framed in terms of such social psychology theories as self-verification. [84] People want to be known and understood by others according to beliefs and feelings grounded in how the self is viewed by itself and through consequent self-esteem. It is because self-view plays a key role in making sense of life that people are motivated to maintain them through self-verification.

To be seen (noticed) and heard communicates that I am worth listening to. In Adam Philips' psychoanalytical study of excess, 'On Balance', he explains excess as a desperate search for limitations by a parental figure who will say, 'no'. Exaggeration is a strategy for gaining attention, to know that somewhere there is a restraining hand and someone to care for us.[85]

Attention is a crucial conduit of value- especially the loving gaze of a biological mother, a 'valuer', the face of one who is pleased to see you and calls you by name. This is a vital part of affirmation, which also has the elements of touch and play. These factors connect emotional circuits that are fundamental to the wiring of a healthy self. The capacity to assert a valuable self may depend on how much affirmation and attention has been paid. Such affirmation leads to the child and then the adult feeling that a secure place in the world is deserved. Supportive nurturing results in positive brain chemistry that continues into adult life. [86]

Disvalue and value are communicated by acts of gazing. How we treat someone results from how we see them. The unformed self is called into explosive being through parental gaze—whether smiling eyes that sustain secure attachment or indifferent eyes that disappoint a baby looking up. It is a century since Charles Cooley formulated the idea of a 'looking glass self'. [87] Neuroscience has since confirmed that we are made in the mirror. The new-born infant endeavours to re-gain eye-to-eye connection with its mother. It becomes expert in scanning facial expressions.[88] Language comes later- and with it the ability to name the world. A whole new branch of neuroscience grew, dedicated to exploring how people come to know the minds of others and their own minds. Elegant studies indicate that infants know something about other minds by making inferences from their own experiences and their experience of others.[89]

It had been proposed by Bowlby that vision is central to the formation of attachment bonding to the mother.[90] Mary Ainsworth suggested that this is internal and not just over behaviour. Imprinting takes place within the child's nervous system.[91] The infant's recognition of the maternal face is crucial for brain-to-brain interaction. The infant uses the output of the other party in the dyad as a template for the hard wiring of circuits in his or her own brain.[92] Biochemical events take place such as release of endorphins and dopamine that promote further neurobiological development.[93]

When the developing child starts to move about, vision is the prime means by which the mother is used as a beacon of orientation. With a secure base, the mother's face connects with the emotionally expressive face of the infant in visual affective communication.[94] Specific areas of the brain- almost certainly the pre-frontal cortex—undergo a considerable developmental change in the infant of around 10-12 months.[95] This is vital for attachment systems to form and is shaped by face-to-face transmissions. However, the secure attachment is the ideal and far from realised. The mother's face triggers high level of endogenous opiates in the child's growing brain. Attachment relationship is a means of regulating entwining the caregiver's mature nervous system and that of an immature infant.[96] It transfers one to the other. Mutual gaze is vital to wire the developing child.

What an amazing sleight of hand is conveyed through vision! The act of seeing magically transforms people and situations. Self-worth feeds self-identity- the way we perceive ourselves. An individual seeks to break free from the all-encompassing way he or she is seen.[97] A social group demands to be seen differently, to have a greater stake in the politics of attention. Perspective means a different way of seeing which counteracts the asymmetry of vision.

I wrote this in South India where homeless Dalits (untouchables) are regarded as being lesser individuals, not to be sited on the same street as Brahmin families, even in a poor village. A wall has been (literally) built so the Brahmin families do not have to look upon their underclass neighbours. Maybe the wall serves a dual function. Perhaps the Dalits feel they are being shielded from superior eyes. Devaluation is closely bound up with the gaze. Someone who does not think they are worthy of respect does so because they do not see themselves in that light. Value and worth are accorded through acts of vision. The gaze communicates either value or disvalue. The act of seeing transmits because it triggers. It reproduces what is perceived. The other rarely looks at the self from the perspective from which it sees.

The gaze triggers a reaction. Sartre insisted that a shared gaze generates a struggle over who is to be subject and who is to be object. "I felt I was repulsive" says someone, who complains of being treated with disrespect.[98] His sense of himself as shameful arises because he perceives himself in the eye of those who disrespect him. It was an act of seeing- or so they thought- that triggered a temporary self-loathing. The client now sees himself in a certain way and that act of vision is intrusive. It rapes, it molests, until the self is seen as worth-less or even worthless.

Meanwhile in the West, new neighbours are installed.[99] They are on benefits. They become aware of those that live next door. "What are you looking at?" is their belligerent assertion, provocative (or reactive) because no gaze was intended. It is rather in their perceived vision of superior eyes that they feel an affront. Their own gaze has misread, misperceived the vision of another, casting their own self-regard on to the perception of their neighbours who they see as 'looking down' on them. The internal gaze has somersaulted next door to attach itself to the face of the neighbour that in turn triggers a reaction. The gaze is devaluing because it is cyclical, interactive. It not only sees what is there, for better or worse it transforms what it sees. The human situation is one where the self is able to see itself. Projectors all, we take up a position outside of ourselves (or so we think) and look at ourselves. The problem is that such reflexivity (which is the essence of self-reflection) can reproduce false images. We see ourselves in the mirror. The capacity to be self-regarding is essential to the human condition yet sometimes, the gaze is too intense. A characteristic of some psychological conditions such as being bi-polar or paranoid is that sufferers are all too aware of the gaze to the point where eyes are everywhere, even to the point of being re-located in a split self. In a condition such as OCD, every action comes under the most intense scrutiny.

There can be too much seeing. Human communication in the contemporary landscape is dominated by the ubiquitous Smart phone. You are seen; your footprint leaves an unmistakeable digital mark. Companies can be fined for excessive scrutiny of activities of its workforce. A State can be all pervasive in its malign observation of its citizens. 'Big brother is watching you' as George Orwell adumbrated in 1984. A sufferer of Obsessive Compulsive Disorder (OCD) comes to realise that his intense scrutiny of the body is greatly exacerbated by a fear of how others will see him as a contaminated person. Fear of dirt is fear of scrutiny. A dearth of smiling eyes and regular criticism has generated panic about how he is seen. In turn, his self-regard has hijacked the vision of how he thinks others will perceive him. Distorted vision communicated by not feeling up to the mark has become a circular problem and a channel for transmission of disvaluing of self.[100]

This is the kind of raw human experience that has aroused considerable philosophical speculation. The desire for 'recognition,' has a long running in western philosophy at least as far back as Hegel's *'Philosophy of Mind'*[101] though Honneth sees an earlier account in Hegel's Jena lectures, *'The Phenomenology of Spirit'.*[102] For Hegel, desire for recognition is crucial. Desire denotes lack and hence the experiencing subject. The desire for recognition is different to other forms of desire. It is a desire to be desired, to be recognised and it is this recognition that elevates the subject into participating in history. We need acceptance by others as we work out our identity.

As Sartre described it, if there is a Me for whom the Other is an object, this is because there is an Other for whom the Me is an object. *"The Other cannot act on my being by means of his being, the only way of that he can reveal himself to me is by appearing as an object to my knowledge".* [103] Two self-consciousnesses collide. A master-slave relationship for instance is colonised by power. It is not just the underdog that is affected. The master *sees himself* as the oppressor.

Recognition leads to the bifurcation of the world. The French philosopher Jacques Derrida comments that the 'I' is never at home in the world, never at one with itself. The self includes the sense of a turning or swivelling mirror.[104] To locate oneself in the world requires the experience of a 'kind of vertigo of place', everything related to everything else (as in Derrida's 'distracted theory,' there is no saturation of context).

As Foucault saw, charting the forms of power in modern western societies, power is a fluid concept. It does not just arise from formal social relations but flows around them. Power does not just accrue to the ruling class. Often the river is reversed. A client reports feeling de-skilled by her partner, her independence now but a memory. [105] This may exemplify the social forces of gender construction shaping the dynamic between them or inter-personal dynamics per se (as if these could somehow be separated). Yet the point is that subversion of this mini-social order within the family (resulting in her having not felt she was worth very much) began with fresh perception of herself (based on prior recognition of worth). Foucault described the techniques of surveillance whereby the technology of power operates through visibility. In feudal society, to be powerful was to announce one's presence or publicly demonstrate the cost of deviance. [106]Today, everyone's life is scrutinised.

The demand for recognition assumes that our identity can be distorted through non-recognition in a way that becomes internalized. Black people or feminists adopt a self-depreciation that then serves as a potent instrument of their own oppression. Due recognition is a vital human need. As Charles Taylor observed, *"democracy has ushered in a politics of equal recognition,* which has taken various forms over the years, and has now returned in the form of demands for equal status of cultures and of genders." [107]The notion of recognition was developed by Hegel as intrinsic to core humanity. Following Hegel, Taylor proposed that *"the struggle for recognition can find only one satisfactory solution, a regime of reciprocal recognition among equals."* [108] Taylor's *'Politics of Recognition'* explored the kind of human communities that can be moulded from human diversity. What lies behind a politics of difference, he argued, was development of a modern notion of identity. [109] Receiving recognition from others is a vital human need. *"Our identity is partly shaped by recognition or its absence, often by the misrecognition of others."*

Following this kind of analysis, it has become more common to talk about a politics of recognition (focused on securing equal respect for hitherto marginalised groups) rather than a politics of re-distribution. One is about social esteem; the other is to do with material goods and income. But there are questions to be asked. Is it superficial to see asymmetrical social relationships as being about perceptions rather than power? The argument is not that humans have been deprived of resources so much as recognition and it is this that reproduces inequality and oppression. The self is able to throw off the weight of history and rise, unencumbered into profound empowerment and mastery of the future. Hannah Arendt observes, *"nobody is the author or producer of his own life story."* [110]

Patchen Markell argues in his discussion of the dangers of recognition that there is no such thing as dis-embodied action or identity. [111] We all come from somewhere; we are not a person in isolation but a person-shaped by significant others. The lure and promise of recognition is, he argues, illusory and even stifling. But this is to go too far, like saying that behind movements for reform and social change, it is not essential to change perceptions. A struggle for recognition may well be the prior shift that is needed in the minds of the powerful before laws are passed to affirm the powerless. It comes down to whether materialism is the crucial explanatory factor in the package of production, legal form and ideas? Materialism is not the only driving force; neither is the economic motive always prime. Ideas always come wrapped up in practices. But such practices are based on ideas. [112]

It is human devaluation that transmits the pernicious effects of social divisions. This is associated with social injustice rooted in practice and actions. The question is how these two aspects interact and which is prior. They are connected. *"I only get £40 per kilo for my shark fins because I am only a fisherman"*, complains a poor African coastal fisherman who is low down the human food chain[113]. The lack of recognition goes hand in hand with the lack of reward that keeps him in poverty. From a wider perspective, the incessant hunting of sharks just for their fins that will provide a delicacy for soup-drinking Chinese is a different question of justice since that is how they see the world.

In 'The Struggle for Recognition,' Honneth argued that there are three distinct kinds of recognition, which support three distinct stages in the development of individuals, each with quite different social and political implications. Critics have pointed to his failure to even consider the significance of the dominant relationship of modernity, the commodity relationship.[114] Together with Nancy Fraser, his subsequent work, *Recognition or Redistribution?* argued for the priority of ethical categories such as recognition over structural social-political categories such as class redistribution.[115] Honneth's later work 'Reification' reformulated this idea in terms of intersubjective relations of recognition and power. For Honneth, all forms of reification are due to intersubjectively- based pathologies and lack of recognition rather than the structural character of social systems such as class.[116] It may be doubted that the problem behind conflict and distress is not in fact ontological misrecognition but there is nevertheless an important topic to be investigated here.

The issue of whether such misrecognition is a major player or indeed comes first is a vexed concept. Is it putting things the wrong way round? Edward Said had shown that western constructions of the Orient as dangerous, exotic and exciting were not only passive descriptions of other places and other people, they were central to their imaginative production. From almost the reverse position, as a Muslim spokesman of Pakistani heritage observed, child abuse grooming scandals in the UK involved criminals who think white girls are worthless. Internet usage in such cases involved pornographic images of rape. Was there a crisis in masculinity involving respect for women. There was a mindset that completely disrespected the female. And examples of the historical gaze continue to surface. In May 2013, in quick succession there were four public and official acts in the UK designed to recognise groups in the Second World War. These were to do with Arctic convoys, Coastal Command, the Battle of the Atlantic and Bevin's Boys (those sent down the mines to produce coal for the war-time economy). Or to take another example, the North Korean State employs the 'songbun', a caste system in which families are discriminated against according to whether they are regarded as friendly, wavering or hostile.[117] In all these instances, lack of recognition seemed to be integral to and constituent of the experience.

There is invariably a prior mindset. The decision to use African slaves was not about profit. Colonists in America could not imagine using European labour in this way. Africans were different. It was acceptable to enslave them. Africans were not fully human but if human, clearly inferior to whites in mental and spiritual faculties.[118] Once slaves were de-humanised, treated as objects, not 'people like us', slave trade helped build racism that became deeply embedded in attitudes to black people later.

"*Please validate me, hear me*", cries a young lady constrained by mental illness. "*Say it's ok to feel like this.*"[119] It echoes the vital need to be heard. Unacknowledged distress is profoundly devaluing. It strikes a blow at the human subject, not just the words he or she is uttering or the angst with which those words are expressed. The need to be heard, to be seen—this is an Emporium of the senses.

Race was a composite concept, built from such an Emporium of the senses. How Africans sounded along with belief that their skin was rougher and their hair coarser and that they smelt different played important roles. But above all, it was visual appearance that was the most important marker of race, especially skin colour. [120]The status of sight became pre-dominant in communicating disvaluing. An African looked different.

But what is that is being recognised? Is it that we see our fellows as equal bearers of moral status, awarding recognition of someone as a person or 'purely' as a rational agent? This is a pressing concern. Throughout history, most humans have been cloaked in invisibility. From the perspective of those who dictate the terms of recognition, the social experience of women, black people, minorities, the disabled, colonial subjects and so on has been invisible—or only partially seen. As Raimond Gaita points out, "*it is only when one's humanity is fully visible will one be treated as someone who can intelligently press claims to equal access to goods and services.*"[121]

The problem of recognition of our value, what in philosophical terms is a question of anthropology, emerges too in discussions about shame. Shame is, Sartre argues, by nature recognition. I recognise that I am as the Other sees me. "*The human being is not only the being by which negatives are disclosed in the world; he is also the one who can take negative attitudes with respect to himself*".[122] The Other has not only revealed to me what I was, he has established in me a new modality of being which was not in me potentially before the appearance of the Other. I need the Other to realise fully all the structures of my being. Sartre considers the phenomenon of shame, a mode of consciousness

"*a shameful apprehension of something and this something is me. I am ashamed of what I am. Shame therefore realises an intimate relation of myself to myself. Through shame, I have just discovered an aspect of my being.*"[123]

The starting point of Jean-Paul Sartre's argument about the nature of Being is that there is a distinction between Beings-in-themselves (non-conscious things that have essences, existing independently of any observer) and Beings-for-themselves (conscious beings whose consciousness renders them different from other things in relation to themselves and to one another). Consciousness is separated from the world of things by a gap, a Nothingness. This enables us to negate propositions, to deny things and to describe things truly as well as falsely. In our consciousness of ourselves, we are thereby rendered conscious of ourselves as different from what is around us. "*The human being is not only the being by which negatives are disclosed in the world; he is also the one who can take negative attitudes with respect to himself*".[124] Sartre goes on to discuss some notion of value, the meaning we attach to things or experiences. "Now we can ascertain more exactly what is the being of the self: it is value. . .human reality is that by which value arrives in the world. But the meaning of being of value is that towards which a being surpasses its being: every value-oriented act is a wrenching away from its own being toward. . . ."[125]

Sartre's phenomenology of vision is not the last word on the subject. A shared gaze can establish shared humanity rather struggle and resistance, an ambiguity that confronts us in this essay. [126] Yet the sensorium of disvaluing is only one social arena where issues of value are generated. There is a curious quality in self-respect. It has the ability to somersault to the social gaze of others so they come to witness (celebrate or be threatened by) this move. The act of self-valuing commandeers the vision of the other. Diminishing, however, goes beyond the gaze of unseeing indifference we have just noted: it is about how the 'put-downs' of everyday life reduce and dwarf.

This is the problem posed by Other beings. As Hegel argues, If there is a Me for whom the Other is an object, this is because there is an Other for whom the Me is an object. "The Other cannot act on my being by means of his being, the only way of that he can reveal himself to me is by appearing as an object to my knowledge". [127]

Was it in the early modern world consciousness that people began to feel they were worthwhile? Maybe it is from Shakespeare that the conscious self began to inhabit itself more self-consciously. Navel-gazers since Descartes have peered deeply into themselves to discover the authentic self to which they must be true. Even so, self-reflection was not a new invention. "*Mirrors were discovered in order that man might know himself*" declared Seneca. In the ancient philosophical tradition, mirrors were essential so that the self seen by others could be improved upon. [128]

Locating a sense of value in the appearance 'stakes'- obsession with size 0- is a major focus in a society where people work on their bodies rather than their souls.[129] Medical technologies to improve appearance are now routine. Bodily insecurity rules.[130] Global marketing of such discontent results in restless personal renovation and self-improvement. Fascination with the celebrity super-class co-inhabits with alienation from attractive norms. Obliged to live in two worlds, the subject dwells in ideals far-out of reach. Distancing carves a place where people live out their fantasy.

This chapter is not just juxtaposing a materialist conception of consciousness with the versions of being human we wrestle with; it is pointing up the problem that such a conception has with regard to the value needed for psychological survival. By what possible means can that be accounted for in a universe where quarks and leptons have built systems that have built everything else? Purely physical processes are hard put to supply this theory of everything. An added layer of existence is surely needed that brings a dimension of value, love and meaning connecting with our personhood.

We are in an existential situation of profound dichotomy. On the one hand a purely physical description of the cosmos derived from fundamental building blocks of matter and energy. There is no room for spirit or metaphysics. It comes down to just physics. On the other hand, there is the cosmos of which we are most conscious, though theoretically a fantasy. This is a cosmos where we need a sense of worth to feel any kind of significance and achievement yet which is a mirage if natural processes are all there are. Our psychological survival requires something that is fundamentally empty. This is an existential contradiction without a corresponding subjectivity.

A fundamental human need seems to be the quest for endorsement, for affirmation. 'Is there anyone or anything out there for me?' Contemporary psychodynamic theorists introduce intersubjectivity into their approach, because they believed that the unconscious realm is vital but that relational therapy approaches were needed. The unconscious structure includes- the pre-reflective unconscious, the unvalidated unconscious, and the dynamic unconscious. The pre-reflective unconscious is where patterns and themes are created and organised and it is easily accessible, unlike Freud's preconscious understanding. It does not contain instinct drives or repressed emotions, but simply stores experiences. The dynamic unconscious works as a 'regulator of the affective experience', which means defending the affects of the unvalidated unconscious, protecting from past trauma and creating resistance patterns.[131]

Humans possess complex social networks that are activated as we observe and interact with those around us. [132]Mirror neurons link observation and action allowing us to learn from others by watching. In this way, attention to others undergirds the role of social processing. As Cozolino suggests, *"our mind reading is instantaneous and obligatory...in biblical terms, it is a reflexive habit of the social brain to attend to the mote in our brother's eye and not to the beam in our own"*.[133]

These issues come to the fore in the question of relational neurobiology. There has been much interest in this as it became clear that in deep psychotherapy, something else is going on beyond therapist and client. Research is on-going about what exactly is taking place in psychotherapy but it seems clear that another subject is facilitating something of depth in the tricky realms within.

The need to be of worth is of fundamental importance and a strong motivator in human dynamics. [134]This is not a fringe concern for the alignment of scientific materialism and personhood. It goes to the heart of the dilemma. How can we find the significance that we need in a universe where we are infinitely insignificant? Human beings seem to need something or someone that validates them, that says they are fundamentally ok. We thrive best even amidst much vaunted self-sufficiency if there is someone there for us. The alternative is existential loneliness.

Chapter Four

Valuable Personhood and The Innermost Gaze

"You can have everything in the world and still be the loneliest man. And that is the most bitter type of loneliness, success has brought me world idolisation and millions of pounds. But it's prevented me from having the one thing we all need: A loving, ongoing relationship."
—singer Freddy Mercury [135]

"That Man is the product of causes which had no prevision of the end that they were achieving; that his origin, his growth, his hopes and fears, his loves and his beliefs are but the outcome of accidental correlation of atoms—all these things, if not quite beyond dispute, are yet so nearly certain, that no philosophy that rejects them can hope to stand"—Bertrand Russell [136]

"Everyone is born ok...there is a profound difference between the intimate worth of our existence and any evaluation of our behaviour. Our being is unquestionable, our actions may not be.....Whatever we do, every life has its own unique value. Clients are helped to restore this belief in themselves as intrinsically worthwhile." [137]

Observing that the methods and justification of empirical science labour under built- in limitations, there would seem to be a contradiction between the materialist perspective and need for real meaning for psychological survival.

Analytical and reductionist approaches cannot offer the whole truth about human beings in the objective way that they claim. A scientific naturalist cannot adequately explain humanity: there are immense gaps of meaning. When "*we contemplate the unique transcendence of a being which, while part of nature, can understand and comprehend its own reality*", [138] there are significant gaps missing to do with value, love, purpose and meaning. It forces the question of whether there is something about human beings we should respect. A mechanistic view of reality suggests a thorough determinism based on initial conditions in whatever field of enquiry we consider.

Our quest is what may be termed, 'the approach from value'; rooted in the value and worth of human beings and the way that is under assault today. Consider the following:

i) The mental health of young people; in particular the prevalence of anxiety and depression due to intensified social comparison;

ii) The crazy politics we are experiencing with massive populist pushback against an elite global system that has seemed not to listen to people;

iii) Concern about the effects of Artificial Intelligence (AI) de-personalising human beings:

iv) The on-going struggle for equality to do with gender, ethnicity, disability, age etc.

v) Reactions to the way that human life is trashed;

vi) In personal life, the kick back against what happens when we are denigrated.

These are salient issues on the contemporary scene. The fundamental proposition is that humans are in some sense wired up to be a valuable self. This is not just becoming a person per se but becoming a valuable person. Indeed, we will argue that being of value is essential to our thriving.

Feelings of worthlessness often arise through traumatic experiences such as abuse and violence (whether directed towards them by others or themselves) which cathartic trauma treatment can help to reverse. The reaction people often exhibit towards experiencing social injustice betrays a sense of feeling relegated, made 2nd class, not standard issue. The latent capacity for Protest against these pressures marks out the strong reflex of

'I'm worth more than that.'. This is important for new social movements in our time. The moral outrage against genocide, famine or torture often leads to demand for humanitarian intervention and cries of "we're not putting up with this anymore." Protest against human rights abuse often echoes the sense that someone must not be stripped of their dignity. They are worth more than that. The reaction is of the inner world. What is it about us that we cry to be of high worth- either for ourselves or we cry for others? What is it that protests?

The notion that the human person has a special value and a dignity deserving of respect has been under sharp attack in the scientific revolution since the seventeenth century. According to much contemporary biological thought, humanity is no more an entity for reproducing genes than any other creature. We have no higher protected status than any other living thing: it's just that we have an inflated notion of self-importance. Rational, scientific investigation might seem to have stripped human life of purpose and significance. The notion that people are important is not part of materialist worldview.

The contours of valuable personhood can be noted and explored for they are food for humankind:

1. The sigh and cry for <u>significance</u>. Humans need to feel they have a purpose even though for so many, their sense of significance is heavily constrained by the subordinate social scripts handed out to them. Even though boxed in, humankind looks to be worthwhile. When people no longer feel there is a point to themselves, something happens and they wither; becoming a shell. In many social interactions, people feel diminished, belittled. Being in reduced circumstances is not just about income; emotional as well as financial constraints make people less than they are and something cries against it.

2. The sigh and cry for <u>dignity</u>. Indignities of all kind represent invasive handling that pierces the emotional skin and does harm. Indignity generates indignation. Indignity and rejection constitute the negation of personhood and a trashing of the value and worth that can be argued to be inherent.

3. The sigh and cry to be <u>listened to; to be seen, to be heard</u>. When this is not forthcoming, something happens and there is an erosion of worth. People do not feel valued if there is an absence of being regarded and recognised.

A key move to thinking about such things is to reconceive the pursuit of high value <u>from</u> being an aspiration <u>to</u> being a fundamental impulse in the dramas through which human beings play out their existence. There is a wide gap between regarding the search to be a valuable person as an ethical concern as if would be ideal and obviously beneficial if only people were treated this way AND between seeing this quest as a driving impetus in human affairs. Where it is present, people flourish. When absent, a sense of self is eroded and the human spirit withers somewhat. [139]

Pursuit of a high value that comes from endorsement can be described in a multitude of ways and across varied landscapes. The quest for such recognition can be labelled 'comfort, reassurance, approval', seeking agreement or just 'love'. Valuable personhood seems crucial to human existence.

The struggle to realise our value against the many factors in social life that erode it is fundamental. Rather than say the psychoanalytic saga of the Oedipus complex, it is this dialectic that lies at the heart of human functioning. Being poor relative to the standard of the day will create harm because it affects the sense of self that relies on high value in order to flourish. [140] People feel 'less than'.

We are compelled to live as if we are worth something. Where that is absent, experiences of devaluation set up a reaction, that at a profound level, we matter. Experiences of devaluation plays loudly in people's lives. A sense of a valuable self is formed in the face of someone who smiled when they saw you. But experiences of devaluation create an energy which fuels the Protest. Anger was often hot collective indignation; the capacity for outrage a test of the bonds of humanity!

In short, the interior landscape cannot be understood without some concept of the struggle to realise our sense of inner worth and what we will call 'a valuable self', fundamental to personhood.

The ream of value, love and meaning can best be approached negatively; through its deficit this is missing in people's experience. Ways in which a negation of value affects people, drawing from client experiences boil down to three types of experiences that erode a sense of value and worth:

i) *Indifference-* the need to be heard, to be taken seriously, to be recognised and given attention. *Attention must be paid- even to a salesman'-* Arthur Miller. [141] Being heard communicates that I am worth listening to. "*I am not an agenda!*"- "*I feel treated like dirt by the system*"—[142] Clients react negatively to not being seen or voice not heard.

ii) *Indignity- at the interplay of indignation* and dignity lies the assertion of a valuable self. 'I am worthwhile.' A narrative about the effects of constant rejection after being laid off from work shows this aspect: "*I can't describe it. It's just like, it is like, the end of the world. I'm not ready for retirement; there is still a lot of work in me. There's no one to blame.*

It's just gone. That's it. Thrown on the scrap heap at 53." [143] Clients react negatively to being rejected, set aside or being subject to invasive handling.

iii) *Inferiority* - the reflex against demeaning talk or being put down, that calls for appropriate respect for a valuable self and affirmation. *"When people say things I feel small. They make me feel I'm not worth very much"* - says a lady about the people at work [144] Clients react negatively to being belittled and made to feel two feet tall in social encounters. This humiliation can be construed as a form of inequality- made to feel less than, written down and diminished. Erosion of our value calls for response.

A fundamental 'engine' behind human functioning is the drive to be recognised, endorsed and validated. Our primary pursuit is to be a worthwhile person living a worthwhile life that matters because we matter. For that will deliver a life with meaning, significance and purpose. This is a primary motivation and not a secondary conceptualisation. The value and worth of people is more than a principle of moral action and duty, calling us to a description of 'this is how we 'ought' to live'. At heart of human functioning is a quest for an answering echo. It is a search for the validation of self, for recognition of high value, for re-assurance. 'Comfort us. Approve of us. Affirm us. Confirm our existence, endorse our personhood. Recognise us. Include us. We are valuable.'

Amidst the complexities of the interior world, the unconscious activities of the mind should include the desire to be valuable, to count and be of worth. Distorted neuroses may be a lot to do with blocked attempts to extract significance and value from our world. Repression may or may not be a disguised factor in pathways towards fulfilment but rejection is an experience that bites people to the core. Core challenges reveal the strength of unconscious influences in human action as the subject is often in the grip of forces that are past all understanding. Yet as a specific content domain in its own right, this core aspect of human identity has been insufficiently theorised as a key driver.

If the whole of our existence is grounded in impersonal principles, all this is meaningless. If though there is a creative and personal intelligence behind everything, our personhood resonates with this.

At least three propositions adumbrate how pursuing a high value for the psyche plays a key role in intra-personal and inter-personal processes.

1. Every biography is a complex mix of varied ways people pursue a high value for themselves against the many factors that devalue the human

Social valuing is hugely important to people. The pursuit of value as a motivation takes us from concern for honour, status and legacy to social esteem, reputation and tokens of recognition. This is a standard observation in social psychology, for example Tajfel's Social Identity Theory where self-esteem is in dynamic relationship to group identity.[145] Yet where does this emanate from? A case can be made that these are species of a drive for personal value that is a vital element in human flourishing. It comes from an internal need, sustained or eroded by group processes. Pursuit of a high value seems a key ingredient of biographies, varying through the life-course but arguably central to what it means to be human in both healthy personalities and pathologies. Psychoanalytic politics offers an example of how this motivation is competitive, a zero-sum game. In the Wednesday society early on, members sparred for position, descended into acrimony or vaunted their originality—yet such praxis did not impact theory. Individual biography can be charted against the drive to accrue social value which reacts with devaluing circumstances and inter-personal put-downs as well as systemic factors that distribute worth in capitalist society. Behind the ceaseless fight for tantalising recognition is the internal struggle to be valued by peers, by history and oneself.

2. The motivation to be of high value and worth is a key driver within the personality.

Client observation reinforces the notion that A sense of self is par for the course in social psychology but how do we classify the impetus towards recognition for a valuable self? The history of psychology is replete with projects to categorise mental structure. One thinks of Freud's endeavour to re-classify the drives into those aimed at self-preservation and those aimed at sexual satisfaction (subsequently elevating aggressiveness into a rival to libido [146]) or Maslow's hierarchy of needs. Self-actualising individuals, he argued, enjoy a reasonable feeling of worth and respect and do not for long have crippling feelings of inferiority or worthlessness. [147] Yet the driver to be of high value seems to be deeply embedded within the personality structure. There can be little doubt that highly prized people feeling that they are valuable human beings possess inner resources that weather the vicissitudes of life. Often, this seems to be as a direct legacy of the security of attachment systems from families of origin, patterned into the templates of adult life. Yet even where insecure attachments, depression or destructive relationships erode self-respect, the impetus to be of worth may be wistful and possibly instantiated into the brain. It is a sigh that can be recruited. Whether described with such language as respect, dignity, self-esteem or the impetus to count for something, people respond to the value placed upon them; either by society generally or through inter-personal interaction. This is not just external; it is an impetus fundamental to our psyche yet how to speak of this impetus is a matter of debate. Arguably, the motivation to be of high value can be construed as a need within fundamental psycho-dynamic forces, largely unconscious and reactive against de-humanising circumstances. This impetus is formed relationally and is sustained through interaction with significant others. It is a key psycho-social ingredient of human flourishing.

3. Experiences of devaluation can trigger a range of demoralising psycho-social effects

Much social and inter-personal life is formed at the collision between how external valuation is experienced and the inner dynamic of personal worth. This could help to explain a range of social experiences about the impact of inequality in society.[148] Responses to experiences of being disvalued are essentially fourfold:

i) *Demoralisation*—in which the ego is dented, often profoundly, because devaluing factors have gone deeper than the actions of the self <u>relative</u> to other selves. They strike at an <u>absolute</u> sense of a valuable self which lies at the core of human action. Some pathologies could perhaps be categorised in this way, e.g. eating disorders or depression. That the self feels that it has no worth need not be the end of the story but the neural pathways are at least formed that way for the time being. This is where different parts of the mind are in constant struggle as, except in cases where clients have lost the point of themselves altogether, a tendency towards low self- valuing is at odds with a wistful sense that one matters.

ii) *Resignation*—where there is unwitting collusion or acquiescence in the denigration, indignity and indifference that assails the valuable self. However, resigned eyes that accept relegation to lesser importance can re-focus. There is always potential towards re-imaging of the self towards assertion of its inner worth, being first class.

iii) *The Protest*—in which the self will not accept second class treatment and mobilises itself around empowerment which is critical towards re-gaining value. The cry of Protest is perhaps one of "I'm worth more than that!" There is that which can be mobilised into the Protest and it is often the task of therapy to re-discover value, mine sources of self-validation and restore self-respect.

iv) *Violence*- as people play out their dramas in the human life-world, we see all too clearly processes in which some want to be the most powerful person in the family, organisation or neighbourhood at the expense of others: they can only feel powerful if someone else is diminished. This is a dysfunctional aspect of needing to be of high worth but it also reflects the aphorism of Martin Luther King that violence is the language of the unheard.

Much social and personal life is shaped by the value society places on individuals and groups. Society thus conceived is a conflict between different forms of value. Economic, financial, social and personal value are in dynamic flux. [149]

"*I'm not here to be pushed around*" says a client, [150] experiencing being belittled but reacting against it. This reflex does not happen automatically in inter-personal life any more than it does in social or political life. People do not always and inevitably react with indignation against the erosion of their value. Clients often collude with the endemic devaluation, embark on self-destructive behaviour or have low self-esteem. even this belies an instinctual understanding that devaluation is unacceptable—we either rebel against it or collude with it and self-destruct, but both show an unwellness to accept it. There is that which can be mobilised, a capacity to respond to being valued which can be aroused into a heightened sense of consciousness.

Recent thinking is showing how the personality is interactive within itself. We are polyphonic. Our selves incorporate different voices in dialogue, voices that need to be heard in order for integration to be realised. This used to be characterised as someone44 having 'different sides' or a side that had not been seen before when they go off the rails. Person-centred therapy, for instance, has begun to use the idea of configurations of self, including the negative parts- '*the 'me' that just wants to curl up and do absolutely nothing', the 'part that wants to go back'; and 'the bit of me that wants to destroy this therapist'.*"[151] This is important for how a valuable self emerges.

She sat the opposite side of the consulting room, her sullen face enlivened periodically with flashes of hot indignation. "*I wish he could just tell me what he wanted*", she said in exasperation about the way her new partner had dumped her. "*He gives me the run-around*", she complained, puzzled about the 'missing- you' texts that belied the thrust of his conversation. "*I'm worth more than that*", she said. It became clear how the sense of a valuable self that had been growing in recent months was, as she put it, "*something to grab hold of.*" [152]

There was that lady who spoke of how devalued she heard in the court battle to obtain custody of her children and what it meant to her that someone finally believed her that her partner was cruel to the children and manipulating the authorities. She was no longer discredited. She had been heard. And with that hearing came a value. "*I'm worth more than that!*"- the strategy of the devalued, a Protest of hot indignation claiming dignity, those written down stating their worth. Within that sense of powering up, there lies an eruption of value. Or there was a client who came from a difficult background. "*Stop misbehaving*", was the daily news until his late teens. "*Don't do this!*" in a way that seemed to flatten him. He went on to become MD of a company. Against an indifferent world, he must have found self-belief from somewhere. [153]

"I had very controlling parents" reports one interviewee. "*Even when you're right, you're wrong!*" "*There were a lot of rough edges in our family*" reports another. "*The sarcasm could get quite nasty*"- [154] "*I was fifteen years married, treated like dirt on the floor. No more!*" says a woman with spirit that betokens a new sense of a valuable self. "*I didn't mean anything to him. I can see that now!*" [155] What is the connection between being treated 'like dirt on the floor' and a subsequent statement of worth-'*I'm not going to be treated like that!*'?

Here is the actress Kate Winslett. "*I've always been very, very aware of wanting to be understood as being the person that I really am*", she said, not wanting to be dismissed as an arrogant young actor which would be devaluing. [156]

The hypothesis is this. We have an in-built psycho-social need to be worthwhile people engaged in worthwhile projects and therefore active in garnering worth from our world. In contemporary life, value is accorded to individuals and groups in a way that is unrelated to inner value or 'value-in-oneself'. What someone is worth is awarded to social participants on the basis of the wage economy (economic value), identity badges (status value such as ownership or appearance) or identity boundaries (social value; being the right sort of person).

Necessarily, valuable personhood is self-aware. My dog is of value to me and has a strong value at species level. Is it, however, conscious of its own existential need to be valuable to itself?

Value and disvalue matter profoundly: this belief is important. Does the value we award to each other correspond to something 'out there' or true? "*The human intuition that our lives are meaningful should be allowed to be a true intuition*". [157]

Is there any description of reality that includes the sense of personal value that seems to be vital to our psychological experience? We count, we matter. Some degree of validation is a crucial component of what it means to flourish as a human being. This is not to say that everyone feels that to anything like the same degree. Patently, and sadly, many live lives that are cramped and confined. The agenda is set by others. To take three facets of the contemporary scene, there is huge sensibility around how far black lives matter, how far society respects the equal status of women and girls but also how far we value in practice all lives and strive to save them in a global pandemic. Consciousness-raising in these domains has been acute. A recent Equity Language Guide discourages, for example, using the term 'disabled' in favour of 'people living with disabilities'. 'People-first language' emphasises that 'everyone is first and foremost a person, not their disability or other identity'.[158] Advocacy here pursues a world without oppression and injustice.

Social and political life—at least in the West—would be unthinkable without these issues pressing in upon us in recent days. It may be that such concerns are modern, bearing no relationship to the swirl of particles and their interaction that contemporary physics attempts to describe. We will discuss the idea that the need for transcendental value is simply an evolution of/extension of the need for social value.

The struggle to realise our value against the many factors in social life that erode it is fundamental. Rather than say the psychoanalytic saga of the Oedipus complex, it is this dialectic that lies at the heart of human functioning. It forms identity within our social location. There are strong psycho-social assaults on dignity (one of the prime ingredients of value) that come from poverty and injustice.[159] Being on benefits or going to a foodbank can be stigmatising for some. Being poor relative to the standard of the day will create harm because it affects that sense of self that relies on high value in order to flourish.[160] We are less than: it underlines the mystery of human personhood.

It is integrally related to the spiritual sense reaching out to a transcendent that is greater than us. The origins of the religious sensibility are perplexing to historians. What is based on? Is the spiritual impulse hard-wired into our brain? Is the sense of something "more than meets the eye" a response to human smallness and weakness amidst cosmic insignificance and indifference? The sense of something beyond the material and empirical world of everyday experience has been all pervasive, even though it has been expressed in a range of belief systems, traditions of numinous beholding and diverse communities of belonging offering spiritual support to the faithful.[161] This book is about the challenge to our conception of the universe posed by the sense of value that is so fundamental to our lives and how mentality and self-reflective consciousness might be at the heart of things.

Mind the gap? The gap is not just between conceptual realities it is within human beings themselves. *"Countries like ours are full of people who have all the material comforts they desire, together even with such non-material blessings as a happy family, and yet lead lives of quiet, and at times noisy, desperation, understanding nothing but the fact that there is a hole inside them and that however much food and drink they pour into it, however many motorcars and television sets they stuff it with, however many well-balanced children and loyal friends they parade around the edges of it, however much contentment they place between it and, their own consciousness, it aches."* [162]

Schopenhauer referred to an existential void; the *"bottomless abyss of its heart,"* and that no worldly satisfaction could fill its infinite cravings. [163] People generally regard feelings of emptiness and loneliness as distinct from themselves and cling to the illusion that their inner void could be eradicated, avoided, or filled. They can spend their lives trying to do so, perpetuating endless internal conflict. Twelve-Step Programs are founded on the premise that cravings and inner emptiness cannot be filled through addictive behaviour, and that relief is spiritual. Bill Wilson, the founder of Alcoholics Anonymous wrote to psychoanalyst Carl Jung who replied explaining that alcoholism was a spiritual problem☒ *"a spiritual thirst of our being for wholeness, expressed in medieval language: the union with God,"* which he believed to be the answer.[164]

Our lives are understood through the stories we tell of them; of childhoods, of weddings and funerals, triumphs and disasters. Story looms large in this enterprise. We dream in stories or infuse the future with narratives of despair, devoid of a reason for optimistic living and empty with the absence of God. Story-tellers all, humans seem driven by the compulsion to assemble what has happened to us into a narrative of meaning-making that can at least attempt to make sense of what is going on. Such disempowered communication adopts a narrative structure in the effort to explain.

A growing body of counselling theory embraces the quest for meaning-making. Humans are not instinct driven so much as personal beings who have value and purpose and who seek higher goals.

The experiences of Victor Frankl, the psychotherapist who went to Auschwitz, would be widely recognised, despite being very much outside everyday experience. *"It is very difficult for an outsider to grasp how very little value was placed on human life in camp"*.[165] Frankl's book 'Man's Search for Meaning' provides a vivid account of an individual's experience as a prisoner in a Nazi concentration camp. The book demonstrates how love, hope, responsibility, inner freedom, and the beauty to be found in both nature and art as means that help one endure and overcome harrowing experiences. Our deepest desire is to search for meaning and purpose in a way that can transcend suffering and find significance in the art of living. Frankl's searing experiences showed that finding meaning deeper than the situation we find ourselves allows us to survive even the worst conditions.

Contending that psychotherapy denied the spiritual side of our humanity, Frankl quotes, with approval, the aphorism of Goethe- *"if we take people as they are, we make them worse. If we treat people as if they were what they ought to be, we help them to become what they are capable of becoming"*.[166] Frankl also showed that the moral worth of the individual was not only vital to retain, even in hell, <u>but that this translated into psychological reactions</u>.

"Under the influence of a world which no longer recognised the value of human life and human dignity, which had robbed man of his will and had made him an object to be exterminated. . . . .the personal ego final suffered a loss of values. If the man in the concentration camp did not struggle against this in a last effort to save his self-respect, he lost the feeling of being an individual, a being with mind, with inner freedom and personal value."[167]

For Victor Frankl, what about human liberty? Is there no spiritual freedom regarding behaviour and reaction to any given surroundings? No choice of action? *"Every day, every hour, offered the opportunity to make a decision, a decision which determined whether you would or would not submit to those powers which threatened to rob you of your very self, your inner freedom; which determined whether or not you would become the plaything of circumstances, renouncing freedom and dignity to become moulded into the form of the typical inmate."* This surely stands as a counter argument to the idea that we evolved a need for transcendental meaning out of social bonding. Meaning is significant survival mechanism but is undermined when we consciously reduce it to just that. There is something that goes beyond the need to be meaningful to other people that can't be reduced to it. In fact, we cry out against reduction because the thought that our needs for transcendental meaning are just evolutionary mechanisms/developments of the need for social meaning works against us and makes us feel devalued.

Anyone, Frankl asserted, *"can even under such circumstances decide what shall become of him- mentally and spiritually, may retain his human dignity even in a concentration camp. Dostoevsky said once 'there is only one thing that I dread: not to be worthy of my sufferings'"*. [168] Psychological observations of the inmates showed that only the men who allowed their inner hold on their moral and spiritual selves to subside eventually fell victim to the camp's degenerating influences. Any attempt at fighting the Camp's influence on the prisoner had to aim at giving him inner strength by pointing out a future goal to which he could look forward. We can only live by looking to the future.

Such are the dramas that play out on the surface of planet Earth; an insignificant island and rocky outpost in an unimaginably vast cosmic ocean but where the people claw and cling to significance to try to get through. It means nothing if we count for nothing and value, love and meaning are illusory.

Deprive a person of their main source of validity and something happens inside that dents their sense of valuable personhood.

This is important for our argument here as valuable personhood, so essential for humankind, needs accounting for within the bigger picture of reality. It is not, as said, just a matter of the conscious observer (tricky though that is to account for) but the added layer of how the sense of human significance of those observers that they need inside themselves relates to a vast cosmos. Notwithstanding the unfathomable immensity of the universe, there seems to be a welcome to our personhood. Something in the scheme of things switches us on. It lights us up.

Where this might take us is that we are called into being by an act of gazing. Within the looking-glass self, there is a feedback loop that generates reciprocation. 'I look at you' you look at me'. This dynamic lies at the heart of psychotherapy. Such mirroring is also central to good parenting.

"The loving eyes of healthy parents enable us to see ourselves as wonderful, special and worthwhile individuals, while the distressed eyes of dysfunctional parents create feelings of shame and worthlessness." [169]

Is there a Cosmic Observer whose acts of gazing are creative, both ennobling and enabling?

Chapter Five

The 'I' in The Eye
Identity snd Personhood

"*An identity is who or what a person or thing is. Your identity is how you define who you are; it is also how others define you (and these definitions are often not the same). That's why we talk about self-esteem and probably don't always realise how important it is to health and wellbeing.*"[170]

'Attention must be paid- even to a salesman' —Arthur Miller.[171]

THE DISCUSSION THUS FAR highlights the dichotomy between an apparently scientific view of the world and the real-life dramas being played out on the contemporary scene.

These seem to be in completely different dimensions. Yet this dichotomy could synchronize with contemporary projects towards rethinking reality. Is the entire universe a single quantum object? In the face of new evidence, some physicists are starting to view the cosmos not as made up of disparate layers, but as a quantum whole linked by entanglement. [172]This will be brought later. Suffice here to relate that to the personal sphere. Our minds could be best described as organs with the kind of processing power as a quantum supercomputer. The deep unity of the mind is translated into a single subject of experience- 'ME'. My mind somehow combines different aspects of what is going on perceptually and emotionally into unified awareness.

It comes down to ways of seeing. The naturalistic philosopher would have us dwell in two worlds with no bridge of meaning between them. Contemporary society is marked by strong concerns about de-personalisation; the loss of the person. Yet if we are the product purely of natural forces the only alternative to complete dichotomy consequent upon reductionism here is to say to say that there are degrees of complexity and reality at which life forms and maybe then consciousness can begin to emerge at that level.

The problem of consciousness and how that fits into the fabric of reality is an immense challenge to a view of science that sees a materialist conception of forces and particles as a complete description of what is out there. Our undeniable sense of significance and need to feel that we matter pertains to a different realm surely, totally different to the stuff that physics talks to us about.

It is interesting to reflect that the palaeontologist and heretical Catholic priest Teilhard de Chardin saw three big leaps in evolution. First came the emergence of life, then the evolution of consciousness and then self-consciousness in human beings. This would be superseded, he thought, by a new form of consciousness based on increased connectivity- what he called 'the noosphere'. [173]

A spiritual interpretation of human existence requires metaphysical explanations that are often religious. Scientific interpretations point to the ontology and methodology of empirical analysis derived from data. Background assumptions or subjective bias shape such enquiry. Recognising others as persons does, however, point to a dimension that goes beyond what can be tested.

The observer is not an instrument making a measurement or neutral entity watching what happens. The observer has an identity. Whether shaped by gender, race, ablism or age, identity is played out on the skin of the observer watching and recording. And there is an inner core, the 'I' inside the eye.

It is widely held that mechanistic science provides a description of reality that if partial, is nevertheless objective. The gap is between such a materialist account of science, or a dualist version in which mind and matter pertain to incommensurable realms and the inner world where human actors have a sense of their own value and worth (in presence or in absentia). Hence human subjects began to feel like aliens, unrelated to the cosmos. Searching for a correspondence between matter and mind, this book assesses the scope for a personal dimension in the universe that can correspond to our own sense of valuable personhood. Humans can feel like aliens in the gap between matter and mind; even more so when it comes to our personhood needing recognition.

This is not just, be it said, about the problem of consciousness. The literature about consciousness and why it continues to elude us is truly vast. Searching for a materialist explanation of consciousness has involved considerable labour of neuroscientists and philosophers as well as resources. It is not the purpose of this monograph to add to it or probe possible solutions.

What we shall seek to do here is somewhat different. It is to explore how notions of a valuable self might conceivably interact with the fabric of material reality. These are not the same thing. One can be conscious on an instinctual level. There are different levels of conscious awareness that enable living things to react with their environment. To think oneself as being worthwhile and significant depends surely on a level of consciousness that is self-reflective; able, not just to react but to draw a conclusion that one is valuable and ought not to be trashed. (Not that it will stop the mistreatment necessarily). This is not just a question of conscious awareness but the 'I' that can look upon itself and dare to claim significance or ponder meaning. Our lives and loves belie any sense that we do not count. Surely, on an existential level we feel it to be otherwise. If the total description of reality is about the swirl of particles- and the first person is only a complex formulation of that -where can there be any basis for these brief human years of ours constituting lives that actually matter?

Looking at the way human beings usually have a single, unified experience of the thinking subject persuaded Descartes that the mind was emphatically not a physical entity. His famous cogito ego sum was rooted in the idea that *"the body is by its very nature always divisible, whilst the mind is utterly indivisible. . . . . .I understand myself to be something quite single and unique. . . . ..this one argument would be enough to show me that the mind is completely different from the body."* [174]

Arguing for the reality of the self as a unitary substance, disclosed to me by my introspective thoughts, Descartes was flawed in the view of Kant. Self becomes an object of its own awareness. I know myself as subject, not as one more object. Valberg argues that 'I' am at the centre of an horizon. My experience plays out within those parameters and it is difficult indeed to enter into another's horizon. [175] Yet we do know ourselves as a unified centre of consciousness. All my mental states and memories endure through time as pertaining to me. As Scruton points out, [176]I also know with certainty that I can give reasons for my actions and answer the 'why question' as applies to me.

A single reality? As an example of the latter, Archbishop Ussher in the 17th century, who famously set a precise date for the creation, asserted that "*a Person is one particular Thing, Indivisible, Incommunicable, Living, Reasonable, subsisting in itself, not having part of another. . . indivisible: Because a Person may not be divided into many Persons; although he may be divided into many parts. . . . .Human personhood and divine personhood must be analogically related*".[177]

Our personal lives protest hugely against de-personalisation. '*Don't dismiss me*' had been the cry of a black writer, Bernadino Evaristo, in the years before she won the Booker Prize for 2019. [178] '*Don't dismiss us*' was the cry of the politically dispossessed in the years before the strange politics of 2016 exposed disaffected populism. There was enormous anger at traffickers who had allowed 39 Vietnamese to die in a lorry in Essex, UK, in 2019. 'They see you as a commodity, as cargo', lamented someone who had survived a similar attempt. '*You are something to make money from, not a human being*'. [179] Why are we outraged by this? Some sense of value seems to be part of our operating system and a storm centre for contemporary issues. In personal life, 'don't dismiss me!' is an instinctive protest when disregarded or when inequality affects us. The mental health of young people is eroded through lack of felt worth relative to others. In politics, strong debates often arise from culture and identity- not just the economy.

The dynamics of valuable personhood are not just an ethical aspiration but psycho-social necessity. Valuable personhood is etched into our very being, in the essence of ourselves that is so often immune from the critical influences that impose. 21st century science can no longer dwell in its silo, in the objectivity and rationality that pervades its method. How do we disassociate our thoughts about the world from trying to make sense of ultimate purpose and value as people?

IDENTITY AND ITS COMPLEXITIES

We now turn to note the quest for identity; so crucial on the contemporary landscape but which is belied by scientific materialism if matter is all there is and explains everything. Ultimately the goal of forming groups based on identities is less about achieving an end than being recognised and valued.

Identity is a sense of 'who', the subject is in our experiences who emerges from our inner states and interpersonal relationships. Interactions with parents and peers shape our sense of self-states. An integrated sense of who we are both as fully embodied and fully relational is vital to our sense of ourselves. Identity is hugely political issue in contemporary society. Identities are essential to the significance of significance. They give each of us a sense of ourselves, of our grounding in the world and of our relationships to others. Who we are, a defined sense of identity, is given to each of us by the specific circumstances of our lives and particularities of personal experiences. Our experience of self does not come from the inside alone. The self is shaped interactively with our culture.

One of the dilemmas of our time is that, instead of society, we have been left with transient groupings of individuals who come together only to best pursue special interest claims based on identity or ask for recognition. Authentic association is based on subjects forming voluntary groups to purse common undertakings. They associate, not because of who they are, but because of what they want. It is based on differences tolerated because of a shared, universal foundation. Relativism shattered that foundation giving rise to a deep intolerance and indifference to others: to groupings based on different identities. The shift towards identity politics reinforced the sense of a more fragmented society in which the old social bonds had snapped. For example, many sections of the working class found themselves politically voiceless at the very time their lives had become more precarious, as jobs have declined, public services savaged, austerity imposed, and inequality risen. Those who feel left out, dispossessed and voiceless have clamoured to make their needs known.

In his *Multiculturalism and the Politics of Recognition*, Charles Taylor, the Canadian social philosopher, underlines the way in which the notion of recognition, developed by Hegel as instrinsic to core humanity, raises dilemmas in the public arena. "*The development of a modern notion of identity has given rise to a politics of difference*". [180]

The politics of identity—to create new struggles for recognition - is a key driver. The roots of contemporary identity politics lie in the new social movements that emerged in the 1960s to challenge the failure of the Left to take seriously the issues of racism, homophobia and women's rights. The struggle for black rights in America, in particular, was highly influential in providing a template for many other groups to develop concepts of identity and the importance of organising. Squeezed between an intensely racist society, many black activists seceded from civil rights organisations and set up separate black groups. In the 1960s, the struggles for black rights and women's rights and gay rights were closely linked to the wider project of social transformation. Disability came into sharp scrutiny also as it was argued that society disables us.

Eventually, the promotion of identity became an end in itself; to which an individual's interests were inexorably linked. The question people ask themselves today is not so much 'in what kind of society do I want to live?' as 'who are we?' The two questions are intimately related. Any sense of social identity must embrace both and offer solutions. In his book, "*Identity: The Demand for Dignity and the Politics of Resentment*"[181], the demand for recognition, Fukuyama proposes, is the 'master concept' that explains all the contemporary dissatisfactions with the global social order. The quest for equal and inner dignity, the human desire for recognition and respect, has become hugely important, especially for those that were marginalised. The enduring question of 'Who am I?' is a vexed issue in personal life and politics. It is not just about race and ethnicity. Ever deeper questions about 'how I look' relate to 'who I am' and are basic to explorations of race. The identity I have is determinant of my experience of the world. How would looking different affect my life experiences and outcomes? How has it affected them until now? Outward appearances are fundamental to how others perceive us, and by extension how I perceive with and engage with the world.

One example that comes up a great deal, especially amongst young people, is those who pay close attention to their on-line body image. There is a fascinating and often troubling interplay between the social gaze of unknown others and the internal mirroring of that. It enables many to feel a sense of achievement and the validation of self: indeed, a high value in their world. Though allowing new forms of human interaction, including on-line counselling, the internet inhabits the dark side of the moon in addition to its sunny face. The dark web is a space where evil smurks, where electronic denizens wait to pounce, where identity theft and cyber-bullying is rife and where trolls leer and smear. Even routinised social media offers a space for harm and for the kind of abuse that is no longer tolerated in public discourse or on the TV. The point is that we seem to think the self matters. The salience of online body image and the gaze of the other on the internet underlines the need to feel valued in the sight of the other.

Identity is loaded with almost unbearable tensions on a contemporary scene. Issues of gender and race have particular salience but so too do disability and sexuality, age and ethnicity. Continuity and discontinuity of personal pronouns have become a flash point and forced new forms of conceptual analysis.

Unquestionably, these are controversial and unsettling times for issues of gender and sex. What is a man? What is a woman? The term 'sex' refers to male or female biology: sperm or eggs whereas 'gender' was the cultural overlay shaped by society that affects roles and behaviour. The growth of Second Wave feminism in the 1960's saw gender differentiated from biology on the grounds that male bias interpreted gender differences as being biologically determined. This was now seen to be historically convenient and a cloak for power. Discrimination became illegal. Biology was banished. Now, debates about sex and gender are deafening and often vitriolic. Gender seems to include identities that do not corresponds to biological sex. The primatologist Frans De Waal stresses that gender di-morphism is patterned in the unconscious and hence generates bias. [182] Or the view can be taken that gender identity is malleable, fluid. [183] Transgendered people, by contrast, usually argue that they have an inherent gender identity that has been mischaracterised hitherto. Biology is back! *"One of my guiding principles is doesn't hurt any of us to treat and honour people with respect as they see and experience themselves"* (a clinical psychologist) [184]

Patently, the experience of race is also sharply debated. Psychological research has studied the devastating effects of racism. Most standardisation samples can skew the generalisations we make about human behaviour—comparison groups were often western, educated, industrialised, rich and democratic (WEIRD). [185] As racial awareness increases, for a counsellor, finding your way through your own stance relates to one's own bias and privilege can make empathy difficult. Fragility might arise from guilt as counsellors come to see themselves in the therapeutic process. Building multi-cultural competence can help as can being able to use system-centred language to describe the systemic and structural factors that support racism. [186]

Identity is therefore a loaded term because it depicts an inner sense of who I am which can be distinguished from the more obvious facts about me. My physical characteristics or my social relationships—father, partner, son, colleague and what I do—are increasingly being seen as not those that define us. With gender identity, that has generated new and often acrimonious debates, there is an 'inner sense' of who I am that usually trumps the external markers. How people go about forging their identity gives rise to enormous political contention on the contemporary scene. Maybe the outward markers of me are accidental and do not reflect who I am? Maybe they are imposed on me by others, be they family or society and do not reflect my true self. If I believe myself to be a woman, then that is what I truly am, regardless of the body I was born into. This is the claim. Yet if we have no significance because the universe is neutral and everything has arisen from matter and energy, we are essentially deluded. In the scheme of things, what I might claim inside, irrespective of whether confirmed by external appearance, is most certainly not confirmed by a purely physical set of systems. How does any sense that we matter arise from natural processes or a materialist brain? The materialist perspective contradicts the almost transcendent claim that my internal identity—my mental, not physical identity—is my true self.

The concept of person plays a highly significant function amidst criteria for personal identity. Who someone is remains central as the unit for intentional, agency that can be held accountable. Moral responsibility adheres to a person who can be praised or blamed. This is a contemporary minefield.

It is no wonder that, theologically, believers make the sacred value of a person a matter of divine appointment. To affirm the sacredness of personhood is more real and solid as a basis than a bald calculation of equality with no reason in its favour. A tramp is as valuable as Michelangelo because God would have it so.But there are problems with this clearly. To define persons as sacred could be to abandon their personality. They could for sure be counted as valuable regardless. But if we assert this prematurely, we seem to make humanity colourless. Could we say though that what God values is His image in us? Would that make us like banknotes, to be valued because the bank is known to be sound? A banknote can be replaced if lost. But a human is irreplaceable surely. The whole point of persons presumably is that they are not equal. It is like parenthood. A parent loves his or her children not the same way but differently because they *are* different!

Oppenheimer argues that each of us knows ourselves to be us, to be unique, to be special. Fact and value are united here. If I am snuffed out, something irreplaceable will have gone. What we have to do is to ascribe this same irreplacability to others. In this way, we speak of the intrinsic value of people. It is about recognition; recognition that we each have qualities, not of some primeval essence we must value. This notion of human value is one that can be common ground to Christians and humanists! (Helen Oppenheimer develops her argument about why we should respect persons 'The Hope of Happiness'[187] as a theological treatise subtitled 'A sketch for a Christian Humanism').

PERSONHOOD AND BEING

Ontology is the study of being in general and has been the subject of considerable debate in metaphysics. Since Aristotle's 'First philosophy' (Book IV of his *Metaphysics*), *it has been much discussed whether* being is the same thing as existence.[188] Following the work of Christian Wolff in the 18th century[189] the term was adopted by the founder of phenomenology, Edmund Husserl. Heidegger in *Being and Time* was prompted to transform Edmund Husserl's transcendental phenomenology of pure essences into an ontological phenomenology of existence.[190] In his influential account of human freedom, Jean-Paul Sartre frequently characterizes human beings in terms of the idea of nothingness. Humans introduce nothingness into being (the ability is implicated to individuate objects because they are constituted by nothingness. "*The Being by which Nothingness arrives in the world is a Being such that in its Being, the nothingness of its Being is in question. The Being by which Nothingness comes to the world must be its own Nothingness*".[191]

What of our own existence? Personhood is a related concept given that the focus is on personal being but which again belies an account of reality is purely physicalist. A suppression of our personhood is something we cry out against yet this is so much sigh and emptiness if the universe is neutral. 'Who am I'? What makes 'me' a person or a unique individual? What traits remain constant so someone is recognisably the same person? A societal emphasis on rational choice might evoke judgements about whether someone is acting out of character and not the same person if they appear to have acted irrationally. "*We may consider that someone who is no longer able to weigh probabilities may not be the same person but we do not think that a person whose imaginative faculties are damaged is a different person*".[192] If the material properties of a person change, or if the brain or other physical states change, is this still the same person?

There is an existential fear of depersonalisation in society—seeing people as objects not subjects that have identities. De-personalisation has haunted society in various forms. It was not just the industrial revolution, which raised the spectre of human beings as machines. Traditional or feudal societies were closely bound to a stratification in which one's place in the world was determined largely by others. We will return to the implications for our theme of collectivism and the relative importance of the individual self. Here it is worth noting that fears for the loss of the person have come into sharp focus with impersonal systems that imprison human beings in bureaucracy and more recently, the rise of Artificial Intelligence (AI). The word 'robots' (originally coined for concerns about mechanisation with industrial era machines) now has strong salience with fears that algorithms and highly sophisticated electronic devices will supplant the human dimension and reduce us to servility. Computerised machines are accomplishing tasks that used to be regarded as requiring intelligence.

Persons are those who make free choices and act towards certain goals. Unique individuals with a degree of autonomy, a person is nevertheless embedded in community; for the most part, people are members of larger groups.

So what is personhood? Here is one definition. A person is *"the kind of entity that has the moral right to make its own life choices, to live its life without (unprovoked) interference from others"*. [193]

The debate goes back for many centuries of human thought when people began to explore the mystery of themselves. Ancient peoples practised their cave art using symbolic behaviour to express their sense of who they were in relation to the world around them. Later, the pre-Socratics, Plato, Aristotle and the Neo-Platonists offered their own versions of what it meant to be a person. For Aristotle, talk of a soul was not about a mysterious entity within (as Plato utilised in his dualism) but the organising principle to make a flower a flower or what constitutes a human. The principle of organisation is to be found in the common nature that humans have and therefore we talk about potential. Acorns grow into oak trees. A zygote or foetus has the potential to become a baby.

Pre-Socratic philosophers through to thinkers of the present time have something to say about a developing story of what it means to be human, and how we understand ourselves as persons. Mostly, ancient world thinkers were substantialists, arising from an ontological understanding of the substance of things. It is what things are in themselves that define them rather than what they are in relation to others. Relationality was considered a secondary since it was unable to exist independently. Christian theorists turned to the concept of the 'imago dei', humankind made in God's image. Ideas of 'persona' drafted in to support trinitarian theology led to the human person being considered as their essence; their very being. Three personas in one ousia (substance) was the formula eventually adopted by the Cappadocian church Fathers. The 'person' came to be understood as the human being itself.

A HISTORICAL GLANCE

When the child gets a soul—i.e., at the point of *ensoulment*. In philosophical and religious history, four possibilities have been noted for the time this can occur: at conception, between conception and birth, at birth, after birth.

The Jews neither had nor needed a specialized term for the unborn, whose humanity they saw clearly. Thus the Hebrew Scripture regularly refers to *individuals* existing in the womb ("I knew *you* in the womb," Jer. 1:5; cf. Job. 10:8-12, Ps. 139:13-16, Is. 44:2). [194]

Aquinas believed that the unborn had a rational, human soul from the time it was conceived. [195] However, following Aristotelian science, he thought that conception was an extended process that did not *finish* until forty or ninety days into the pregnancy: "*The conception of the male finishes on the fortieth day and that of the woman on the ninetieth, as Aristotle says in IX Book of the Animals.*" [196]

Other religious views are that ensoulment happens at the moment of conception; or when the child takes the first breath after being born;[197] at the formation of the nervous system and brain; at the first detectable sign of brain activity; or when the foetus is able to survive independently of the uterus (viability).[3]

The concept is closely related to debates on the morality of abortion as well as the morality of contraception

The possession of the soul at all stages of development follows from understanding what a soul is. The soul is the life principle; being. From an ultimate perspective, a human is comprised of a human soul serving as the substantial form of a human body as indicated in Genesis 2:7. The fact that a soul is needed to turn a human body into a human has sufficiently become part of the popular consciousness to believe that the presence of a soul is tied to the right to life. [198]

The question then is one of being. At what stage does a human become 'a human being'? f a newborn baby has no soul (even an undeveloped one), then it isn't really a full human being.[199] Ford argues that 'when does a human being begin?' is an ontological question, and that attainment of personhood is a fact which calls for appropriate moral and legal attitudes.

Theories of human nature, personhood, and the self have had a long running in the history of western philosophy. There have been many ways of arguing for metaphysical underpinnings for what is often been characterised as a philosophical anthropology with a focus on the basic constituents of the unified self. Being human encompasses what all humans share—a pattern of living with traits such as biology, emotional, rationality that set them apart from other living things. [200] Some headlines were:

- Plato - human personhood defined by a capacity to think and rational thoughts
- Augustine of Hippo - humans are soul and body, relating to other persons and God

- Thomas Aquinas - nature not existence determines personhood. Humans are persons because of their ability to participate in community
- Existential philosophy—we are defined by how we act
- Contemporary ideas such as characteristics for personhood e.g. linguistic and operational
- The quest for validation demonstrated by the incessant need for 'likes' on social media.

As Descartes observed, possessing a good mind is not enough. [201] What is crucial is how the mind applies itself. Living bodies without reason are not persons in this view. For the subsequent philosopher John Locke, personhood includes a conscious awareness of self as self. A person is defined as a thinking, intelligence being that can reason and reflect. Locke argued for consciousness as criteria for personhood: consciousness is essential to thinking. Personal identity is linked to the survival of consciousness after death rooted in a criterion of personal identity through time. John Locke argued that personal identity is a matter of psychological continuity. He considered personal identity (or the self) to be founded on consciousness (memory): not on substance of either the soul or body. [202] In a more contemporary mindset, physiological attributes do not equate to personhood.

For Locke, as distinct from Descartes, his account of personal identity is that of a legal theorist and a physician of the mind. He is less concerned with 'who am I?' than what is the origin of the notion of a person? The self has individuated subjectivity defined by consciousness, its memory of its own sense-perception. Consciousness ensures the continued identity of an individual only if the contents of that consciousness remain the same. A person cannot be held responsible for something of which he or she has no knowledge. [203] With Locke, a person is defined as *"a thinking, intelligent being that has reason and reflection, and can consider itself as itself, the same thinking thing, in different times and places"*.[204] This introduced the idea of a stream of consciousness which is now integral to how we think of personhood. Attempts in philosophical history to downplay the significance of memory thus implied have met with considerable opposition. Memory is clearly important but perhaps as one element to say that a given person is still there or indeed still alive!

Bishop Butler, in his criticism of Locke, argued that those who reports their memories already have a self-conception as proper claimants of those memories. [205] He would have criticised Montaigne who mocked pretensions to self-knowledge. "Whom shall we believe when he talks about himself?" At one time, he is serious. Another he is merry. There is no existence that is constant. [206]Butler would say, 'but who is who is doing the remembering of such states?'[207]

A later 18th century writer, Kant, defined humans as noumenal realities because they are persons, not things. Persons qualify as ends in themselves rather than means to an end. [208] Only persons deserve moral respect and appreciate the moral law and its demands. [209] Postmodern philosophers find that problematic. Someone may not qualify as a person because they have not gained fundamental attributes by which personhood is defined. Rights and responsibilities are key. There are collective societies where responsibility is located in the larger unit; the family or clan.

Defining personhood by consciousness alone is problematic because it extends the concept to all living things. But if we define persons on the basis of moral responsibility might lead us to allow inclusion of non-humans such as AI robots. Could machines achieve the kind of moral status that allows them to respect others and be respected in turn as persons? [210]

A brief summary of personhood has to note the work of Soren Kierkegaard in the 19th century. He thought of the human self as an achievement, a goal to strive for rather than a metaphysical substance. Humans exist in the world, as do physical objects. But for human persons, the self must become what it is to become; we play an active role in the process by which they come to define themselves. Our self-consciousness means that humans still contain possibilities to be actualized. Kierkegaard's *'Sickness Unto Death'* depicts how humans fail to internalise contradictions such as the finite and the infinite, the temporal and the eternal; the necessary and the possible. We fall into despair, not just as an emotion of depression but in a position where the self fails to become a self, living in a world of imagination disconnected from actuality. As self-conscious beings, humans are able to "step back" from themselves and "relate themselves to themselves."[211]

The first relationship with another human being is clearly vital for the infant to be co-participant in a dynamic system of reciprocal interchanges. [212] The self-organising brain occurs in the context of another self, another brain. What happens when the caregiver is emotionally unresponsive?

Social referencing is clearly a highly visual set of experiences. The maternal face is a biological mirror but also amplifies arousal and emotion. But such positive vision may not be available. For numerous infants, the transformation of external into internal regulation is markedly absent. Early relational trauma in the form of childhood abuse or neglect may compromise development. Such disorganised attachment bonds are weak; the loss of an ability to regulate emotion. [213] Type D attachment patterns [214] are risk factors for pathology and mental disorders that show up in adult life such as post-traumatic stress disorder.[215] Either the maternal facial response varies or it is not forthcoming. The foetus is mainly asleep, although it shows vigorous continual activity, including breathing, eye openings, and facial expression.[216] The newborn is also able to differentiate between self and nonself touch, express emotions, and show signs of shared feelings. Yet, it is unreflective, focussed on the present moment and makes little reference to any concept of him/herself. Infants display features characteristic of what may be referred to as basic consciousness and they still have to undergo considerable maturation to reach the level of adult consciousness.[217]

What seems vital for development is the maternal gaze that helps to build the wiring for pathways in the brain for the infant. That does not activate the brain and begin the process of forming the mind. So what switches on consciousness to begin with and launches the infant on the journey of being a 'me'? Consciousness requires a sophisticated network of highly interconnected components, nerve cells. Its physical substrate, the thalamo-cortical complex that provides consciousness with its highly elaborate networking begin to form between the 24th and 28th week of gestation.[218] Many of the circuit elements necessary for consciousness are in place by the third trimester. Research suggests that brainstem mechanisms are integral to the constitution of the conscious state.[219] It is hard to pinpoint when consciousness is 'switched on' or if that concept is meaningful. Development of neo-natal awareness is not the same as consciousness of personhood. The substrates and neuronal capacity for eventual consciousness may arise gradually like a dimmer switch. Glimmerings of foetal awareness and responsiveness may come around 6 months.

Though acuity of vision in the full-term newborn infants is only 1/40 that of the adult, newborns can process complex visual stimuli, recognize faces and imitate. Infants at birth prefer images of attractive faces, are sensitive to the presence of eyes in a face and have a preference to look at faces that enjoy them in eye contact. They have 'face detectors' that require the infant not only to be awake and attentive but also to be sensitive to a "social" eye-contact relationship.[220]

The face is a crucial component of the developing sense of self. The 'I' I present to you lies behind my face and looks out through my eyes at others who are disclosed through their face. This is the way of being in the world that the infant quickly learns. It will be foundational to social development.

It is a century since Charles Cooley formulated the idea of a 'looking glass self'.[221] Neuroscience has since confirmed that we are made in the mirror. Mirroring is vital in human relationships. Martin Buber in his 1924 book 'I and thou' understood the human person as a being constituted by the other. The 'primary word' of 'I-thou does not signify a thing but relations with the other. [222] He sought to derive the universal essence of relationships (among individuals and nations as well as human interaction with the environment) as sources of meaning or alienation. This had special resonance with increasing outpouring of anti-semitic hatred after the First World War. [223] Its stress on mutual recognition of equal worth militated against notions of alienation as the human condition. The 'I-you' relationship is distinctive of humans but it is also constitutive. Asking human persons to express reasons for their actions is addressed to 'me' as my response seeks the 'I' in you. [224]

Personhood is a relational status. An understanding of human personhood was expressed in relational terms ('we are what we are in ourselves only in relation to others')[225] The self is constructed in relationship to other selves. It is a Xhosa proverb. 'I am because of you'. Persons depend on other persons to be persons. Social scientists, and indeed theologians, tend to argue for a relational and social view of personhood. This is where we encounter the differing perspectives of some major psychoanalytic theorists from Freud, to whom relationships were the secondary arena for discharge of bodily needs, to people like Bowlby and Fairbairn who stressed the importance of connection.[226] Different schools of psychology elaborated an understanding of human personhood differently.

Personhood seems to require a level of complexity that permits the mind to engage in language, memory, a theory of mind, conscious agency and an orientation towards the future. These qualities are important for humans to enter into relationships at every level. [227] Humans utilise language in highly sophisticated ways not just for daily tasks but as a vehicle for ideas, beliefs and feelings. We have an ability to reflect on and communicate the episodes and memories of our own story. A theory of mind (TOM) enables humans to attribute with some accuracy the mental states of others.

The relationship between soul and body, debated for centuries, has in the last century or so been re-configured as one between mind and brain. How is the former generated from the latter or is the mind merely brain in action? Dualism in this context is the belief that although consciousness might be caused by brain processes, it is not reducible to them. The dualism of Descartes has for the most part yielded to some form of monism, that the only kind of substance is physical. Mind IS brain. But while brain is clearly necessary for mental states such as consciousness, language and thought, this does not entail the reductionist perspective that the mind is nothing but the brain. Few brain states can be mapped precisely on to a specific event in mentality. It may be more accurate to suggest that new properties of mind can emerge out of a physical substance. Such emergence may indicate the development of a sense of personhood.

Configured another way, the essence of human personhood may be proposed as consciousness, creativity, communication and conscience. These are embodied tasks; derived from body systems that are functioning to some extent. A way of expressing the mind-body relationship is "the neural basis of the self" in tandem with brain systems.[228]

A contemporary psychotherapeutic writer, Dan Siegal, puts it like this: brain and mind are to be differentiated. While the brain can be understood as neurons that relate to other neurons and that transforms electrical energy into chemical flow, the mind has not yet scientifically been defined. It is an embodied and relationship emergent process that regulates the flow of energy and information. The mind is in constant rewiring. Siegel and associates create a triangle where brain, mind and relationships all work together. The mind regulates internal energy flow while the brain is the embodied mechanism and in relationships is where the flow is shared. It is through relationships that our brain and minds are shaped. The mind has a set of patterns of behaviours that work on auto pilot, patterns that have been influenced by relationships and stored in the unconscious mind. Unlocking such patterns by accessing the unconscious can result in a change of structure and function of the brain, bringing rewiring for positive change.[229]

Is the nigh on universal tendency towards spirituality fundamental to our personhood? It has been a source of considerable debate why humans have this compulsion to worship something outside themselves. Former zoologist at Oxford, Alistair Hardy, hypothesised that 'the divine flame of religious awareness' evolved into universality. [230]

Why do we have this innate spirituality? *"To the psychologist, the religious propensities of man must be at least as interesting as any other of the facts pertaining to his mental constitution."*- William James. [231] Freud considered religion as an illusion, a kind of neurosis that should be treated. Yet why are humans biologically prepared to seek ultimate reality beyond ourselves and beyond the material world of which we are part? David Hay argued that children have spirituality that cannot be explained through enculturation or environment and becomes suppressed though secular society. [232]

For the most part, neuroscientists have argued for a focus on the brain as generating mind and any sense of personhood. Brain is all there is. Identifying the functions of each part of the brain has become important through powerful brain scans. For example, a recent study (Solms and Turnbull 2018) study on the right and left hemispheres of the brain, investigated how much we live in consciousness or unconsciousness. A source for such theorising is case studies, especially looking at brain injuries, as a way of connecting what is lost in the patient's mental life with the part of the injured brain. [233] investigations in neuroscience have indicated the ability of the brain to see patterns and generate hypotheses; the 'interpreter', (a third force?) located in the brain's left hemisphere.[234] Emotion occurs through a number of brain structures in the limbic system (hippocampus and hypothalamus) operating on both amygdala and indeed the body generally in psychosomatic ways. Then there is the unconscious; a self with different layers; the whole of which can lay claim to be part of one person. Arriving at his seminal 'Interpretation of Dreams', Freud quoted Virgil - *'If I cannot bend the gods above, then I will move the Infernal regions'.* [235] The unconscious is not just a version of ourselves that we only have to discover and surface for all to be well. It is a swirling mass of contradictions and conflicts that can at times seem at odds with our own interests. 'Part of me wants this; part of me wants that' often reflects a divided self suggested by R D Laing. [236]

The best-known example of brain damage affecting someone's personality is that of Phineas Gage, who in 1848 experienced an accident where a railway rod went through his skull and out the other end. Although living another 11 years, he underwent a personality change such that 'he was no longer Gage' as his friends reported. [237] In such conditions as locked-in syndrome, the person seems to be aware of their environment and their identity is intact. With persistent vegetative states, there is no sign of being conscious. With coma, the person is still there though asleep.[238]

On the contemporary scene, in other spheres, there are not only battle-lines around identity as a storm centre for political debate, but personhood is also much contended.

Human rights became a huge issue in the 20th century. [239]The perspectives of modernity also include how far the concept of personhood shapes the bioethical or legal literature. [240]Conceptions of personhood often rely on mental capabilities in contrast to those relying on membership of the human species. [241] Disability raises questions about membership of the moral community of persons. [242] Euthanasia has sharpened contentious discussion about personhood and when that should be surrendered. [243]Debates about abortion reference whether the foetus can grow in personhood like a switch can gradually dim- the so-called gradient theory. Animal rights generate strong contention about the moral status of animals. [244]The astonishing of artificial intelligence has pointed to candidates for non-human persons i.e. robots. Arguably, being human equates to personhood—though not everyone agrees that these concepts coincide. Some postmodern theorists like Michael Tooley have concluded that human beings deprived of higher brain capacity lack personhood while some higher primates should qualify as persons on the basis of behavioural characteristics. [245]

Whatever and wherever the distinctive human essence is located, the versions of self-hood and identity that have so much salience stand as potent adaptations to social and cultural systems. Human selfhood and personhood seems to be radically different from what has been observed elsewhere in nature. The question is what might have produced such radical discontinuity?[246] Clearly, the brain does not need a self or a person in order to carry out its functions. The differential is how and on what basis the subjectively aware creature participates in culture and language. [247]

In short, much is wrapped up in our concept of personhood. We cannot have access to how pre-modern humans saw the world and experienced self-individuality. *"If..personhood- at least in the sense that we experience it today- is necessarily based on the capacity for self-reflection, then human beings have experienced this only as long as their cognitive mode has allowed it"*. [248] For modern humans, personhood is not solitary. It is held in relation to others. There has to be some sense of continuity of being: there is only one of you/us. Only one individual can be that person.

It must be stressed again that these storm centres about identity and personhood are completely at odds with a materialist philosophy that sees us as nothing but a swirling mass of sub-atomic particles. We are forced to live in very different boxes. In one box is the idea that physical processes alone count for the generation of life and being. In the other is the idea that we live, move and have our being in a universe where mind matters; where value, love and meaning are significant arenas for human action and are different kinds of entities. The observer of physical processes is a person too; he or she has an identity. The experiencing self is the 'I' in the eye, looking out at what is going on and sensing a variety of phenomena as a subject observing objects. If the brain is mind, do brains equal persons? If the mind is something else, is personhood extractable from body?

What can be said though is that the human consciousness carries with it very often an unbearable weight of being. Persons can choose to undertake actions that will be destructive yet which will incur accountability. Guilt, remorse and regret stalk our existence and much effort goes in to assuage them. We dwell in the gaze of others but self-scrutiny leaves us weighed in the balance and found wanting. Accountability adheres to us as moral beings. Such is the mainspring of the desire to live a righteous life. That is how we face our community and endeavour to face God.

PERSONALISM

What is real is the personal. Basic features of personality—consciousness, free self-determination, directedness toward ends, self-identity through time, and value retentiveness—make it central to all reality. Personalism averrers the ultimate reality and value in personhood—human as well as (at least for most *personalists*) divine. The idea that humans have a unique quality and dignity that gives rise to moral requirements such as respect for human rights is a feature of the movement in philosophy that separates personal from non-personal beings that is Personalism. Interacting with personal beings involves completely different rules from dealing with non-personal beings. The monthly journal, Espirit, founded between the wars by Mounier, a Personalist philosopher, proposed the human person as the measure by which a solution might be found to the de-humanising crisis of economic and political disintegration. The key to the new thought was to be the human person. Mournier and his colleague were joined by leading lights such as Jacques Maritain who contributed to the UN Declaration of Human Rights. At the same time in America, Personalist philosophers such as B. P. Browne, G.H. Howison and A.C. Knudson took the human person as the starting point for understanding the world. All moral truth arose from the absolute value of the person. In Germany, Personalism was closely associated with the phenomenology developed by Edmund Husserl. The human person was, argued Husserl, competent to penetrate by intuition into the essence of a thing. Husserl's student Max Scheler, was in turn read by the young Polish priest intellectual, Karol Wojtyla, known to history as Pope John Paul 11nd. He wrote his doctoral thesis on Max Scheler, laying out his philosophy in such books as '*Love and Responsibility*' [249] and '*The Acting Person*.' [250] But it was as Pope John Paul 11nd that he had greatest influence, invoking Personalism in a number of addresses and encyclicals that stressed "*the need for theological renewal based on the Personalistic nature of man, that is a defence of the fundamental rights which are consequent of that dignity.*" [251]

Catholic social teaching has stressed that the absolute character of the person provides scope for ethical norms. It provides for the possibility of justice- "*Rendering 'to each his due' hinges on one's understanding of what each deserves, which cannot be correctly ascertained without comprehension of the worth of the individual person and all persons, by the very fact of their personhood.*"[252]

These ideas were brought into a project for a moral sociology. Bauman sought to awaken people to their responsibilities for others. A postmodern constituency of isolated strangers makes us act like cultural tourists. The remedy is to encourage communication and creative action, not in the direction of individualism but when 'I' enacts care for the 'Other'. Bauman wishes the postmodern habitat to be as humane a place as it can possibly be. His strategy is to challenge its inhabitants to live up the highest standards of the Enlightenment." [253] In a world of conflicting authorities, multiplying choices and declining principles, ethical questions grow even as social production of ethical resources shrink.

Reality is an interacting sphere of persons. Only self-conscious agents and their states exist. Personalism, a variant of which is described here under the title 'valuable personhood' denotes the self inhabiting itself with value. As a philosophy of metaphysical idealism, personalism was a reaction against impersonal modes of thought perceived as dehumanizing. In philosophy, "*personalism always underscores the centrality of the person as primary locus of investigation for philosophical, theological, and humanistic studies. It is an approach or system of thought which regards or tends to regard the person as the ultimate explanatory, epistemological, ontological, and axiological principle of all reality.*" [254] "*This personalistic framework permeates our everyday understanding of ourselves and our social relationships.*" [255] Everything revolves around the image of the person [256].

PART TWO

Ways of Seeing

"*Materialism is the philosophy of the subject who forgets to take into account himself*" —Schopenhauer

"*There is no lack of open fundamental questions we must tackle today: the nature of the Higgs boson, the structure of quarks and leptons, inflation, the cosmic baryon asymmetry, dark matter, dark energy, quantum gravity, and more. But there is also a widespread feeling that our theoretical tools—which have been so successful in bringing particle physics to its present stage of maturity—are becoming inadequate to address the next layer of open questions. A new paradigm change seems to be necessary*"
—Gian Guidice, Head of Theoretical Physics CERN [257]

Chapter Six

All by Itself
The Limits to Scientific Naturalism

"*The brain and its satellite glands have now been probed to the point where no particular site remains that can reasonably be supposed to harbour a nonphysical mind*" —Edward Wilson [258]

Is there an anything out there (that corresponds to what's in here?) Does the cosmos give any personal value to our lives—or has the questioning mind between our eyes risen higher than impersonal forms of matter and ultimately energy that has apparently generated everything?

The book probes what ultimate realities are suggested by the drive towards what we are terming 'valuable personhood'. Are there steps <u>from</u> the ways in which, in our experience, personhood needs affirming through recognition and practice <u>to</u> a universe where our personhood is validated? Could this open up an approach to theism grounded in our psychological experience?

The human person thrives on 'I-thou' encounters. There our personhood is called out; there we prosper and grow psychologically; there we do our best work. It is as we are seen that our being lights up. This does not necessarily point to a cosmos where psyche is fundamental but it could do.

Somehow the universe has generated beings who not only think they are significant but, in order to flourish, need to live as if it were true. Some kind of systematic explanation is surely required in order to give a complete, or at least expanded, account of the cosmos. We will probe various options for alternative hypotheses about the nature of the natural world that can take this into account.

Our quest takes us to probe a realm beyond space and time that might possibly provide a template for value, love and meaning where our personhood thrives; linked inextricably to a moral vision.

We are the creatures that must interpret ourselves. What gives us life and makes us special, different from other beings and from each other has been the search of the ages. Why do scientific accounts of the world not include the sigh of significance? How do we correlate the physical laws that shape the universe, with the inner world? The view of the physical world that emerges from contemporary science about how the cosmos works is based on measurable understandings of matter and energy. There is a need to harmonise physicality with the sense of human significance, with emotional dynamics. How does the human consciousness fold back into the physical laws? A richer description is needed. There are limits to how far scientific explanation can extend.

Some of this is due to the reality that physics can only describe things in physical terms. The natural sciences delve with astounding scope and precision into what can be measured. Physics is a quantification project. Sciences uses methods that are not equipped to recognise or explore things that cannot be detected in instruments. Its methodology cannot probe an additional layer of reality.

ALL BY ITSELF

Scientific naturalism asserts that no external agency is needed. There is no non-physical reality. As DNA discoverer Francis Crick said: "*The Astonishing Hypothesis is that 'You', your joys and your sorrows, your memories and your ambitions, your sense of personal identity and free will, are in fact no more than the behaviour of a vast assembly of nerve cells and their associated molecules*".[259]

We will use in this book the term 'naturalistic philosophy' or scientific naturalism on the grounds that its guiding principle is the presupposition about natural processes being able to account for the cosmos as we see it and indeed ourselves as rational representatives of life on earth. Everything happens through self-organisation invoking the principles of physics, chemistry and biology. These are the natural sciences or 'natural philosophy' as they were once labelled. It is true of emergence.

But this must be nuanced. There is a methodological naturalism by which, whatever we make of ultimate reality ontologically, in practice we do science as if natural processes account for all things.

How the physical world of matter generates perceiving minds and a felt sense of needing to be significant is a mystery on these terms. Is the human mind incapable of comprehending itself? Perhaps not. For now, we are left with an immense gap to probe. The gap is between our psycho-social experience as 21st century people and a description of physical reality that has no room for it.

Some limits to explanation derive from the reality that reality itself is highly complex. The trend towards reductionism, scientific naturalism and mechanistic ideas has been potent in forms of explanation in psychology.[260] Yet scientific naturalism describes reality in terms of the physical universe. Nothing exists beyond matter and energy. Brains are physical objects.[261]

There are competing versions of science at stake in this issue. How we see the fabric of reality depends on different ways of seeing. It used to be said that if you were interested in a religious perspective, that was not a story that tells us about the external world. For that we needed science and mathematics. With the rise of modern science came a growing faith in the explanatory power of mathematics, the new language of the cosmos. Galileo argued that scientific theories had to be accepted or rejected entirely on the basis of empirical evidence. Consciousness and the standpoint of the observer was expelled as irrelevant and unscientific and impermissibly subjective. Experimental tests were sufficient, regardless of the intuition of the observers or how they were feeling. Demonstration through experiment was the only route to establishing scientific conclusions, not authority. '*You will go to heaven if you are a good person*' or '*Jesus Christ died for the sins of humanity*' is not a testable proposition. A theory making testable propositions can be regarded as valid as long as it is not just the result of a one-off result through experimental observation. A scientific theory is only tentatively reliable: it might be disproved or falsified.

Galileo sought to describe the world "*in the language of mathematics and its characters are triangles, circles and other geometrical figures, without which it is humanly impossible to understand a single word of it; without these, one wanders about in a dark labyrinth*". [262]

The problem is not the methods of science per se but the philosophy that often accompanies it. 'Scientism' postulates that the only kind of description that mattered is to do with aspects of size, shape, location and motion that can be described mathematically. Sensory and interpretive qualities are in the mind of the observer.

Galileo's error- suggests Philip Goff[263] - was to limit the frame of reference for scientific investigation. Science felt it should limit itself to changes in the position of an object, such as falling objects under the influence of gravity. 'Hard science' would not deal with questions of value, meaning and morality or indeed consciousness generally. Those are not so much off-limits as inaccessible. [264]

The worldview underlying the new science was resolutely clear. Only physical things exist. Everything happens through nature by itself doing it. Any sense of being valuable is but the product of physical processes and is therefore illusory. In a materialist science, matter is everything. Everything yields to hard science. The riddle of consciousness is solvable because Mind is a spasm of the brain. This is the philosophy of Monism: everything that exists is fundamentally one substance. Material things, or bodies, move around static space and bump into each other via laws of inertial force. The realm of subjective qualities that the mind perceives is secondary to the objective qualities of nature. Such a system of mechanics allows the isolation of consciousness and the free will with which it is normally associated from the domain of the physicist's enquiry. There is Mind; there is matter. The person we are is merely a projection of a functioning brain and body. Qualitative experiences, on this view are simply a matter of brain chemistry. Only scientific study of the brain will enable us to determine the nature of consciousness. Everything in the cosmos derives from matter and energy. The very existence of mind, let alone its self-reflective significance and rationality, is supposed to be derived from that. Anything that gives our lives coherence, meaning and value is illusory. Purpose is understandable but artificial. Kant's three big questions—'what can we know, what should we do, what can we hope for?'—are ultimately meaningless. Such were the claims of scientific modernity.

By contrast, the realm increasingly disclosed to us by contemporary physics is one where non-local phenomena takes place, where signal- less communication is the norm and where, instead of matter being everything, there are waves of possibility. In this post-materialist science, a universe suffused with energies and energy is far more prominent than matter. how do we define energy scientifically? Is energy really that philosophically different from matter though—it is a different, less inert substance but it is ultimately physical? We live in an energy-verse. The fundamental nature of the universe is that layers of reality are collections of force fields. As in a quantum computer, electrons jump from one state to another without passing through the space between. 21st century science has not stressed particles and bodies so much as relationships of energy; interpenetrating energy fields. The nature of the related thing derives from these relations.

'Scientific materialism', 'physicalism', 'naturalistic philosophy'—these terms are reasonable interchangeable except that a thoroughgoing materialism might want to say that matter is the only thing that counts. Products of the mind are essentially to be reduced to interactions within the brain. Science seems to be the only universally valid form of knowledge in our culture.[265]

'Methodological naturalism' has been developed as a contrast to 'naturalism' in general. [266]This permits a convention of the natural sciences, while leaving us free to embrace a reality that transcends naturalism. [267]*"If science really is committed to methodological naturalism, then it automatically follows that the aim of science is not generating true theories. Instead, the aim of science would be something like: generating the best theories that can be formulated subject to the restriction that those theories are naturalistic".* [268]

This philosophy is linked to scientific positivism. A J Ayer and his school of thought in 'the Vienna circle' at Oxford rejected metaphysics. No proposition can qualify as meaningful or true/false unless it is empirically verifiable. [269] This position was opposed by philosophers such as G.E. Moore and J.L. Austin as erecting an extreme empiricism; ungrounded since it failed to satisfy its own verification criteria (therefore 'secretly in love with the metaphysical enemy'!)

Much has been written about the limitations of scientific materialism or naturalism. There are indeed doubts about whether fundamental aspects of human life in this world can be derived from within nature as a complete account of reality. [270]Most participants in the human drama presumably acknowledge that physical sciences cannot describe the texture of life. But with what shall we supplement a naturalistic world view—or even replace it with?

There is a hard problem with materialism, the theory that everything can be explained by material entities that can either be observed at the present time or have the potential to be with superior instruments. [271]The universal principles without which nothing was made that was made can in principle be stated mathematically. Should new physics give us more fundamental levels of reality, these will in time yield surely to mathematical precision in their description of forces and particles.

If there is only matter, then consciousness is a product of brain and essentially of physical particles. Any sense of worth that I have is also the result of physical particles: a biological entity governed by fundamental laws of physics and chemistry. It is but a comfortable illusion.

From the very birth of enquiry, the search has been on for a comprehensive view of reality. It led from the speculations of hunter gatherers and neolithic farmers, early religion and through the religious and practical philosophers of the axial age that witnessed such a leap forward in the human imagination. The search for what is real haunted the Greek philosophy of the Ionian thinkers and thence to Plato and Aristotle. In the East, it led to the Dao, to Buddhism and to the Upanishads.

It underlay the birth of empirical science in the early modern period. The scientific method of experimentation to test the claims of material reality became the royal road to establishing the truths of scientific disciplines as we know them and led to the astonishing endeavours of the last five hundred years to understand and harness the world. A purely scientific approach became entwined in the minds of many with what became known as 'materialism', that only what is material and objectively verifiable could be valid. Scientific knowledge was the only way of acquiring truth about the cosmos and indeed reality at every level. There was no other content beyond what could be derived from natural processes.

The understanding of material reality that emerged in the 17th, 18th and 19th centuries seemed to be clear. Even as technology had allowed the globe to be circled and material forces harnessed, it also indicated that the basic principles of nature had been conquered and grasped. The elements seemed to be eternal. Evolution of living things was derived ultimately from non-living matter. A historian of science sums this up.

"There are no purposeful principles whatsoever in nature. There are no gods and no designing forces that are rationally detectable.... There are no inherent moral or physical laws... humans are marvellously complex machines. The individual becomes an ethical person by means of only two mechanisms: deterministic hereditary interacting with deterministic environmental influences". [272]

In 19th century halls of learning, theistic science began to be distinguished from natural science. Academic silos policing of disciplinary divisions grew and solidified. Then came Einstein and the picture of reality that had been given to us was upended.

Quantum mechanics further complicated the understanding of reality as comprehensible and measurable. Today the contours of the physical universe are clearer than ever and at the same time more mysterious than ever. This is apparent at the level of the very large scale and the very small.

The quest for the secrets of matter, the fundamental building blocks that could not decompose into anything smaller, took us to the atom and then within the atom. For the most part, atoms were comprised of empty space. A miniscule nucleus vastly smaller than the atom itself was built from subatomic particles. New forces of nature, such as Planck's constant and the nuclear force, described the structure of material reality more effectively. In the Quantum revolution, light is not just a wave but acts like a packet, a quantum particle. Electrons were found to act like waves, not just the particle stream in a single electron beam. In the celebrated double slit experiment, seemingly electrons interfere with each other as if they move through both slits at the same time. This was the basis of quantum mechanics and was completely incompatible with a Newtonian universe. Schrodinger explained the motion of such particle waves. Only electrons that form discrete wavelengths can form stable atoms. Understanding of the fundamental building blocks of matter has moved away from atoms and then electrons along with protons and neutrons. That was replaced in the 1970's by a model of leptons (electrons) and quarks.

The wave equation proposed by Paul Dirac combined special relativity and the speed of light. It also theorised the existence of anti-matter. Electrons and indeed all subatomic particles had a spin that created such phenomena as magnetism. The celebrated but totally baffling uncertainty principle courtesy of Heisenberg meant that an observer is unable to determine the velocity and the location of an electron at the same time. It behaved as a wave function: a set of possibilities. Determinism and fixed laws of nature had to vacate the room; future events could not be predicted with any accuracy. Subatomic particles such as quarks and leptons began to spill out of Hadron colliders aiding fine-grained empirical observation. How the fundamental forces could be combined into a single account, a field equation continued, however, to be the quest for theory of everything.

Everything? What has been termed 'the standard model' cannot be the whole answer to what the universe is made of. The standard model cannot at this time include the dark matter that holds galaxies together and enabled large-scale structures in the universe. It struggled to explain why there is more matter than anti-matter. Will a new physics, new particles and forces, point to the next layer of reality?

Some of the limits to scientific explanation are due also to the fact that science is always expanding, always restless, always probing and pushing boundaries through hypothesising and testing. Scientific knowledge grows in dynamic flux; often at the graves of its leading theorists at one time as Karl Popper suggested. The body of scientific knowledge in one generation will be leaped over in the next. It may well be that such observations as the mystery of dark matter and dark energy will yield its secrets before long. Consider some baffling mysteries that are often cited; scientific discoveries that shift paradigm and draw out questions about the limits of materialistic worldview assumptions.

<u>Dark energy and dark matter</u>—unseen forces of nature which, if found, would open the door to a realm of the universe currently hidden from view. Evidence is sought for a new fundamental force that forms a bridge between the ordinary matter of the world around us and the invisible "dark sector" that is said to make up the vast majority of the cosmos. This is postulated to drive the universe's runaway expansion. Should such a force be found it would rank among the most dramatic discoveries in the history of physics. The best theory of reality that physicists have explains only 4% of the observable universe. The rest is a mystery made up of dark matter, the strange material that lurks around galaxies, and the even more baffling dark energy, a substance called upon to explain the ever-accelerating expansion of the universe. Gravity acts as a brake. But something is pushing it apart. We may not see dark energy but 70% of the universe seems to consist of it. When the universe doubles in size, dark energy doubles. And we have no idea what it is. It may be that Einstein's theory of gravity fails to describe how it behaves over the cosmos's vast expanses.

<u>Gravitational waves</u>—Predicted by Einstein but until recently undetected, scientists have made (at the time of writing—June 2023), an astounding discovery about ripples in space-time, called gravitational waves. But because the distortions they create in space-time are so minute, they were not detected until eight years ago. Now it emerged that there was a "cosmic background" of ripples in the structure of space and time. A team of astronomers from around the world, working together as the North American Nanohertz Observatory for Gravitational Waves (NANOGrav), made the detection using rapidly spinning glows of once-massive stars called pulsars. Over 15 years, the NANOGrav scientists tracked tiny changes in the burst patterns of 67 pulsars scattered across the Milky Way. It seemed these ripples were not from one discrete source but from a din, a hum, the overlapping echoes of disturbances scattered across the universe. The implications are

astounding. *"Every gravitational wave in that background the NANOGrav team found is humming through the very constitution of the space you inhabit right now. Every proton and neutron in every atom from the tip of your toes to the top of your head is shifting, shuttling, and vibrating in a collective purr within which the entire history of the universe is implicated. And if you put your hand down on a chair or table or anything else nearby, that object, too, is dancing that slow waltz."* [273]

A fifth force—Physicists have, until recently, known of only four basic forces of nature. The electromagnetic force allows for vision and mobile phone calls, but also stops us falling through our chairs. Without the so-called 'strong force', the innards of atoms would fall apart. The 'weak force' operates in radiation, and gravity—the most pervasive of nature's forces—keeps our feet rooted to the ground. But there may be other forces that have gone unnoticed. These would shape the behaviour of the so far unknown particles that constitute dark matter and could potentially exert the most subtle effects on the forces we are more familiar with. Then comes (April 2021), a new study suggests subatomic particles called muons are breaking the laws of physics. [274] This may mean a mysterious force is affecting muons, which would make our understanding of physics incomplete. It could be the same force that is responsible for dark matter, which shaped the early universe. The most ubiquitous subatomic particles in the universe, muons, are deviating so much from what the laws of physics suggest that scientists are beginning to think there is some force in the universe of which we are ignorant. Muons are like fat electrons: They have a negative charge but are 207 times heavier than electrons. Thanks to their charge and a property known as spin, they act like tiny magnets. So when muons are immersed in another magnetic field, they experience an infinitesimal wobble. But physicists at the Fermilab in Illinois have reported a discrepancy between how much muons *should* be wobbling and how much they actually *did* wobble during a lab experiment. The difference is substantial enough that many scientists are convinced particles or forces we have not yet discovered must be involved. The finding, in other words, offers new evidence that something mysterious has played a role in shaping our universe—something missing from the existing rules of physics. The hint is that the muon might be sensitive to something that is not in our best theory.

Parallel universes - One of the most exciting and enticing topics to speculate about is the idea that our reality—our Universe the way it is and the way we experience it—might not be the only version of events out there. Perhaps there are other Universes, perhaps even with different versions of ourselves, different histories and alternate outcomes, than our own. When it comes to physics, this is one of the most exciting possibilities of all, but it is far from a certainty. The reason the Universe appears finite in size to us—the reason we cannot see anything that's more than a specific distance away—is not because the Universe is actually finite in size but is rather because the Universe has only existed in its present state for a finite amount of time. That limit is set by the distance that light has had the ability to travel since the instant of the Big Bang. But this does not entail there are no more Universe out there beyond the portion accessible to us. Parallel universes are one of those intriguing ideas that is imaginative, compelling, but very difficult to test. They first arose in the context of quantum physics, which is notorious for having unpredictable outcomes even if you know everything possible about how you set up your system. If you take a single electron and shoot it through a double slit, you can only know the probabilities of where it will land; you cannot predict exactly where it will appear. One idea — known as the many-worlds interpretation of quantum mechanics — postulates that all the outcomes that can possibly occur actually do happen, but only one outcome can happen in each Universe. This interpretation is as valid as any other: no experiments or observations rule it out. Even setting aside issues that there may be an infinite number of possible values for fundamental constants, particles and interactions, and even setting aside questions such as whether the many-worlds-interpretation actually describes our physical reality, the number of possible outcomes rises so quickly that unless inflation has been occurring for a truly infinite amount of time, there are no parallel universes identical to this one.

<u>Quantum entanglement</u> - Einstein famously challenged any notion that quantum mechanics should allow two objects to affect each other's behaviour instantly across vast distances: *"spooky action at a distance"*.[275] Decades after his death, experiments confirmed have this mysterious behaviour. Measurements performed on one system seem to be instantaneously influencing other systems entangled with it. Quantum entanglement has applications in the emerging technologies of computing and cryptography and has been used to realize quantum teleportation experimentally. It prompts some of the more philosophically oriented discussions concerning quantum theory. But, to this day, it remains unclear exactly how much coordination nature allows between distant objects. Researchers now say they have solved a theoretical problem that shows that the answer is, in principle, unknowable.[276]

Many examples could be listed of the limits to scientific explanation at a cosmic level. Or we could go to the challenge of accounting for the origins of complex life. Self-replicating cellular life forms MAY have arrived through interventions in the natural world that are non-physical—such as argued famously by William Paley with his flawed analogy of inferring a watchmaker from the discovery of a watch. [277]OR natural processes could account for this as Darwin argued with his 1859 theory of natural selection—adopted by Richard Dawkins as the 'blind watchmaker'. In essence, an unconscious, automatic, blind process supplies the only answer to the biggest question of all: why do we exist? [278]

The range, power and predictability of scientific explanation is immense. Through mathematics and observation from an insignificant planet, humanity can reach across time and space. Yet science cannot say that we are worth nothing or that our psychological need to be worthwhile is but an illusion. [279]

A unified natural order that brings everything together on a set of common scientific principles is vital to a proper understanding of the world. But how shall we construct a unified natural order? A more complete understanding surely has to include mind, consciousness and what people label a spiritual realm. Crucially too, it must encompass the sense of valuable personhood to which we draw attention in this book. An expanded view of the natural order must surely observe the natural world of flowers, shrubs and teeming insects as I write these words from my garden but also the observer: that is to say 'me'. Can the existential questions that humans notoriously wrestle with- questions of purpose, meaning or value—be accommodated by a naturalistic process involving only physical law?

The sense of valuable personhood to which we are calling attention to here seems to go beyond forms of explanation that depend on the physical laws. Human personhood is, as noted in Chapter Four, vital to ethical and spiritual dimensions of reality. Science has limited authority to speak on such matters. Humanity cannot be reduced to purely genetic, cognitive or physical constituents.

This is more than the universe becoming conscious of itself as in the much-discussed anthropic principle. Living in a quark and lepton universe needs to account for the internal demand to be validated, to be recognised. This requires a larger picture of the natural world.

Or do we resign ourselves to bi-polarity and a split-world experience?

Today, we speak of a 'post- mechanistic paradigm; a mindset that represents a break from the notion that the physical universe is but a collection of physical particles and the whole thing functions as a machine. The perspective is changing. Slipping away is the previous paradigm of materialism and a cosmic mechanistic process we got from the days of Isaac Newton—though the great man was a well-known theist and alchemist, pursuing the fundamental properties of matter.

Those committed to a naturalistic philosophy might disagree about whether consciousness is completely equated with activity in the brain or whether there is an emergent property; something new that appears. Naturalism does not usually deny the reality of mental events though some think they are illusory. Most naturalistic thinkers would stress that mentality is generated by electro-chemical impulses. Science can explain how the world works and this applies to the human mind! Thoughts, feelings and spiritual impulses can be attributed to and localised within mechanisms within the brain that are physiological before they are psychological.

It is widely held that mechanistic science provides a description of reality that if partial, is nevertheless objective. The gap is not just between that and the world of our experiences. The gap is between such a materialist account, or some kind of dualist version in which mind and matter pertain to incommensurable realms and the inner world where human actors have a sense of their own value and worth (in presence or in absentia with corresponding psychological effects). Hence human subjects began to feel like aliens, unrelated to the cosmos.

The considerations in this chapter point to the conclusion that materialism is inadequate as a theory of everything and that there is a need for a new approach so that we do not live in a split world of consciousness and matter (bringing in the problem of consciousness).

Let's now probe deeper into what this could look like.

Chapter Seven

Field Theory and A Conscious Cosmos

"The deep structure of the universe may be a globally self-consistent assemblage of the empty set. We, like mathematics, and like it or not, are elegant, self-consistent, re-organisations of nothing"
—Peter Atkins[280]

THE IMPORTANCE IN PSYCHOLOGICAL and interpersonal life of a sense of value (and with it, linked concepts of Spirit, significance, meaning and morality) seems at completely at odds with reductionist emphasis on natural processes through physics and chemistry. We have considered the limits to scientific methodological naturalism that is inimical to what we most care about as human beings.

Yet somehow, the realm of value, love and meaning in which we actually live must fold into the overall scheme of things. Now we are to try to give an account of what this could be conceptualised.

A realm where our personhood is validated may belong to a bigger dimension of reality than what see empirically. It is, however, a question that we might be able to infer something about.

It seems clear that empirical proof of such a dimension is not open to us in the same way that we can find something that can be quantified, tested and validated. A dimension of reality that endorses or maybe even generates our personhood does not show up in the Large Hadron Collider. It is not demonstrable as a conclusion of mathematical equations.

Contemporary science specialises in working out how the parts work. What is much more elusive is the big picture. How can we know that there exists something hidden; as yet not showing up in the tools we have for measuring things? As the only entity we know of where the universe becomes conscious of itself, the human person should be central to however we conceive physical reality.

What humans look for is the validation of the self. This can come in varying ways: the significance of a career, the excitable welcome of a pet, the loving mutuality of a high-quality relationship and most of all, the experience of divine love and affirmation.

It has certainly been an argument of philosophical theology in the monotheistic tradition that God is not another object in the universe. Anyone in the nursery school of philosophical theology knows that God is understood as having being in itself—aseity—and therefore not part of the world as we understand it. By contrast, the God pictured by the vociferous atheists of our time is a product of nature, not its creator. God is simple, not complex, in the sense of needing to arise by natural selection. Simple agents in the world can be the cause of more complex entities.

It was Kant who sought to show that reality as we see it is a product of our way of thinking. The categories by which we structure reality, such as space and time and change, are in our heads. Knowledge pertains to appearances of things, not to the reality of things themselves. The realm of value, love and meaning would not, according to Kant, have spatio-temporal properties.

Since Kant, it has been common to split the world. To science belongs empirical process and the measurement of physical phenomena. Talk of God, Kant argued, lay beyond the phenomenal world of our senses. The human mind is unequipped to go beyond this to what he called 'the noumenal' world. We are aware that the noumenal world exists. Human sensibility is merely receptive; responding to what is beyond phenomena. But the noumenal world is not itself open to our physical senses and must therefore remain otherwise unknowable directly by direct apprehension. The noumenal world is the realm of things as they are in themselves: things we seem compelled to believe in, but which we can never know as we lack sensory evidence of them. By contrast, our sense of the phenomenal realm is constructed by the mind to impose order and make sense of what we see. The mind interprets sense-data. Rejecting the notion of an objective world independent of our mind, the world was a creation of the mind.[281]

A theistic realm that corresponds to human personhood and significance is not thought to be one that is open to direct observation. That has not stopped a train of philosophers in the tradition of Thomas Aquinas coming up with empirical proofs, most notably the 'Five Ways', endeavouring to demonstrate the existence of a supra-personal realm, namely God. Nevertheless, theistic 'proofs', despite looking like scientific inferences, have limitations in that they treat God as we treat nature.

There has been debate about whether such approaches are deductive or inductive. For 'proofs' of God's existence to be deductive, they would have to flow inexorably from the premise. If the truth of the premise definitely confirms the truth of the conclusion, it is deductive. Apart from the first part of the cosmological argument, the Five Ways are inductive in character. They are a posteriori (post experience) because it depends upon empirical (derived from the senses) evidence and experience that leads to a possible conclusion.

Induction is a general problem of knowledge deriving from cognitive resources we have as human beings. We move from some observations to conclusions which could then be universally valid. Our ordinary ways of knowing things from everyday effects are extended into scientific theorising to make these observations and draw such conclusions. The challenge to science, philosophy and some forms of natural theology is how we might learn from experience. It was challenged famously by David Hume in the 18th century. In his Book 1 of his 1739 *Treatise of Human Nature* he could not see a way that *inductive reasoning could be justified. Why should similar causes produce similar effects. All such inferences assumed that the future would be like the past.*[282] *They cannot be justified by mere logical reasoning. What has not been experienced as yet lies beyond our reasoning.*

Bertrand Russell's homely example stands as a caution: the chicken cannot assume that just because it has been well-fed yesterday it will be the case today. [283]

Scientific reasoning has proceeded in this way. In his elaboration of optics, Isaac Newton did not probe the problem of induction as a general species of reasoning, but he did think hard about what he could reasonably infer from his observations about prisms and rays of light. In his 'Opticks', Newton claimed that the rays of the sun were susceptible to refraction as they passed through different mediums. [284] He did not seek to explore whether in theory the rays of the sun might differ the next day or behave differently if he went from Cambridge to the Royal Society in London. The general problem of induction was not in his sights so much as the specific set of experiments he was performing with prisms and what could reasonably be concluded. Might his experiments go wrong? What would happen if some elements were different? Perhaps there were possibilities of error in the particular way his experiments were set up? These were his principal concerns.

Since Newton's day, scientific reasoning has advanced through such routes as Karl Popper's notion of falsifiability. Theories are the most corroborated and valid that have survived testing through means of demonstrating that they could be false. Popper began to formulate his philosophy of science in 1919, when *"the air was full of revolutionary slogans and ideas, and new and often wild theories"*. [285] On the basis of whether a theory is testable and what evidence might count against it, Popper regarded verification of Einstein's theory of general relativity that year as good science but not Freud's theories. Although Popper regarded it as of considerable importance, he thought that psychoanalysis appeared so flexible it could be reinterpreted in the light of contrary evidence. *"There was no conceivable human behavior which could contradict it"*. [286]

In the late 20th century, astronomers began to infer the existence of thousands of exoplanets—planets orbiting stars beyond our own solar system. Then there came actual photographs, courtesy of the telescopy power of James Webb: for example, HIP 65426 believed to be a gas giant planet, a half-dozen times the size of Jupiter. It orbits its host star at a distance about 100 times greater than the Earth-sun distance. But the inference came first.

A contemporary challenge both to those who advocate induction and falsification is the problem of underdetermination. There is a logical gap in that the connection between the hypothesis being tested and the relevant data is not direct. [287] An additional premise, or auxiliary assumption, is needed to establish that the data is true. Theories are underdetermined by the data alone. Something more is needed.

Abduction is a form of induction and possibly relevant here. Exercising human rationality in general is a combination of deductive but also inductive reasoning to form what the 'best possible explanation' (or inferential best explanation—IBE). [288] If to postulate something might account for a range of observable but also unobservable phenomenon, then aspects of the given reality might seem to *"severally cooperate in favour of a conclusion"*. [289] In arguing for the applicability of this approach to the web of evidence, experience and beliefs humans encounter when it comes to ultimate realities, Peacock suggests we need to draw on a combination of:

- Comprehensiveness
- Fruitfulness
- General cogency and plausibility
- Internal coherence
- Simplicity and elegance[290]

In short, a postulate has to do a better job of explaining phenomenon than other explanatory hypotheses. Applied to the present task, this entails building a picture of reality that can take account of scientific methods and consequent explanations but also the psychological data (readily observable) about the vital role of being of value that humans seem to need. This is a picture that can be examined not merely from a scientific perspective but also from a philosophical cum theological lens on that picture. However, as considered in the previous chapter, it is also a picture that can take is reference from human experience regarding our sense of worthwhileness (or its deficit) that can claim to be common possession in contemporary culture.

We might approach such a conceptualisation through a process of inductive reasoning. We have few tools with which to produce a deductive process based on existing theory that is then subject to:

Testing hypothesis—data collection—data analysis—verification or amendment of hypothesis

Inductive logic is intended to be a range of arguments that provide indicative support for their conclusions but do not give certainty such as found in the logic of deduction. The logical positivists stressed the importance of induction as error is always possible. *"Hardly any of the arguments and evidence that we confront in everyday life and science carry the kind of guarantees found in deductive logic. Even the best kind of evidence we can find for a scientific theory is not completely decisive."* That does not stop scientific claims that they are supported by evidence. Science, however, rarely reaches absolute certainty.[291]

Inductive reasoning by contrast is based on observations. The main difference between the two approaches is that inductive reasoning entails developing a theory while deductive reasoning aims at testing an existing theory to see if conclusions are valid. A conclusion on the basis of an inductive approach cannot be 'proven'.[292]

Much science has proceeded indirectly rather than through empirical verification[293], examining, for example, indirect evidence that might support the Big Bang such as microwave radiation. The planet Neptune was discovered by inferring a new object that explained deviations in the orbit of Uranus from a perfect ellipse. Then comes new discovery and challenges to theory that alter the conditions and potentially a new paradigm is in the making.[294]

This style of reasoning is linked to the idea of probabilities. Rev Thomas Bayes, a generation or two after Newton wrote 'An Essay towards solving a problem in the Doctrine of Chance' arguing for a conditional probability. 'Bayesian inference' refers to a distinction between probability that a belief is correct from probability based on frequent occurrences or repeat trials. [295] Machine learning for Artificial Learning has utilised Bayesian optimisation to infer inverse probability based on how a game could have continued or a belief is correct (what would optimise the situation). Quantum computing is based on mathematical probabilities. Quantum physics is derived from multiplicity of possible outcomes that gets resolved into a specific outcome that does actually take place.

Consider again dark matter and dark energy. We cannot detect dark matter but we can see the effects as we can for dark energy that is causing everything in the universe to repel everything else. As I write, the European Space Agency has launched a telescope especially designed to detect both. [296]On the basis of the amount of mass we see, the Milky Way should fly apart in a puff of instability. Yet it, and myriad galactic companions, have proved remarkably stable. We infer then an unseen object keeping galaxies together. Perhaps the answer lies in weakly interacting massive particles (WIMPs). Our world moves within a shower of what have been called 'photinos', partner to the photon. Collision with protons would result in myriads of sub-atomic particles that can be detected.

The principle of sufficient reason is also relevant here as an adequate basis for what it is. Mackie argues that this need not apply to the universe or the ultimate issues posed here: it is just based on our experience. Though it might apply within the world, our reasoning is limited to explaining the world as whole. It leads us nowhere to argue that somethings happen or exist for no reason at all. [297]

Emergentism is a more recent inference for showing how mentality can be derived from non-material factors and forces when physical processes achieve a degree of complexity. At a certain point of complicated interaction of material forces, the human consciousness emerges. This has been welcomed by many working in the field as having potential to explain the origin of consciousness. This stance is in contrast to the inferences of reductionism where reality is 'nothing but' the interaction of far smaller parts. Emergence suggests that reality is 'something more than nothing but' and is essentially an inference from epistemological unpredictability—to cite weaker versions.[298]

So what then could be inferred about the bigger picture of reality? The main phenomena to account for is the challenge of consciousness and the observer but here another dimension is being added; that of valuable personhood that somehow seems indispensable. Consider for example, some of the moves that have been made about how consciousness might be integrated within material reality and the equations that describes the universe.

STRATEGIES FOR INCLUDING CONSCIOUSNESS

The standard model and descriptions of the cosmos proposes that the universe is a lifeless collection of particles interacting with each other and obeying preset rules. The main problem involves life: how to account for its generation remains a scientifically unknown process though subsequent adaptation could develop along Darwinian mechanisms. The even bigger problem is that life contains consciousness: a difficulty for physics as well as biology. How can a group of molecules in a brain create consciousness? As previously discussed, our experiences are known to scientists as human beings but are puzzling to science per se. Scans can track where in the brain sensations of sunsets and sex arise, but not how and why there is any subjective personal experience to begin with.

Three approaches might be noted that have been adopted by thinkers past and present relevant to an account of reality that includes some sense of consciousness.

There is the claim by <u>metaphysical idealism</u> is that mind and consciousness is fundamental to the nature of things. [299] The position in philosophy usually labelled 'idealism' entails two fundamental conceptions. The first is that something mental (mind, spirit, reason, will) is the ultimate foundation of all reality, or even exhaustive of reality. This was the stance held famously in Western thought by Bishop Berkeley in the 18th century and German idealists in the 19th but various branches of Indian philosophy have long since espoused the idea that reality is spiritual or mental rather than material.

Articulating one strand of such thinking, is the American philosopher Josiah Royce at the end of the nineteenth century. Metaphysical idealism, he says, "*is a theory as to the nature of the real world, however we may come to know that nature,*" such as "*belief in a spiritual principle at the basis of the world, without the reduction of the physical world to a mere illusion*". [300]

The approach of metaphysics cannot be 'proven' but could be the subject of inference based on philosophical arguments. Predictions cannot be made; nor can any science be conducted on its assumptions. It is way of seeing the world based on the ubiquity of mentality.

There are various moves here, such as conscious realism as a description of nature—"*The objective world, i.e., the world whose existence does not depend on the perceptions of a particular conscious agent, consists entirely of conscious agents.*" [301] Chalmers labelled this form of idealism one of "*the handful of promising approaches to the mind–body problem.*" [302]

There is attunement with the development of process philosophy. In Whitehead's view, the dualism of Descartes had led to the contradictions of scientific naturalism. There should not be a disjunction between mind and nature. [303] Drawing on William James, Whitehead constructed a view of reality based on experiental events forming an 'ocean of feeling'. Experiences come 'in drops' and are ultimate constituents.[304] There are no enduring substances underneath: events enjoy 'subjective immediacy' but are then swiftly replaced by their successor. [305] This is a world of endless becoming and, in the metaphysical addition of Charles Hartshorne, God is subject to it and has a limited and consequent nature (the 'moved mover' rather than the 'unmoved mover of Aristotle's proposal). [306]

That there is consciousness somewhere in the cosmos is an inference deployed by those who favour panpsychism through which metaphysical idealism has found resurgence. Panpsychism is the notion that everything is alive with consciousness; that the consciousness which to some extent is shared with sentient beings, is also shared with inanimate matter. If you cannot explain consciousness in terms of the interplay of subatomic particles and forces and dualism, a way to go is that consciousness itself is a fundamental property. It is 'degreed'. Everything in the universe is conscious to some extent. The rationale for is the difficulty that seems nigh on insurmountable of giving an account of how any kind of self-awareness can be generated from tissue in someone's head or indeed any kind of matter. A strict scientific materialism that nature by itself is generating this appears to fail as much as a dualistic explanation that only recasts the problem of where the psyche originates from as a different kind of substance.

It is an umbrella term for variations on a theme that argues for the ubiquity of mentality in the cosmos. Contemporary resurgence in the philosophy of mind is associated with Thomas Nagel, David Chalmers, Galen Strawson and Philip Goff. Collectively, this has brought an older theory of mind into a model of consciousness that seems more plausible and joined-up. *"The basic physical components of the universe have mental properties"* suggested Nagel. [307] This was in contrast with older metaphysics that spoke of immaterial substances. Nagel argued from ontological materialism or monism, from mental realism (that consciousness is a property of the human organism and hence of material beings) from no reductionism to physical properties alone and from non-emergence. Mental properties cannot be reduced to the organisation of material parts. The constituent parts must be posited as including non-material aspects that help to explain consciousness.

As Coleman summarised, *"there must be some secret properties of matter with a direct connection to consciousness such that when you put matter together in the right way, as a brain (and perhaps a body too), you get a conscious being"*. [308]

Chalmers argues for consciousness as being 'the hard problem'; that whatever we can explain about brain and body, we will never have explained why any of this is accompanied by experience. Consciousness must be designated as fundamental to the material world rather than a mystical force. *"There is nothing especially transcendental about consciousness; it is just another natural phenomenon. . . to embrace dualism is not necessarily to embrace mystery"*. [309]

Taken together with the work of Galen Strawson and latterly Philip Goff, these philosophers have made it impossible to ignore panpsychism. Strawson contended that 'something akin to panpsychism is not merely one form of realistic physicalism but the only possible form. . .'. [310] Every concrete phenomenon is wholly physical; consciousness is a real, concrete phenomenon. Consciousness must therefore be wholly physical. By this he means that even physical phenomena cannot be described fully by physics. Consciousness may be neurons firing but there is more to neurons than we grasp.

The strict panpsychist would argue that only well-integrated systems of particles—such as in the human brain—are fully conscious. One answer then might be that of Goff, who argues that a concept of far smaller particles and constituents of matter having consciousness is not needed. What counts is the combination of smaller aspects of matter into an integrated system.

[311] It is possible to locate various functions within say a split-brain patient where surgery has taken place. Nevertheless, there still seems to be an underlying unity between these different aspects of experience such that there is a ME. This appears to be true even with bipolarity and a divided self; the feeling that there are different parts of us wanting conflicting things.

Units of consciousness are, on this reading, widely spread and globally participatory. Everything is alive. Many religions have shared this perspective—such as Japanese Shinto with its multiple kami spirits and forms of animism that have permeated indigenous peoples for centuries. Yet so too have philosophers and scientists. Indeed, there is a venerable and respectable history which has recognised that mentality, mind, is integral to how the universe functions. But how do we know if non-sentient beings are conscious? I have just watered the plants in my garden. For all I know, the plants are having some kind of experience as the water falls on them and revives them on a droopy, hot afternoon. At a basic level, is a hosepipe experiencing something?

Panpsychism has definite merits as a philosophical position. It also has flaws. How can predictions be made and any science conducted on its assumptions? The notion that sentient beings have awareness is tautologous. What would it mean though to claim that material things like rocks and hosepipes possess units of consciousness? The DNA in living things is very different. How can the very existence of physical laws of nature be accounted for and why do they have to be so precise?

Endowing a form of consciousness to all material entities might seem to remedy dualist deficiency. However, that stance has no account for how more advanced forms of consciousness might evolve. It is also clear that consciousness has only been observed in physical, sentient systems. Perhaps the different internal states in elementary particles (by which they can have experiences) become relevant only when in combination with other particles in large collections (unobservable to us).

However, it is worth noting that Sabine Hossenfelder in her exploration of Existential Physics can see a place for panpsychism on the grounds that consciousness is not binary but emerges from systems that process more information. It could therefore be more gradual than either-or.[312]

Another possible pathway is bio-centrism- the idea that consciousness is continually present in the cosmos and can exist without connection to a living organism. Totalising theories of everything that generate scientific narratives do not take into account an essential factor: we are creating them. "*It is the biological creature that fashions the stories, that makes the observations, and that gives names to things. And therein lies the great expanse of our oversight, that science has not confronted the one thing that is at once most familiar and most mysterious—consciousness".* A more accurate understanding of the world than current models is that we consider it biologically centred. Life creates the universe, instead of the other way around. Advocates point to indications that consciousness exists beyond the brain, such as when the brain is temporarily incapacitated, as well as to the survival of consciousness after death. Life after death or such phenomena as near-death experiences is for the most part dismissed by scientists as they cannot be accommodated by a materialist view of reality. Spirituality and religion embrace the continuity of consciousness and ascribe it to a nonmaterial spirit or soul that is immortal. This is a re-evaluation of the nature of reality that goes far beyond anything we could have imagined. It brings physics and biology together rather than keeping them separate, and places observers into the equation.

And yet as a total explanation, it falls short for the same reason as panpsychism. How do we account for the framework of physical laws that govern the world and the remarkable fine-tuning of these constants? How were the lights turned on in the human entity?

The hard problem remains. Where and how do we locate the phenomenon of experience in the universe. "The mind-body problem" says Nagel, "*is not just a local problem. . . but that it invades our understanding of the entire cosmos and its history*". [313] Evolution cannot be merely a physical process.

THE PROPOSAL HERE

The approaches above could lead us to aver that there is no independent external universe outside of biological existence. It is consciousness that has created the universe, not the other way round. The key proposal here is that ultimate reality, the deep field behind all other fields, is personal. This can reasonably be inferred from our own sense of personhood. It is personhood at the cosmic level (divine personhood) that is behind interactions of matter and energy and which validates our own. This goes beyond metaphysical idealism where spirit per se is the ultimate constituent.

The stance here could be languaged as a variant of personalism, general affirmation of the centrality of the person for philosophical thought. Personalism posits ultimate reality and value in personhood—human as well as (at least for most personalists) divine. Amidst many schools of thought, the common thread is the emphasis on the significance, uniqueness and inviolability of the person, and the person's essentially relational or social dimension. To be sure, there is a difference between a theistic personalist rather than classical theist conception of God: the latter arguing that God does not 'have' personhood or intellect or such qualities but IS all those attributes in essential nature.

Here we probe the implications of a form of personalism for the scientific understanding of material reality. The emphasis we will make is that of personhood being 'valuable.' In other words, humans are not just conscious observers but have some sense of themselves as:

- Being worthwhile and significant
- Spiritual beings possessing a sense of the spiritual and eternal dimension
- Thriving on hope and purpose
- Requiring the designates previously discussed; the contrast pole of indifference, inequality (or inferiority) and indignity against which humans tend to react.
- Flourishing when there is love and relational connection.

ANTHROPIC PRINCIPLE

The idea that the universe is conscious might seem to find an ally in the anthropic principle: the universe is favourable to the consciousness of observers because of the intricate and fine-grained tuning in the natural world by which human observation has come about. A welcome given to observers like ourselves has been the focus for this. Does that demonstrate that personhood is at the heart of cosmic concern?

Since at least the work of Robert Dicke in the 1960's, it has been a scientific conundrum as to why the physical laws are so finely tuned. The exact strength of four kinds of forces (the gravitational, the electromagnetic, the strong force and the weak force—and maybe dark energy) are set within very narrow values. The appearance of fine-tuning in the cosmos needs explaining. Why the initial conditions of the universe were such that could allow for the possibility of life has been estimated at below one in in a billion, billion. A big metaphysical question is what Derek Parfitt called 'the puzzle of reality: why the universe exists'? Does this point to a Creator? "*We may be tempted to dismiss this answer thinking it improbable that God exists. But should we put the chance as low as one in a billion? If not, this is a better explanation.*" [314]The rival explanation is to be many worlds theory where there are so many big bangs, it is not surprising life and conscious observers crop up in one of them.

Patently, life exists, intelligent life capable of making observations about the universe and pondering the scheme of things. Aspects of our universe are vital for supporting life, such as the longevity of stars, the abundance of carbon, the availability of light for photosynthesis and the stability of complex nuclei. The universe seems remarkably adapted to humankind, not merely that humankind is adapted to the universe.[315] Our own existence seems to hinge upon a remarkable set of coincidences. The anthropic principles attempt to connect aspects of the overall structure of the universe to those conditions necessary for living observers to exist. There are numerous aspects of the cosmos that are coincidences, derived from the numerical values of the fundamental constants that define the gravitational and electromagnetic interactions of physics.[316] Physical constants permit the cosmological fine-tuning that allows for the development of sentient life.

Much debated and much critiqued, the anthropic principle encompasses two versions; the weak and the strong.[317]

The weak anthropic principle is based on the idea that observed values of physical constants are not equally probable but derived from sites where carbon-based life can evolve and that the universe is old enough for this to have happened. A weak version has it that the properties of the universe were conducive to the emergence of conscious observers because that is how things happened to be (a 'brute fact') without which we would not be here to witness and reflect on our witnessing. Even if the notion of multiverses be allowed, observers such as ourselves could only have arisen in the subset where development of carbon-based life could take place. We would not be concerned about this unless the fundamental constants of nature allowed for it.[318] This is a self-selection effect due to the very fact of our existence.

The strong anthropic principle, introduced by Carter, states that the universe needs to have the properties that allows life to develop at some stage. The strong version is that the universe was in some sense hard-wired for human observers. The properties of material reality were favourable because there was an intentionality about it. The constants of nature must be such that allows life to develop. To say that there is only one possible universe which has been designed with observers in mind continues the tradition of the historic design arguments that date back beyond Aristotle's notion of a final cause (the end for which that cause exists and is operative). This approach has strong teleological aspects; observers must play a vital role in cosmic development. There have been strong dissenters across the centuries to any idea of premeditated design—and hence deity. Darwin's work undermined the application of design in biology as natural selection had shaped local environments. 'Coincidences' in the physical laws that were fortunate, to say the least, have had a different reception, however, and have led to the Anthropic Principles.

The physicist John Wheeler proposed a version of the Strong Anthropic Principle in which observers are necessary to bring the universe into being. [319] Physical reality does not exist independently of the observer. This 'Participatory Anthropic Principle' is reminiscent of the philosophical idealism argued by Bishop Berkeley. If a conscious observer like ourselves can bring into existence which way an electron spins, could there be a yet more conscious and intelligent observer that brings into existence the electrons themselves? The implication of this is that there is an Ultimate Observer who coordinates the observations of all observers and brings the whole universe into being.

More recent discussion has underlined the 'many worlds' interpretation of quantum mechanics in which the wave function never actually collapses. This approach stresses that humankind as observer of an experiment is an essential part of physics (certainly the Copenhagen interpretation discussed above points to this). The observer measuring something changes the wave function and thus knowledge of the system. [320] This was a radical departure from the passive role in classical physics. But an implication of quantum mechanics could be that a range of different universes potentially exist in which ours is the one necessary for the existence of life.

This is associated with the notion of a multiverse, that "*our universe, with all its hundreds of billions of galaxies and almost countless stars, spanning tens of billions of light-years, may not be the only one. Instead, there may be an entirely different universe, distantly separated from ours—and another, and another. Indeed, there may be an infinity of universes, all with their own laws of physics, their own collections of stars and galaxies (if stars and galaxies can exist in those universes), and maybe even their own intelligent civilizations.*"[321]

All the special features of the universe that seem to support life are typically not the case if one random universe amongst many exists. In a multiverse, there are enough random chances for life to appear in at least one of them. Yet that is pure conjecture and it remains highly improbable that conscious life would develop anywhere in the universe unless it were fine-tuned for precisely this.

Where these considerations might point is the role of consciousness, the astonishing phenomenon that sentient life is not just conscious and indeed self-conscious aware of itself, but in fact needs to be recognised and dignified. A physical description of reality cannot account for the realm of value by which humankind lives. The conscious observer seems to be necessary somehow for quantum weirdness to materialise. Consciousness itself is an immensely tricky issue to solve. The inference is that there is a total field at a deeper layer of reality to which our personhood is responding. Clearly there are elements to our existence that are far more than quarks and leptons. What could we infer then about the realm that give our lives value, meaning and significance?

BEYOND THE DEEP FIELD

The quest for what the universe is made of and what lies behind everything has haunted philosophers, scientists, religious people and human beings generally.

The notion of 'field' can be invoked to describe a realm which has certain discernible effects, with which we interact and which potentially lights up our minds and supplies meaning to our existence. The Hubble Space Telescope and then the James Webb provided some stunning imagery of the deep field. Behind what can be seen by even the most advanced telescopes before Hubble lay deep fields of galaxies and yet more galaxies. The deeper we probed, the further we saw as countless galactic inhabitants were revealed.

When it comes to cosmic personhood, an additional layer of reality can be supplied by the notion of a field. Invoking a deep field poses huge conceptual questions. What could we infer about it?

How we infer the presence of a wider field generally is to chart the effects of activity, of phenomena that enable us to say that this is being acted on by a broader sphere of operation. The concept of field is everywhere in our understanding of reality. It is well grasped that phenomena take place within a field of some sort on which forces act.

Historical analysis often proceeds on the basis of field definition; famously in the 'Study of History' by Arnold Toynbee.[322] Dissatisfied with micro-productions of detailed analysis of localised events, Toynbee sought a field that was broad enough to encompass what was taking place on a wider canvas. He put into world history the concept of a civilisation as sufficiently large as a unit of analysis that it could include forces operating in that field and enable an interpretation.

The history of economics went through various phases according to the unit of analysis, whether mercantilism, free markets, the theory of the firm, supply and demand, the demise of capitalism, monetarism or John Maynard Keynes' notion of how demand in the economy is linked to unemployment. He labelled his magnum opus a 'General Theory' as it sought to explain how the whole capitalist field of economic activity operated rather than the working of an individual firm. His solution *advocated the use of fiscal and monetary policies to mitigate the adverse effects of economic recessions and depressions.*[323]

Field theory in the social sciences is an approach whose essence is the explanation of regularities in individual action by recourse to position in a field. The position in the field indicates the potential for a force exerted on the person that impinges 'from the inside' as opposed to external compulsion. Motivation is a paramount example of social structure in action, as opposed to a residue of chance or freedom. [324] For Pierre *Bourdieu, fields* denote arenas of production, circulation, and appropriation and exchange of goods, services, knowledge, or status. [325] Systems theory is a way of discerning the operations of social forces across a field. Sylvia Walby dismantles the conservative versions of systems theory and provides a new way of approaching the dynamics of intersectional change by considering the field within which they operate. This generates significant insights into the ways in which modernity is contested and the construction of equality and inequality in how social democratic and liberal states. [326]

In psychology, field theory is an approach which examines patterns of interaction between the individual and the total field, or environment. The concept first made its appearance in psychology with roots to the holistic perspective of Gestalt theories developed by Fritz Perls. [327]

Similarly, when it comes to change management in education, Kurt Lewin's field theory rule states that 'analysis starts with the situation as a whole'. By gaining an overview as early as possible, we intend to broaden the perspective from which we as scholarly practitioners engage with the general characteristics of the challenge or opportunity facing organisational clients. Interest in it declined significantly until the 1990s when a variant, force field analysis, became widely used. [328]

Observation and analysis of physical forces moved into a completely different mode when gravitational fields began to be understood through the ground-breaking work of Newton in the latter half of the 17th century in a given frame of reference. The concept of field though really goes back to Faraday. The work of Maxwell 150 years later provided a way of understanding how electricity and magnetism could be combined invoking the notion of an electro-magnetic field.

The notion that fundamental layers of physical reality are force-fields rather than solid lumps of matter was at odds with previous conceptions such as those of Lucretius. [329]"*All nature as it is itself consists of two things— bodies and the vacant space in which the bodies are situated and through which they move in different directions. . . nothing exists that is distinct from bodies and from vacuity*".

Einstein proceeded to show field equations that could show how fundamental components of physics such as time and light were affected by the frames of reference in which they moved. The special and then General theory of relativity brought a new window on celestial mechanics that transformed our view of the universe. Although we speak of a gravitational field, gravity is not a force like others. As the 20th century unfolded, discovery of the laws of quantum physics revealed properties of the very small that were best understood as operating in a particular field. We are surrounded by quantum fields. Quantum field theory helps to explain the life and death of particles.

The discovery of electromagnetism was a huge conceptual leap forward. From brains to stars, this was the force that holds everything together and it operated in fields. Reality is not only made up of particles that move about; there is another actor, albeit in the background, that of the field. When we see trees and people in the park, there are invisible waves happening between all the objects of perception. Einstein's advance demonstrated that the cosmos comprises of particles and fields; space is neither an additional dimension nor an empty container. It is a real entity that moves and pulsates. This is the legacy of his description of the world. Space is not a rigid container but an enormous entity akin to a mollusc. Space and time are not something else but fields which move on other fields. According to quantum ideas, time emerges from the processes of fields of space. Space-time is a substratum of quantum fields and is generated from them.

The discovery that led to the Higgs boson discovery was the realisation from research in the 1960's that wherever the symmetry of apparently empty space is broken, there is a hypothetical field involved. It seemed that there was no quantum field without a quantum particle, the Higgs boson enabling clustering and the acquisition of mass. This mass generating mechanism was swiftly dubbed 'the God particle'. In physics, the standard model- complete with Higgs bosun—is responsible for what we call mass. The properties of all particles - mass and electrical charge - is connected to how their fields interact with other fields. Electric charge is about how an electron field interacts with the electromagnetic field. Mass is how the electron field interacts with the Higgs field.

The Fermi theory shows how the interaction of the electron with the electromagnetic field can create photons. Electrons and photons can be created. Particles are excitations in their own field. The concept of field reflects the physical world is being a web of interactions—some are attractive and others are repulsive. This is rooted in the spin of the mediating particle being odd or even.

On the contemporary scene there is field theory, quantum field theory and gauge theories. Many problems in physics can be discussed as field theories. Each entity lies within a field. Each field has its own dynamic and is influenced by other fields, according to proximity and force strength. A quantum field forms part of the fabric of physical reality. Like currents and waves in the ocean, energies within the field can oscillate and pulsate. In addition to electrons, *"a large number of further fundamental particles also have associated fields and the combined structure of these fields is both rich and beautiful, like a tapestry shimmering with a variety of patterns all interleaved together"*. [330]

A quantum field is unified whole of space and time. The notion of quantum entanglement could point to a deeper field within which two entities play out their non-local connection. A deeper field might be a form of explanation that allows for a background that is operating against which the two entities are linked. In the same way, there could be a spiritual realm that is greater than the purely material realm described by physical science. It will be objected that there is no evidence for an eternal, spiritual realm. But this could be countered by the evidence that is universal in human culture of the search for something beyond ourselves and that will outlive us. It is not just a question of perennial religious experience. It is the presence, as being argued here, for the psychological necessity for value without which humankind implodes.

The inference here is that the optimum way of accounting for the realm of value, love, meaning and spirituality by which supplies the emotional content of our consciousness of valuable personhood is that there is a deep field of reality to which it responds in some way. This goes beyond consciousness as a mental event which may be connecting with some sense of an ultimate Mind. What needs to be accounted for is that human significance is not only a philosophical and existential enquiry but the inner milieu by which we live. Take that away and human being lose the point of themselves.

Why would the sense of significance that seems to be hard-wired into our DNA, point to and possible require a larger field? Our very sense of ourselves as worthwhile, is totally at odds with either the vastness of the cosmos or a description of reality in terms of natural processes that are inherently neutral and blind. Our psychological make-up seems to require more; a reality that somehow recognises us and which answers the cry of the human heart that there is someone or something 'out there' for me and that will endorse my existence. This can be described as a realm of meaning and value beyond ourselves, possibly writ large into the scheme of things to which our lives connect. What might count as evidence for personhood being validated by something bigger than ourselves?

- Being worthwhile, having the potential for being worth something
- A sense of human significance
- A felt subjectivity of being 'me' to whom respect is due
- Our personhood that requires I-thou encounters.

The inference is that there is a field operating beyond the material realm validating our personhood, that our personal sense of ME connects with. What does it say about the nature of ultimate reality? Crucially for our concerns here, can that connect with the question of observation and what it is that permits the role together with the internal dynamics of the observer? A physical description of reality cannot account for the realm of value by which humankind lives. Valuable personhood is inseparable from contemporary debates about why anyone should care about segregated societies or the value of the human.

The conscious observer seems to be necessary somehow for quantum weirdness to materialise. Consciousness itself is a really tricky issue to solve. But so too is the self-consciousness by which the self becomes self-regarding: consciousness becoming conscious of itself and deeming itself to be worth seeing because of what appears to be an in-built psycho-social impetus to be valuable.

So where do these considerations take us? The possibilities on an ontological level seem to be:

- BL 1–3]That despite all the points against it raised in this volume so far, cosmos and brain are completely explained by a naturalist conception of things; that mind is matter in operation;
- That the universe and human participants are bound together in a single quantum reality or energy field; one variation of this being panentheism or that the universe is conscious as in panpsychism
- That the universe is best explained by a single, purposing Mind; a conscious Being who is the ground of all being and who calls personhood into existence by multiple acts of seeing.

At issue here is the very nature of reality and to this we must now turn.

Chapter Eight

The Topography of Reality

"Why does the universe go to all the bother of existing? Is the unified theory so compelling that it brings about its own existence?"
—Stephen Hawking [331]

IF TWO PEOPLE ARE playing chess, where is the game? A single film shot or glance of the eye at sees individual actors acting and interacting but are part of a single screenshot.

What is real? What is ultimate reality?

The universe we actually live in is a combination of different levels of reality. There is a gap between these. How these realms fold into one is an immense mystery. The fabric of physical reality generally presents huge conceptual challenges. The two chief equations—special relativity and quantum uncertainty - do not fit together well. Particles can pop out of a vacuum and then disappear.

Have we come to genuine insights about the nature of things, what they fundamentally are?

Life is often described in a functional way. Science deals with mathematics. But mathematics only describes. As Hawking says at the end of 'Brief History of Time', what is important is what breathes fire into the equations. [332] The material world is an object—mathematics is one way of describing it but not the only way. Physics tells us what matter does—not what matter is. It could be that there is nothing beyond what matter does. Yet our sense of our personhood surely affirms that there is something more to us than matter. If asked 'who are you?', we would describe our mental state.

Science has limited things to say about questions of love and value, or meaning or morality. Here we want to examine this especially from viewpoint of value of people: the inner reality that confronts us. Different maps of reality are surely needed. Philosophers have often argued that that branches of knowledge are like maps—each answers a different set of questions. Not everything can be 'reduced' to physics. [333] For a personal universe, we start with consciousness and try to get matter out of that. Conscious entities—or ultimate, pervasive mind - interacting in certain ways are how we get physics.

Perspectives change. There is a view of reality - the simulated universe hypothesis - proposing that what humans experience is an artificial reality, akin to much like a computer simulation, in which they themselves are constructs. This has emerged from information physics, which suggests physical reality is fundamentally made up of bits of information. Melvin Vopson has previously argued that information has mass and that all elementary particles—the smallest known building blocks of the universe—store information about themselves in the same way humans have DNA. In line with the Second Law of Thermodynamics, the entropy in information systems should increase over time. Vopson's research on the evolution of these systems indicated that it remains constant or decreases. (This led to articulation of the second law of information dynamics, or info dynamics). [334]

Key findings include:

- Biological systems: The second law of info dynamics challenges conventional understanding of genetic mutations, suggesting that they follow a pattern governed by information entropy. This discovery has profound implications for fields such as genetic research, evolutionary biology, genetic therapies, pharmacology, virology, and pandemic monitoring.
- Atomic physics: The paper explains the behaviour of electrons in multi-electron atoms, providing insights into phenomena like Hund's rule; that the term with maximum multiplicity lies lowest in energy. Electrons arrange themselves in a way that minimizes their information entropy, shedding light on atomic physics and stability of chemicals.
- Cosmology: The second law of info dynamics is shown to be a cosmological necessity, with thermodynamic considerations applied to an expanding universe supporting its validity.

This approach, where excess information is removed, resembles the process of a computer deleting or compressing waste code to save storage space and optimize power consumption. And as a result it could support the idea that we are living in a simulation. Vopson's work had suggested that information is the fundamental building block of the universe and has physical mass. He even claims that information could be the elusive dark matter that makes up almost a third of the universe, which he calls the mass-energy-information equivalence principle. The second law of infodynamics lends support to this principle, potentially validating the idea that information is a physical entity, equivalent to mass and energy.

So what is the ultimate ground of reality? It could be argued that just because the need is there, and points to being met by an external field of meaning, that does not necessitate that the objective outside world corresponds to that need. Could psychological needs correspond to objective truth?

The philosophical difficulty has been that a realm of value, of spirit, meaning and morality has been conceived as being of a different order than physical reality. The latter is the order of empirical proof that can be verified, measured and described through both theory and replication.

Physics can only describe things in empirical terms. Modern science has separated mind from matter, treating it as something in a realm separate to the physical dimension. This stance undermines any attempt to see into the real nature of things since the aspect of reality we do grasp is what we live with each day: our own self-conscious experience and the need to be worthwhile.

Science has enabled us to calculate what things will do and how they move but not what they actually are. The nature of scientific explanation is to give an account of one thing in terms of another. A negative charge is contrasted with a positive charge. A frame of reference is needed to offer contrasts or smaller entities.

The human body is explained in terms of its constituent parts yet we ourselves are more than this. This is the black hole of reductionism to which forms of explanation are notoriously prone. Micro-reduction is the idea that everything is reducible to fundamental building blocks of matter. A quantum state or how 'a thing' is 'at bottom' can be expressed by a number or mathematical picture. The feeling of consciousness and of being 'ME' is an incredibly complex pattern of particles. What is troublesome for micro-reductionists is the notion of quantum entanglement that received experimental confirmation in the 1970's. Seemingly what shapes entangled particles in superposition is the whole system rather than its parts. The system is greater than the sum of its parts. [335]

A collection of parts where each has its own self-contained nature is not, however, the whole picture of reality. It is not like myriads of small bricks combining together so much as overlapping waves of the sea. As Briggs, Haslverson and Steane note, *"It can hardly be overstated how great is the change in our understanding of physical reality that takes place in transition from classical to quantum"*.[336]

The 20th century discovery of quantum physics in addition to classical physics has given rise to a new description of reality. Entangled particles and molecules are integrally connected no matter how far they are apart. Distance seems to be no object; regardless whether we are talking across the universe or the human brain. The latter points to the way that a human being is a fundamental unity rather than a collection of parts. There is a difference between physical reality -reducible to number- and self, irreducible to numerical value.

Almost impossible to prove, the notion of wormholes indicate a non-local property of space-time. There are interesting moves in physics to describe space-time as *"a geometrical picture of how stuff in the quantum system is entangled."*[337] These ideas seem to point to a bigger picture of fundamental unity beyond space and time. Space-time is a consequence of entanglement, now often understood as *"the world-making relation"*. [338]

Quantum Field Theory (QFT) depicts not just the individual behaviour of particles but how they behave together in space and time. This points to a field that has a spatial dimension. Quantum mechanics describes the operations of a single electron. The motion and behaviour with other electrons and with photons involve the branch of QFT called quantum electrodynamics (QED).

These ideas were supplemented by the theory of decoherence, in which *measurement can be* brought into a system larger than that in which the measurement occurs. Every system is coupled with the state of its surroundings and simply loses 'information'. A quantum system is interacting with a much larger system. As the quantum system evolves due to these interactions between the system and the surrounding environment, coherence is lost. On this reading of reality, matter may turn out to be emergent rather than being fundamental. It is the bigger picture that defines 'reality'.

It became clear in the Quantum revolution that reality is deeply strange and puzzling. 'Complementarity' became a centre piece of the Copenhagen view of the quantum world. *"Opposites do not contradict but rather complement each other,"* Niels Bohr declared. [339] The quantum revolution was founded on the principle of complementarity. As Niels argued, the notion of dualism is the existence of both wave and particle of light and matter. A full description requires both. Pairs of complementary properties cannot all be observed or measured simultaneously. [340] The nature of reality had shifted fundamentally.

Here now, it is how the inner, existential and not just quantum world marries up with the external world shaped by physical laws that is the question. For giants of these matters, such as Einstein, Dirac or Hawking, the vast chasm of their own inner world runs in parallel with their discoveries. Kant suggested that the realm of the physical universe and the moral world of meaning, refer to two different and incommensurable realms. But surely there should be some tie up?

What material reality actually is has been hugely disrupted by 20th century physics.

Space-time can be re-framed as an outcome of entanglement. In his General Relativity theory, Einstein's great legacy was that gravity is not a force like other forces. It is embedded in space and time taken together. *"Time and space appear to be aspects of a single four-dimensional reality."*[341]

Special relativity was rooted in the realisation that two observers moving at different speeds will not agree about the timing of two events or which took place first. With his by now famous example of a witnesses in a railway carriage observing lightning bolts in conjunction with observers on a platform, Einstein probed whether two events (two strokes of lightning) *"which are simultaneous with reference to the railway embankment, are also simultaneous relatively to the train?"* [342] Space and time can be stretched. But space-time distances, conceived integrally, stay independent of an observer. It depends on frames of reference.

As Einstein's mathematics mentor, Herman Minkowski, remarked, *"Henceforth space by itself, and time by itself, are doomed to fade away into mere shadows and only a kind of union of the two will preserve an independent reality".* [343] Earlier in his career, Einstein had showed that space, time, matter and energy were part of a four-dimensional symmetry that was s larger dimension. However, that symmetry had nothing to say about gravity and acceleration. The key would lie in unification; the unification of space and time and matter and energy. Einstein failed to find a unified field theory partly because he was missing a vital piece of the puzzle—the nuclear force.

There are twelve fields relating to matter, electron, muon and the tau—three neutrinos and four quarks. There are also four forces. The field associated with gravity is space-time. Bundles of energy are the electron, waves of the same underlying field. Even when the particles have been taken out, there remains a quantum field. Nothingness is a quantum field. There are no particles. The basic building blocks are fluid-like substances we call fields. The field is constantly fluctuating. Just like the waves of the sea are features of the same underlying ocean.

String theory began to develop as a set of disjointed equations that were then brought into a unified field theory; a field theory equation. String theory seemed to unify gravity with quantum theory. How relativity and quantum theory might be aligned has puzzled physicists. The symmetry between fermions and bosuns, supersymmetry was a way of combing these two.

The search for a unified field theory pre-occupied many of the giants of the 20th century- Schrodinger, Heisenberg, Pauli and Einstein himself who had sought a guiding principle. Combining Dirac's theory of the electron with Maxwell's theory of light became Quantum electrodynamics (QED) that obeyed both quantum mechanics and special relativity. Schrodinger held that the code of life itself lay within a secret molecule that followed the laws of quantum mechanics. It fell to Watson and Crick to discover DNA but they used the methods of quantum mechanics to identify the structure of life in every cell. The quest for ultimate reality continued through various forms of explanation. A field is localised. Yet the astonishing puzzle is that the laws of physics seem to operate across the universe as we know it. The search in 20th century cosmology for unification could reflect that there are the same set of particles behaving in the same way because there is a unified field. The role that entanglement plays in quantum field theory suggests a single reality with everything entangled and connected. Equations for the same fields for particles are similar. Three forces could be combined into one force- unification. In models of supersymmetry, matter and forces are related.

Strip away the veneer of 'hard' objects we encounter from day to day; objects that have spatial-temporal existence with their own frame of reference in the mechanics of forces. The objects that have physical reality are, on closer inspection, layers of material compounds of all sorts; some organic, some inorganic. Go deeper and we will encounter molecules and then atoms. Have we arrived? By no means. For atoms are composed of a nucleus and electrons circling around in primarily empty space. What binds atoms together is electricity; the charge that is constantly in exchange between particles. Look even closer and we find that quantum forces mean everything is in flux. There is little that is constant. The world of the very small is populated by quarks and leptons in dynamic interaction. Sub-atomic particles operate with a cloud of possibilities, not fixed positions.

Differing interpretations of quantum mechanics point to views on reality that are hard to put together. "*The quantum reality problem is, strictly speaking, not a physics question at all, but a problem in metaphysics, concerned as it not with explaining phenomena but with speculating about what kind of reality lies behind and supports the phenomena*".[344] Ultimately, this is a question of metaphysics because we cannot see the reality behind phenomena.

In Quantum physics, objects are so completely merged that it becomes impossible to say something about the constituent parts. Quantum cosmology can lead us to the view that the fundamental layer of reality is the universe itself. A hidden reality behind the phenomena is a valid prediction. But can there really be an integrated whole without personhood? There are considerable difficulties explaining reality without reference to self-conscious personhood- (since observers have an effect in quantum physics)? Though there could be numerous multiverses or many worlds predicted through quantum cosmology, there is always a more fundamental layer of reality behind everything. The Standard Model, General Relativity and quantum mechanics would all be derived from this. Yet the foundation of science surely needs to include the personal dimension for a complete description.

In short, scientific materialism has been challenged by:

- Relativity
- Quantum physics that shows matter has much less substance than thought and imposes a limitation on what can be known and 'pinned down'.

- Chaos theory throwing light on dynamic systems which can be self-organising and where the future is open.
- Organisation, complexity and especially information. It is powers of mind that are in the transcendent over matter. What counts is a cosmic network of forces and fields.

WHERE IS IT?

The origin of the word 'reality' lies in the Latin word 'res' which means 'a thing'. To be real is to have the quality of being 'a thing'. In turn, 'res' is linked to the Latin verb 'reri'; to think. The real thing, though, has to be more than what can be imagined. Humans can experience impressions and fears as being incredibly real. A mental image or representation can be created through imagination but what is thought about has to have independence from our thought in order to count as 'the real'.

As we are exploring, a theory of everything needs to account for the value in human life without reducing it to matter, which is in itself not able to account for quantum uncertainty and strange wave behaviour. There is no realm of meaning and value and especially love that confers a sense of value on them which can be explained in quantitative, physical terms; unless that is, feeling loved or worthwhile is purely the result of neurons firing in our brains.

There is a Quantum world, the world of the very small.

There is an inner world within human beings and which surfaces in their interaction within fields of behaviour.

The inner world is detectable though interaction of thought and feeling; aspects of reality that will be evident to some extent on a brain scan except that those are very one dimensional.

There is also what is usually described as a spiritual realm.

It is immediately clear that it is not appropriate to speak in terms of the location of the spiritual realm or that of the inner world that appears to respond to it at some level.

It is hard to argue that the spiritual realm is in a mathematical or topographical relation to physical reality. It is not perpendicular to it or slightly beyond the clouds! *Here we* draw a parallel between the quantum fields overlapping and the spiritual/physical world. It may be, however, that there is a causal/ontological link between the quantum and the spiritual.

We could take the view that it lies within material reality. Or that it surrounds us. It is the template, the circuit board against which all else happens. Or that is pervasive and immanent.

Quantum fields are not thought to live within spacetime but on top of other fields. The universe represents the spacetime continuum observable in every direction.

The topography of reality might offer some scope for a holistic dimension in which value, love and meaning reside in a way that our personhood and spiritual quest latch on to and connect with.

Some physicists speculate that there are many parallel universes, existing within a multi-dimensional hyperspace. Perhaps they are separated from our universe by a single quantum event that made the universe bud up and inflate massively in the first place.

In the topography of reality, we could speak of a 'deeper reality'. Or we could use the notion of height and speak of a 'higher principle that is above us' which connects perhaps with the higher self. Our tiny minds that are so so human and far too inadequate to fathom the reality that transcends our capabilities.

Another way of describing reality is to invoke the notion of things being alongside each other in parallel. It could be therefore that the realm of significance and value somehow sits alongside material, practical world of the everyday. Unconsciously, we invoke it to derive meaning but we have no vocabulary or conceptual tools with which to articulate the how these might align.

Recent years have witnessed a buzz about the notion of a mathematical shape called an 'amplituhedron'. This geometric shape has its own Facebook page (with the bold statement "*I am the shape of the universe*"). Its discoverers Nima Arkani-Hamad and Jaroslav Trnka in 2013 coined this expression as a clue to the very nature of space-time and reality.[345] In theoretical physics, space as a real entity is redundant. It is a description beyond space-time as we know it.

The topography of the universe has given rise to much scientific discussion. The universe might be shaped like a doughnut, not like a pancake. A 1997 paper from Juan Maldacena of the Institute for Advanced Study suggested that our universe could be a hologram. Much like a 3-D hologram emerges from information encoded on a 2-D surface our universe's 4-D spacetime may be a holographic projection of a lower-dimensional reality.[346]

All observations so far though suggest the universe is flat. In geometry, "flatness" refers to the behaviour of parallel lines as they go out to infinity. With a tabletop: Lines that start out parallel will remain that way as they extend along the table length. In contrast, look at Earth. Lines of longitude begin perfectly parallel to each other at the equator but eventually converge at the poles. The fact that parallel lines initially intersect reveals that Earth is not flat.

The same logic applies to the 3D universe. For instance, the cosmic microwave background (CMB)—light released when the cosmos was only 380,000 years old—now sits over 42 billion light-years away and features tiny fluctuations in temperature across the sky. Astronomers have calculated the predicted size of those fluctuations compared with observations. If their measured size differs from predictions, that means those rays of light, which started out parallel, changed directions over space-time, indicating that the geometry of the universe is curved. But those same measurements have revealed that, ignoring small-scale deflections from galaxies and black holes, the overall geometry of the universe is flat.

There are different ways of being flat. Parallel lines on a piece of paper wrapped around one end of the paper to connect with the other form a cylinder. The lines remain parallel as they circle the cylinder. In the language of mathematics, any cylinder is geometrically flat but is said to have a different topology. With both sides closed, there is a doughnut shape. A thin strip of paper wrapped in a circle with a 180-degree twist in one end results in a Möbius strip, which is still geometrically flat.

Astronomers have measured the topology of the universe in multiple ways. All evidence suggests the universe is both geometrically flat and has a simple unwrapped topology. If the average density of matter in the universe is less than 1, there is enough matter and gravity to reverse the cosmic expansion, the universe is open and the curvature implies it is saddle shaped.

DIFFERENT DIMENSIONS?

Our view of reality is restricted and limited. Mathematical physicists can create a model of reality that seems to be the true reality. But how and why would we claim that our model is the true reality? This is what Ward refers to as 'the fallacy of misplaced consciousness'. [347] Conceivably, the realm of value, love, meaning and spirituality lies in another plane of reality—what Hick calls 'the fifth dimension'. [348]

The basis behind 'M-theory' is that there is an eleven-dimensional reality behind everything. Proposed by physicist Edward Witten, this was a mathematical construct demonstrating how there were five different string theories in ten-dimensions within ten-dimensions. This theoretical work, amplified by a crowded field of papers drawing on the postulates of Juan

Maldacena, showed that there were fascinating dualities between gravity and other physical forces. [349]

Interestingly, there has been much discussion in the scientific community of parallel universes or even of the metaverse. It is hard to know where metaverse begins and metaphor ends as both could be describing a realm of reality that conceivably are not geographically located but run in parallel with what we observe and can manipulate experimentally.

As soon as we allow for one universe being created, we open a theoretical door to many universes being created in parallel. The universe could exist in numerous quantum states. In principle, entirely new laws of physics and a new reality could co-exist.

The idea of superstrings vibrating in ten-dimensional space-time has been advanced as a theoretical construct ever since German mathematician Theodor Kaluza wrote a paper in 1919 he showed to Einstein demonstrating that electromagnetism and gravity could be unified in a single theoretical framework. However, four spatial dimensions were required. Seven years later, Oscar Klein argued that the extra dimension could be rolled up so small it would forever be hidden. There could though be more potentially. String theory as it evolved required no fewer than nine dimensions in which the hidden strings could vibrate. As a refinement to this mathematical construct, at every point in our three-dimensional space there could lie a six-dimensional shape (the Calabi-Yau). These hidden dimensions are so minute, they are beyond probing by any scientific instruments.

A more recent development is supplied by the ideas of holographic imagery. Shining a laser beam at a flat sheet that had three-dimensional data encoded within it and the three dimensions stand out (much like the holograms in sci-fi). All the data is present within the two-dimensional sheet: it only needs the light to reveal it. Along with time, we think we are three-dimensional beings. Maybe we are moving within a much larger field of reality.

In the idea that reality can be thought about in a reflective way and probed through empirical means lay the birth of modern science. Physics rather than metaphysics was the best route for understanding what the earth was made of and how the heavens went. As foreshadowed by Plato, mathematics was the best language for discovering the cosmos. Mathematical laws can be calculated that define the movement of objects that are celestial but also objects on earth. Precise equations could be calculated that showed fundamental cosmic laws in action.

When we walk in the park on a sunny day, our shadow pursues us. We are being followed by a two-dimensional object that is ourselves. However, we live as three-dimensional people replete with subjective thoughts and emotions. Humankind cannot in practice live out a materialist worldview.

Our existence could be played out within our 3 or 4 dimensional world (if you include time's arrow) but that other dimensions frame it or represent some kind of backcloth. Analogously perhaps, fish in my pond can swim in their micro-marine world aware at times of feeding that another dimension above them is somehow breaking into their reality. Most likely, they have very little sense of it but they feel the effects.

FORMS OF REALITY

One type of explanation for how the different realms cohere is that of stratification of reality. Philosopher Roy Bhaskar was the founder of the school of Critical Realism in philosophy; the prospectus for which was laid out in such works as 'A Realist Theory of Science' (1975), [350]'The Possibility of Naturalism' (1979) [351]and 'Scientific Realism and Human emancipation' (1986)[352] and 'Reclaiming Reality' (1989). [353] His subsequent 'From East to West' (2000)[354] and 'Reflections on Metareality' (2002)[355] pointed to different layers that are hierarchical. In any phenomenon, there are always more basic levels of explanation. Understanding medical phenomenon such as symptomology can be understood at various levels from purely physical explanations to associations and influences that are social. To say that influences upon a patient are social could invoke the notion of systems, in which there are effects from participation in something bigger. A system is a pattern of actions and influences that is visible in their impact but which are largely invisible.

The point is that each hierarchical level requires a different form of analysis appropriate to the level of phenomenological reality under discussion. Methods that study disease, for example, might not tell the whole story of how that disease could affect someone in their situation. Reality is multilayered. A condition such as bipolarity can be studied in terms of biology.

It is commonplace to observe that reality is layered in that higher level forms of complexity required higher -level laws. Not everything need be reduced to the laws of physics.

Relationships of different kinds of reality are described by the idea of emergence. Not all realities are equally fundamental. Some only make sense if more fundamental realities constrain what is possible. Higher level descriptions rely on previous building blocks. Social organisation and psychology are shaped by the biology of life: fundamental particles do not rely on biology or social life. As Paul Davies argued, *"there exists a propensity in nature for matter and energy to undergo spontaneous transitions into new states of higher organisation...there must be new general principles—organisational principles over and above the known laws of physics- which have yet to be discovered".* [356] Many contest this, arguing that what we know about and deal with in our lives is emergent. It derives from deeper level fundamental theories or forces such as those governing atomic nuclei. As theory about materials derives from the way their constituent parts behave. Arguing this point, Sabine Hossenfelder suggests that what seems fundamental will turn out to emergent from a yet deeper level.[357]

But what counts is information. If a school fires a teacher, the school remains the same. The larger unit (the school) is not limited by the smaller entity (the teacher). Information is not discarded by whether the teacher is male or female. The more fundamental an entity or a description of reality is, the less information it discards. If something is intact, it has low entropy; when broken or messy, iy has high entropy.

At some level, the inner, existential world, needs to be folded into the objective world of scientific laws. Does this require talk of God? Presumably these aspects of reality fit together since that is how we experience the world. I sit writing this amidst many other humans overlooking a stormy sea. I am in my thoughts, my mind ranging far across the ocean to private dramas playing out. Though different kinds of entities, swirling sea and swirling thoughts at least seem to blend together. They are at least part of my reality

Penrose suggested that the concrete world of physical reality seemed to emerge out of the ideal world where mathematical laws applied. The other two worlds—the physical and mental worlds- are but shadows of the mathematical world. [358] How the one (the underlying unity of the universe) relates to the many (the world of multiple concrete things) has been the philosophical and religious quest down the ages. What links these two? Heraclitus, for instance, argued that everything was in flux, thus giving rise to plurality and engendering motion. His debating partner Parmenides took the view that the real is what is unchanging beyond change and chance. The Many only express the One.

Unless in cases of considerable splitting and internal fragmentation, humans do tend to experience reality as a whole. We have an interpretive, integrating lens that sees the world holistically.

So what might be said about a more accurate theory of everything?

1) <u>Reality has different substances</u>, different aspects such as matter, mind, abstract norms, value and so forth. How these types of 'realities' interact is the big metaphysical question. The rational, human self-consciousness is different from anything else in nature. The real world

is not only the content of what science talks about but the human dimension. Reality must of necessity incorporate such aspects as:
- An objective, physical world we rely on daily
- A conscious self capable of purposing
- Spirituality and religion
- How our minds can influence our bodies and generate action
- Other minds like our own (i.e. a theory of mind)
- Objective, rational standards
- Language capability, the complexity of which seems universal
- The reliability of our sense data

2) <u>Reality is multi-layered</u>- there are forces and operations appropriate to each field. Just as in disciplines and sub-disciplines. The deeper you go, there is another reality. Just as in the human field, there are multiple realities corresponding with multiple perspectives, there are as many frames of reference which supplies a larger perspective. An adequate worldview has to encompass all this and answer the question of whether everything developed from purposeless energy.

3) <u>Reality is dynamic</u> and in a state of constant flux. This is the legacy of quantum mechanics; that the more we look into the details of what is around us, the greater the movement within. The more fluctuation, the less constant. Vibration we do not easily see yet lies at the heart of things we can see. Indeterminacy and probability are mean that the future is not a straight predictable line from the past. In accordance with the ideas of quantum mechanics, everything is in process, in transit from one state to another. There are some basic structures- homologies. Yet also, there is the property of indefiniteness (from human perspective—such as wave/particle duality).

4) <u>Ultimate reality is ultimate mind.</u> There is information written into the scheme of things; an intelligibility, a rational cosmos and deep order in the world that allows for rational enquiry. This information seems to contain *"a purposive development towards self-consciousness, ability to master the environment, and complexity"*. As a result, there are *"whole communities of complex beings with central nervous systems and brains that can store information, have consciousness and purpose and can come to an awareness of what they are and direct their own future"*.
359

5) <u>Reality is relational</u>—substance and the relational character of the observable universe. General Relativity offered a single, integrated account of space, time and matter. There is a wider field where these aspects combine be it superstring theory or whatever. Relationality is built into the nature of things. All events we perceive are interactions; they occur in relation to another field. Phenomena only manifest themselves through other interactions. There is a whole movement in philosophy concerning this and how far we can know substances in themselves apart from related entities. Until this movement, most western forms of explanatory category privileged substance over relation. They focussed on the essence of things. It was Aristotle who developed an account of predication that differentiated accidental properties of things from their substance.[360]

6) <u>Reality is more than just subjective</u>. Many contemporary philosophers echo David Hume's insistence, denying the possibility of subjective knowledge. As Richard Rorty argues, truth does not need to correspond with reality.[361] On the basis of such relativism, we cannot know anything objective about external reality, however. Relativism surrenders any idea of universal truths or the significance that imparts value to our lives as being mere constructs. If the subjective self reigns supreme, there is no objective knowledge.

7) <u>Reality is personal</u>- the notion that ultimate reality is personal goes beyond panpsychism. It infers that there is a dimension to which our personhood corresponds. Humans are indeed made of the same substances as suns, seas and stars. Yet there is an aspect of our existence which goes beyond material reality. If ultimate reality is impersonal—a life force of some kind—where is that which our own personhood and worth can relate and which is endorsed by it? An impersonal universe does not endorse or validate our personhood. Neither does it affirm our person as being valuable.

8) <u>Reality entails an observer</u>- the position of critical realism

9) <u>Reality gives a loving backcloth as a frame of reference</u>—a welcome to human entities as witnessed by the anthropic principle and the valuable personhood argued for in this volume.

10) <u>Reality is indivisible</u>—as Democritus grasped, the world is made up of far smaller, indivisible particles. It cannot be broken down an infinite number of times. Whether molecules, atoms, quarks and leptons or even strings, at some point you have to stop; something made up of

particles of a certain size. You have reached the point from which fundamental building blocks of everything else begin to scale up.

The inference is that there is a transcendent reality that holds everything in place. Science has limited things to say about questions of love and value which lie beyond material reality. There are several conceptual moves that could be made about how the realms fit together.

1. we could say that the realm of value, love, meaning and spirituality has no ontological status except for being part of the interpretive world we construct so as to navigate life;
2. we could say that that which endorses personhood as worthwhile does not exist and that we read off our experience of the world erroneously if we suppose it does;
3. we could say that the realm of value, love and meaning is so bound up with cultural meanings such that there is no status independent of ourselves which could possibly be a referent;
4. we could say that it is not possible to 'locate' such a realm as having a field of reference in relation to material reality. It is not another observable dimension.
5. we could say that although the realm of value, love, meaning and spirituality is not directly detectable empirically, it does, however, show up in evidential studies of everyday life.
6. we could say that material reality that seems to be clear cut under the conditions of human existence, is impossibly fuzzy and imprecise in the realm of the very small but also the large-scale structures of the cosmos (like dark energy and dark matter). We see very little.
7. We could say that this 'spiritual' realm is located (though not spatially) in God and that a personal being is what is needed to correspond to and endorse this.

This aspect of our discussion is entangled with ways of speaking of the divine. The concept of God according to traditional Judeo-Christian-Islamic theism minimally includes the following theses: (i) There is one God; (ii) God is an omniscient, omnipotent, and morally perfect agent; (iii) God is the creator *ex nihilo* of the universe and the sustainer of all that exists; and (iv) God is an immaterial substance that is ontologically distinct from the universe. Proponents of alternative concepts of God, such as pantheism, panentheism, religious anti-realism, developmental theism, and religious naturalism, exclude at least one of (i)–(iv). Each of these stances have generated spatial metaphors. We have then a choice for how we speak of the realm of value, love, meaning and spirit that validates human existence. [362]

We could speak of the ground of existence as denoting something underneath us and which upholds us. [363] It could be a 'higher' imaginary, denoting transcendence, or a 'deeper' field.

The realm of value, love, meaning and spirit could lie <u>within</u> physical reality but, topographically, is more likely to be '<u>behind</u>' it as best fit for a spatial metaphor. It will not be detected within the Large Hadron Collider in the same way that the Higgs Bosun sprang out of theory and into observation. It has no spatio-temporal existence; however, it might interact with it. The problem with such a metaphor is that if such a realm lies 'behind' everything, how is there any interaction with physical reality? What and where are the points of contact?

The situation might be analogous to the relationship between brain and mind and how one affects the other. A dualistic account of things is that these are different types of substance that clearly cohere but in ways so far hidden from view. My mind is active through my brain in tapping these words on a laptop but how it is directing the work of fingers is unknown. To see this as a monist, composite whole takes us further possibly but an account is then needed of the different types of operation and how these intersect.

Maybe there are other universes, replete with different numbers of spatial dimensions. We find ourselves in an area friendly to life. The idea of the Multiverse is complemented these days by the 'ugly verse'; the notion that structures and symmetries are messy, leaving us unable to make sense of the universe.

Does one of these encompass the spiritual realm? If this is purely energy, how does that answer the personal realm that validates our personhood? As I write these words (August 2023) the film 'Oppenheimer' has won global critical acclaim. The atom is split and enormous amounts of cosmic energy is released. Audiences are reminded of the awesome power at the heart of things yet there is the reality too of the private lives of the participants. It is how you out these factors together that is the theme of this book. There has to be some tie up since both happenings are played out on screen yet this is projected on to a depiction that is both sign and signifier. The happenings are integrated as is patently the case in the reality experienced by us human observers. This metaphor, however, requires an intelligence bringing both material aspects of the physical world together with private dramas to make one, composite reality. To return to the metaphor with which we began this chapter, if two people are playing chess, where is the game?

It is along these lines possibly that there lies some explanation of the evident truth that human beings are around who not only have the capacity for consciousness but perceive themselves to be of worth. Are these possibilities inherent in the fabric of reality? Self-evidently, there is an order of things that governs the natural world, whether from within or externally and this has given rise to intelligibility about our place in the universe.

This would challenge the assumptions that have governed physics. There may well be new physics that lie beyond the Standard Model but the Large Hadron Collider (LHC) is not seeing anything at the moment. The next layer of reality has not yet been observed. To go beyond the Standard Model, a new description of physical reality has to take account of such mysteries as dark energy and dark matter. A materialistic science can never give us the complete truth. With Monism, the whole is greater than its parts. The wood is greater than the trees.

Who or what fixes the world as it is? Maybe there is no one or nothing and we inhabit the one universe we live in—or we dwell in one in with a multiverse of plurality. But what is surely needed is to account for both the quantitative data of testable phenomena together with the reality of our subjective experience. How also do we account for the laws of mathematics, of logic and morals? The world of our inner experiences - our emotions, beliefs, desires - is integrally connected to the way we live, move and have our being in the external landscapes of hills and trees and living things. What creates a unified whole? What though is the relation between the material universe and spirit?

Polytheism and dualism are not viable interpretations of the scheme of reality since the universe is one entity. If there is a unity behind everything, how can that leave room for contradictory beings? If we are to form an impression of the reality of relating the material order to personhood, we have to come again to the starting point of our knowledge; the sense of ourselves and of our need to be of worth. Human personhood exhibits spirit and matter in intimate combination; or mind and body, according to definitions and categories used. The facility of separating ourselves from ourselves (self as subject from self as object) is what we label self-consciousness or reflexive capability. We are thereby relating ourselves to something we might call 'immaterial'. In the moral sphere we encounter this as knowledge of conscience and taking responsibility. 'Spirit' or 'personhood' (we might use these terms interchangeably here as long as a personal force is denoted) could be argued to be 'immanent' within matter. With regard to our environment, we discern the contrast between spirit and matter as composite parts of reality, in our capacity, for good or ill, to mould the external world to our use. It all hinges on our worldview as to having a fragmentary approach to reality.

It is of course just at this point that much contemporary thinking is at odds, seeing a separation between ourselves and the environment as responsible for the degradation of the latter. As David Bohm, for instance, argues, it is how we see reality that shapes action. If we regard humanity as the basic reality and as separate from nature, there will not be a harmony within an individual or society. An analysis of the world into independently existent parts does not work well in physics generally. We do not have to see the world this way, however. Our fragmented worldviews lead to the view that reality is fragmented. The whole world is of comprised of separate building blocks. Yet relativity theory and quantum theory, however, imply more orderly ways of seeing composite reality. [364]

Bohm's approach was to suggest that a vision of the wholeness of reality led to Eastern religious views rather than Western modes of thoughts that emphasised division and separation. [365] But this leaves little place for personhood. Personhood can though lay claim to be the most real entity of which we are aware. What affects us personally and persistently is arguably the most real of our experiences. Each person has their sphere of reality which includes everything in relation to it: material things are 'ours' and we wrap layers of meaning around them.

As we saw, there is a oneness between the observer and the observed. We can go further. Between the conscious observer and the inner eye of consciousness, personhood shapes reality (the anthropic principle it could be said). From these considerations, we move now to a way of looking at what lies beyond our observable physical reality to include something that activates our personhood. We are concerned here with the wholeness of inferential reality, a forming dimension in the Aristotelian sense of the cause of the growth of things; the inner movement in the cosmos that is essential to how things are. Our quest here is not, be it said, to probe some particles or an entity located in a particular space or place. It is rather to infer a field; a field where consciousness speaks to consciousness, personhood calls to personhood and deep calls to deep.

Chapter Nine

Wifi Universe

"*We can't avoid some anthropic component in our science, which is interesting, because after three hundred years we finally realise that we do matter*". —Physicist Paul Davies [366]

THE QUESTION BEFORE US is whether matter and energy have an innate capacity to self-organise and become self-conscious? Or is there a larger sphere of reality that is creating the potential for organising and imparting the information needed and endorsing our personhood?

This could be interpreted as some form of dualism. Although the brain is a natural object, something more is going on, over and above the laws of physics. Yet it could also lend itself to a form of monism in which Mind and Mentality lies behind everything and that there is a cosmic consciousness. The philosophical difficulty has been that a realm of meaning and value has been conceived as being of a different order than physical reality. The latter is the order of empirical proof that can be verified, measured and described through both theory and replication.

It is a particular type of universe that is capable of producing systems of complexity sufficient to sustain conscious life. Our minds are able, through mathematical equations, to peer into the deep structures of the universe. Over an immense period, something has *"turned a ball of energy into the home of saints and scientists"*.[367]

So what do we do with this? We could just accept as Kant did that the physical construction of reality and our existential life are incommensurate realms and our ways of knowing not up to the task. Or we could try to probe further, restlessly recognising that where we live from is our inner world.

And besides, we are betrayed by secret knowledge.

Consider the case of Erwin Schrodinger, who helped transform the landscape of the new quantum theory in the 1920's. His wave mechanics sought to dispense with particles altogether and replace with wavelengths of matter. However, there is a field of behaviour that his theories have to be set against: namely his private life. This physicist of immense stature, who will forever be associated with the thought experiment about the cat in a sealed box that might be dead or alive, was also a human being. He exhibited considerable turmoil in private dramas in relationships to his wife Anny and numbers of other girlfriends. There is the map of reality Schrodinger was looking to recast. But there were his own endeavours to find value, love, meaning and spirituality generated by the need to find his own significance as a scientist before he got overtaken by younger figures. [368]

This highlights the paradox in the behaviour of humans who may believe/think of reality as material and ultimately meaningless but are nevertheless driven toward pursuing meaning. The secret knowledge is that whatever we think of God or the structure of ultimate reality, we KNOW we are a people of worth and significance (unless life has dented that sadly); that knowledge of the outer world is meshed in somewhere with our need to derive some purpose and meaning. We will search in vain for a God-particle.

Yet we dare maintain human significance in a universe that stretches on and on into the night. The strong anthropic principle responds to this concept but so too does the valuable personhood discussed here. Therein lies the paradox, a paradox that illuminates the dilemmas of relationality (and indeed relativity) in which things are explained in terms of something else. Sentient beings are perhaps picking up on a realm of information potential much as an internet-ready phone picks up on the field of information and communication such as Google.

This is not speculative. We actually interact with the realm beyond this one a great deal. Indeed, our very sense of self might be responding to it everyday. It is what we live by.

Most religions teach that immaterial realms exist transcending the reality we know. Rather than focus on the spiritual dimension per se, this is a proposal for how the realm of value, love, meaning and spirituality (VLMS) interfaces with the physical reality. A strictly materialistic and quantitative science cannot capture the reality of either consciousness or self-reflecting valuable personhood which is inherently subjective and qualitative.

Personhood is not something to be levered into the physicalist account of the world. It belongs surely to a complete picture of reality. An impersonal universe (or divine essence) is inadequate. It is of the nature of personhood that we respond to acts of seeing, of recognition. Being human requires the affirmation and endorsement that comes from this. We seem to flourish best when our lives have some significance; when there is a 'why?' as well as a 'what?' to live by. The realm of VLMS is surely not an illusion—or if it is, it is a fiction that humans have evolved for survival in order to get through.

The impulse towards VLMS looks to be one of responsive capacity: the capacity to be of worth, to love and be loved and to find meaning in our world. These are human capabilities that emerge under the right circumstances.

Personhood responds to the personal. VLMS reflects essential personal aspects of human existence. They do not equate to a machine like or neutral environment. Impersonal AI or purely forms of energy do not need value, love, meaning and spirituality. They are redundant. Through them, however, something happens inside. Humans are called into being.

An example seemingly indispensable to contemporary life might help to make sense of this layer of reality. A Wi-Fi field explains how communication is possible given personalised connection. As I write these words, the Wi-Fi field is 'down' in the surrounding venue. For a while now, the attempts to re-establish network connection have proved fruitless. We could infer the presence of a Wi-Fi field through our electronic devices connecting with it such that connection and communication becomes possible. The range of that field will be limited, according to the strength of signal, rooter and so on. If our phones are not informing us of the presence of a given field of potential connection, we would not infer its existence or at least we might consider that the field is not available to us.

In the 21st century, Wi-Fi is pervasive. A Wi-Fi field is generated by means of a rooter that can pick up an available network. For a price and pass-key, a smart device can tune in and receive information and phone calls. The rooter and phone is enabling the human voice to be converted into electronic signal that can be picked up across thousands of miles. A person does not need to speak loudly to be heard across this distance. The electronic signal, disassembling and re-assembling across radio waves, mobile data or landline is able to transmit with high accuracy.

There are two aspects of this, what is now every day, occurrence that are relevant here. One is that the Wi-Fi source is available within its field to anyone able to access who is within range. To be attuned requires a passkey which can result in responsiveness to what is available. The signal is there to be picked up. Human personhood may then be activated by having the right means with which to respond to the cosmic realm that enables that.

The second aspect of Wi-Fi that calls for attention is that the electronic equipment is acting as a transducer. A transducer is a device that converts variations in physical pressure or brightness into an electronic signal. Energy is being converted from one form into another. A microphone does this but so also does the phone. One idea is that the brain is a bidirectional transducer. The laptop on which I am writing this links wirelessly to a router a short distance away and the router connects to the internet service provider. A phone cable runs from the router to a wall socket. The cable leads to dozens of other network points through which representations of my voice pass. If we are also using video to communicate, cameras are sending images to screens, again through many transition points, and in both directions. These images and sounds pass through thousands of miles of copper or fibre optic cables or are being transmitted to satellites in orbit above the earth then re-transmitted to receivers on the ground. Such pathways are bidirectional; shared simultaneously by numerous different conversations. The pattern of sound waves produced by my voice is being converted by the microphone into a similar pattern of electrical activity. The better the microphone, the more accurately it duplicates the original pattern.

Transduction is part of us. Our sense organs transduce distinctive properties of electromagnetic radiation, air pressure waves, airborne chemicals, liquid-borne chemicals, textures, pressure, and temperature into distinctive patterns of electrical and chemical activity in the brain. The brain then could be special kind of transducer that translates signals from the physical world to a different, immaterial level of reality.

The unexpected return of mental clarity and memory shortly before death in patients suffering from severe psychiatric and neurologic disorders, which we have called 'terminal lucidity', has been reported in the medical literature over the past 250 years. [369] Researchers have explored this brief paradoxical clarity and it has not been uncommon for medical journals to publish credible reports of highly impaired, uncommunicative people who became lucid for a few minutes before they died. Those with dementia, advanced Alzheimer's, schizophrenia, and even severe brain damage who have not been able to speak or to recognize their closest relatives for years—suddenly recognized their loved ones and spoke normally. Surprising activity levels in dying brains may help explain the sudden clarity many people with dementia experience near death. Such terminal lucidity is defined as the unexpected return of cognitive faculties such as speech and "connectedness" with other people, something like the 'old self' emerging." According to Peterson, a researcher of bioethics and consciousness who co-authored a study of the phenomenon commissioned by the National Institutes of Health, "*it suggests there may be neural networks that are remaining, and/or pathways and neural function, that could help potentially restore cognitive abilities to individuals we otherwise think are permanently impaired.*" [370] Such episodes need to be handled with care. The state of research on the dying brain is in its infancy. Yet it could point to mind beyond brain function.

A recent study found a surge of organized brain activity in two out of four comatose people who were undergoing cardiac arrest after being removed from life support. The activity was detected in the so-called hot zone of neural correlates of consciousness in the brain, the junction between the temporal, parietal and occipital lobes in the back of the brain. This area has been correlated with dreaming, visual hallucinations in epilepsy, and altered states of consciousness in other brain studies. [371] Reports of near-death experiences—with tales of white light, visits from departed loved ones, hearing voices etc are common enough but the fact that these reports have so many common elements raises the question of whether there is something fundamentally real underpinning them. Are those who have managed to survive death providing glimpses of a consciousness that does not completely disappear, even after the heart stops beating? How vivid experience can emerge from a dysfunctional brain during the process of dying is a neuroscientific paradox.

THE LIGHT OF SIGNIFICANCE

This idea is of course found in many religions and is there in the Bible of Christian belief. *Consider, for example, John's gospel chapter 1v9—"the true light that gives light to everyone was coming into the world."* (New International Version).

It is found in Christian theology, witness John Calvin's insistence that the knowledge of God and knowledge of self are conjoined from the start. *"Our wisdom, in so far as it ought to be deemed true and solid wisdom, consists almost entirely of two parts: the knowledge of God and of ourselves. But as these are connected together by many ties, it is not easy to determine which of the two precedes and gives birth to the other. . .the endowment which we possess cannot possibly be from ourselves."*[372]

Knowledge of God, knowledge of the self and knowledge of the world are entangled. Knowledge of the divine is not just an inference from knowledge of the self nor to an inference drawn from nature. Humanity exists in a creation-context.

John Calvin, was, however, a creationist when it came to the soul. Each human soul is created by God directly. Only the human body is supplied by our parents. The contrasting viewpoint was traducianism (Latin 'lead across' or 'propagate'); the idea that both body and soul are generated by human parents.

But the notion of an external lighting of human existence is also found in some psychological ideas.

Henri Bergson suggested that our brains do not generate mind and consciousness but rather act as valves that reduce the 'bandwith' so to speak of perceivable reality. [373] Aldous Huxley also proposed that the brain limits external experience. It mediates a realm beyond itself.[374]

William James was a prominent Harvard philosopher and also arguably America's first psychologist. In 1898, James his book entitled *'Human Immortality: Two Supposed Objections to the Doctrine'*, in which he praised his contemporaries for boldly using scientific methods to investigate providential leadings apparently in answer to prayer, instantaneous healings, premonitions, apparitions at time of death, clairvoyant visions or impressions, and the whole range of spiritual capacities.[375]

James asserted that a universe-wide consciousness beamed human consciousness into our brains 'as so many finite rays,' just as the sun beams rays of light onto our planet. Our brains, being limited in their capabilities, he said, generally filter and suppress real consciousness, while sometimes allowing 'glows of feeling, glimpses of insight, and streams of knowledge' to shine through. He called this idea 'transmission-theory.'

What that spiritual impulse is and how we should describe it is of perennial interest. It seems to reflect a profound foundation of the human situation that we are reaching beyond ourselves. The question is if this is located at the very birth of human identity and self-awareness that lies latent until developed? A neuroscientist Mario Beauregard used sophisticated technology to peer inside the brain in a way that lead him to the surprising conclusion that spiritual experiences are not a figment of the mind or a delusion produced by a dysfunctional brain. Beauregard and O'Leary argue that the mind cannot be simply reduced to physiological reactions in the brain, exploring attempts to locate a "God gene" in some of us. The claim is that our brains are "hardwired" for religion. [376]

Deeper aspects of reality, of conscious life are becoming illuminated by the developing field of neuroscience. There is more to the brain than what neuroscience tells us. Just because nothing happens without a brain does not mean that the brain is all. Numerous advances are pointing us in a direction that is at odds with the materialist view of reality that believed matter and energy is all and that there is no spiritual dimension. There is an alternative view now proposed that the brain is not a self-contained information processor but a transducer for the realm of mind (akin to a microphone passing on sound and converting voice and volume). This might help to explain such phenomenon as blindsight (blind people being aware of objects in their environment that they cannot consciously see), mindsight (near-death experiences of congenitally blind people where they are able to see normally), terminal lucidity (a brief period of clear consciousness that sometimes precedes death in dementia patients), hallucinations and such diseases as schizophrenia could be explained by the inference that the human brain focuses and transduces consciousness rather than generates it. [377]

Unlike string theory or theories of parallel universes, the theory that the brain is a bidirectional transducer is directly testable. Empirical support for this theory has the potential to profoundly change our understanding both of ourselves and of our universe. Neuroscience has been hamstrung for half a century by its reliance on the information processing model of the brain - a metaphor that has shed no light on how the human brain actually works. Transduction theory appears to be consistent with three core theories of modern physics - string theory, inflation theory, and quantum theory - each of which predicts the existence of alternative realms of reality.

At the back of material reality is something that imparts light to the human brain, a light that gradually grows and glows like a dimmer switch. Something in us is responding to spirituality, to purpose, value, love and meaning that do not lend themselves well to a naturalistic explanation. It is this dimension outside ourselves that accounts for the observer influence in the nature of physical reality. It accounts for the emergence of personhood, the 'me', the 'I' between the eyes. It accounts for consciousness and reflexivity.

As the philosophical/theological notion of traducianism affirms, the sense of personhood does not need to be directly created one soul at a time to be linked to cosmic reality. The ingredients from which the 'person' can emerge can be passed on by the parents. But at a certain point, 'personhood' emerges from nascent consciousness which then reacts and interacts with the environment to form the self. That would take a full psychosocial account of the self and human person to demonstrate.

The suggestion of a Wi-Fi universe to which we respond could be a helpful metaphor here. Our personhood being regarded as valuable emerges from the birth of worth, to attachments. Yet there is a mystery as to how a sense of worth and significance can emerge even from situations where there has been little affirmation and cultivation of attachments. Where this has been conspicuously lacking, there is still something that can be mobilised, waiting to be born. It must surely be related to the potential for love and also spirituality that can leap upwards in response. It seems to be incorporated into the human DNA at species level definitions of what it means to be human.

The proposal is that Mind and consciousness are a fundamental property of cosmos, arising from the very Ground of Being. [378]the subjective experience of the cosmos and indeed of the ego. Before Descartes and modern subjectivism, the human soul was one entity amongst others—despite being the medium for experiencing all else, it was not the basis for their reality. Kant placed all knowledge of experience on the foundation of the ego's consciousness. Fichte went a stage further in deriving all forms of knowledge from self-consciousness. [379] This was formulated by Hegel in his idea of how the consciousness of self and the consciousness of objects fit together:

"The truth of consciousness is the truth of self-consciousness, and the latter is the ground of the former, such that in existence all consciousness of another object is self-consciousness". [380]

One vital fruit of that self-consciousness as posited here, the cry for endorsement- is there someone out there for me?—is answered by the echo of the cosmos. Personhood and significance is imprinted on our being at some level. A WIFI universe is a metaphor for a key idea, that of a realm where our personhood is activated so to speak much as a transducer is picking up signal and enabling our mind and spirit to connect. Our significance and personhood is latching on to something out there which is personal (namely God). An impersonal universe does not enable this any more than a cosmos generated by artificial intelligence.

Personhood is integral to the cosmos. Many religions and forms of spirituality work with the notion of an impersonal energy that supplies the unifying dimension behind all dimensions. Yet this view and philosophy does not account for ourselves as personal beings. Does that point to the need for God to be personal? That will be the subject of Chapter Ten. For now, we need to ponder how matter and spirit cohere. This dynamic may supply the key to an underlying cosmic personal impulse; something that is influencing mentality.

A question inevitably suggests itself. A transducer magnifies communication from elsewhere. A WIFI field generated by a rooter is replete with latent capability; awaiting a device that can connect with it. On this analogy, does that take us to our consciousness being filtered via the brain (the 'device') from that which is imparted from elsewhere; most obviously the divine Mind and ultimate Personhood? If such an analogy offers clarity, it raises a subsequent question about how then our individuality might arise? An account is needed about this.

MATTER AND SPIRIT

'Mind and consciousness' is a more contemporary formulation but 'body and soul' has ancient metaphysical pedigree as has 'matter and spirit'.

The dynamic between matter and spirit lies at the heart of our view of reality. Whatever religious thinkers and philosophers may have speculated in past centuries, it is our contemporary scientific equipment that has enabled us to peer into the heart of matter. The closer we observe, however, the more 'hard matter' seems to dissolve into electricity and other forms of energy. Electrons are very far from their nuclei and there is little between them.

We know matter and what we might term 'spirit' in combination. What is meant by that is that, as Kant demonstrated, our knowledge of the world is filtered through the constitution of our minds. Sensory effects percolate the mind, which gives both structure and meaning. It is our mind that interprets both the colour and meaning of a sunset. Our way of being in the world is refracted through matter as it affects our minds. Matter is fused with mind. It is when it is when matter is brought into relation to our minds that there is both sense and sensibility. Matter and mind are only known in combination. We cannot know much directly as independent realities except through the prism of our own minds; they seem to us be co-ordinate aspects of the one reality through which we encounter the world. It seems to us though that although spirit and matter constitute aspects of our experience, they are separable in concept. "*The fundamental characteristic of spirit, as far we know it in human personality, is self-consciousness, the power to make mental distinctions between self and other things, and to regard all other things as objects over and against our subjective self*".[381]

Inasmuch as spirit chooses its own purpose as having a value for itself, this is in contrast to matter whose reason for existence lies in relation to other entities.

Could matter be adapted to personhood at least in the form of the conscious observer (as some interpretations of quantum physics propose)? Matter seems to subserve spirit, as brain enables consciousness. "*We attribute an absolute worth and dignity to spirit, simply because it possesses the power of purpose, purposeful thought, purposeful action, purposeful love. Purpose is our standard, our inevitable standard of value. . . . ..the free determination to realise a foreseen end.*"[382] Purpose is the key to existence; the systems of nature are purposeful in going somewhere. This idea is what has often been labelled 'final causes'. Such teleology used to be viewed with suspicion; perhaps because it was confused with physical causation. This does not mean that we can conclude the utility of every individual part of the system. But we could infer that the cosmic system as a whole is guided by a spiritual Being, a personal will of commensurate capacity. The entire material order ministers to spirit, to Mind. Our spiritual nature can roam across time and space while matter moves in its own local frame of reference.

The realm of external nature has influenced spiritual conceptions of the cosmos since time immemorial. "*The heavens declare the glory of God and the firmament shows his handiwork*".[383] Theological literature and religious liturgy alike are profoundly influenced by nature. This reflects the spiritual reality behind materiality and is true in all religions. For Christian and indeed the theology of Abrahamic religions, the cosmos is not God's body but God's work.

DIVINE IMMANENCE

The preceding chapters have argued that it is possible to infer a deep field that influences behaviour. This is for three reasons. Firstly, there is something that activates consciousness. Secondly, there is something that disposes our kind towards a sense of significance that is not existential only but pertains to the psychology and sociology of human functioning. Thirdly, the anthropic principle points (in its strong version) to the validity of a cosmos wired up for the likes of us.

Human worth is, on this reading, a sign of significance; the highest development of consciousness and reflexivity. It is closely allied with conscience, a sense of moral responsibility and guilt, that serves as categorical imperative. In its absence in felt experience, there remains only wistfulness.

The metaphor of a Wi-Fi field that is pervasive—and which we can pick up - invokes the idea of immanence. This maybe a more satisfactory metaphor than invoking spatial representations with reference to coordinate systems. With immanence, presence is pervasive. 'In him, we live, move and have our being' observes Paul, quoting Greek philosophy (Acts 17v28).

Human beings exhibit a kind of immanence in that they indwell their bodies in full. The ability of all parts of our frame to respond to the impulse of motor neurons reflects a pervasive immanence expressed through personhood. All of our embodiment expresses who we are. In Christian theology there is a careful contrast between a God who is both perfectly transcendent and truly immanent—infinitely beyond us and yet personally with us. *As usually drawn, transcendence* is that aspect of God's character that recognizes his position above and beyond all that he created. God is great, impenetrable, and matchless. By contrast, *immanence* recognizes that God enters into creation, working and acting within the world created by divine action. The idea of incarnation seeks to hold both of these together and it matters whether we think of these things 'from above' or 'from below'. Christ is a highly localised presence reflecting and being a point of reference for a transcendent God.

But there is another sense of immanence which is to do with omnipresence. Religions of most varieties hold that the divine is everywhere rather than a localised presence. Ubiquity denotes the notion, usually divine, of being present everywhere at the same time, all-enveloping and pervasive. In classic Judaeo- Christian thought, God is described as a being that possesses omnipresence.

> *Where shall I go from your Spirit?*
> *Or where shall I flee from your presence?*
> *If I ascend to heaven, you are there!*
> *If I make my bed in Sheol, you are there!*
> *If I take the wings of the morning*
> *and dwell in the uttermost parts of the sea,*
> *even there your hand shall lead me,*
> *and your right hand shall hold me. (Psalm 139v7–9)*

Chapter Ten

An Impersonal Universe and A Theory of Correspondence

"*Man is the product of causes which had no prevision of the end they were achieving; his origin, his growth, his hopes and fears, his loves and beliefs are but the outcome of accidental collaboration of atoms*"
—Bertrand Russell [384]

THE QUESTION WE ARE probing is this: 'is there anything out there that corresponds to what's in here?' This may be illegitimate to ask as any talk of an ultimate realm could be the ground of being and is deeper than personal beings: the frame of reference sustains self-conscious humankind. Yet that is only to re-cast the question. Is there an ultimate realm that supplies meaning and value for people?

Put another way, this is to do with correspondence and supposes some analogy of being. it is how the inner realm that is existential and above all, personal not just quantum world marries up with the external world shaped by physical laws. For giants of these matters, such as Einstein, Dirac or Hawking, the vast chasm of the inner world runs in parallel with their discoveries. At the same time as Einstein was developing his General Theory of Relativity, his personal life was in turmoil. He had discarded Mileva, his first wife, and was on the brink of marrying his second, leaving little space in his personal cosmos for his sons. [385] The human frame of reference is not just about different physical systems moving and being interactive in our environment but how we relate to ourselves.

Our newly enlarged understanding of the universe (alongside the on-going quest for dark matter and dark energy) continues to pose huge questions about a Theory of Everything that can place it into a framework of explanation. Yet there is a considerable gap to do with the absence of the inner world of the only conscious observers we know about so far—ourselves.

Perhaps there is no external world 'out there' and our minds are structured to interpret our existence and construct material reality as we perceive. Immanuel Kant suggested that the realm of the physical universe and the moral world of meaning, refer to two different and incommensurable realms. But surely there should be some tie up. The linkage between the two realms has long since fascinated philosophers. As Kant remarked in his Critique of Practical Reason, then *"Two things fill the mind with ever-increasing wonder and awe, the more often and the more intensely the mind of thought is drawn to them: the starry heavens above me and the moral law within me."*

This followed from Kant's reading of the physical and the moral sciences, both of which grew out of reflection on self-evidence sources of wonder. Kant thought that a true understanding of either has been mired in superstition and blind conjecture. The physical sciences were finally reaching a point where they were developing on empirical and rational grounds. Moral philosophy lagged behind but Kant hoped to pioneer a scientific, rational approach to ethics. The method Kant uses in his Analytic philosophy reflected this. Separating the a priori foundations of ethics from anything empirical before proceeding through a series of proofs to the most fundamental moral principles, Kant believed he had improved on a method of how we do ethics.

The essential point in Kant's philosophy is that it is the human mind that structures our experience of the external world and providing the categories for both knowledge and action. Our experience of being human is a mediating screen between an external world and an inner world of observation and significance. Essentially, the mind does not just mirror the world, it actively constructs it.

The philosopher Hilary Putnam endeavoured to show that meaning in language was not solely about what is intended. Identical twins, he hypothesised, live on identical planets that differed only in that water on one of them was not H2O but another substance with similar properties. Each twin refers to water, intending the same meaning but they would be referring to two different things. [386] Putnam went on to adopt externalism; the idea that meanings 'ain't just in the head'. We are meaning-seeking creatures, but our interpretation of the world is not just constructed by what happens in our heads. [387] Our brains are wired for meaning but that is based on something.

Whether considered external or not, the underlying reality to which we might claim to respond, arguably needs to be personal in some way in order to 'match' our personhood. How else would it validate our personhood? Does our personhood even need to be aligned with that which is beyond ourselves—there could be a disparity due to the particular way we have evolved.

In this chapter we will probe how far the considerations we have been exploring point to the existence of a divine realm that is personal. The concept of a transcendent and spiritual God who is personal is a postulate to our sense of value.

Such a reading of the physical world as containing rumours of divine purpose constitutes a form of natural theology. This is not the same as theistic proofs that Aquinas and Anselm proposed but a more modest role of offering theistic belief as an insightful account of what is going on. This position is not a rival to scientific explanation but seeks to complement that explanation by setting it within a more profound context of understanding. An account of this sort does, however, draw psychology and faith closer together.

I am going to use the term 'analogy' rather than 'argument' which carries the connotation of a 'proof' for the existence of God. To suggest 'an argument from value' is not helpful - as if God is the result of an equation. Proposing an argument for the existence of anything within our range of empirical proof cannot be equated to the existence of a being beyond our imagination. Following on from the philosopher David Hume, Immanuel

Kant is thought by many to have demonstrated the weakness of theistic proofs and natural theology. Hume sought to show that while design arguments, for instance, might point to the existence of something that caused the universe to exist, it is quite another step to say that this is a personal God who loves and cares.

Rather I will suggest that there is an analogy of being between personhood as we try to articulate it and a personal divine realm which instantiates the cosmos. There is a quality of existence in the cosmos of which our personhood is a pale reflection. Our sense of meaning points to a personal being outside of ourselves who supplies a at least a frame of reference but maybe in some sense transmits personhood and allows us to connect with it.

It is beyond the scope of these proposals to reference the dialogue between science and religion. A recent (2023) exploration of relationships between them charts the usual landmarks, demonstrating the nuances and complexities that go beyond ideological propaganda and polemical politics. [388] Science has probed restlessly the age of the natural world together with the mechanisms that resulted in the array of living things and the human place within them. [389]

Our own sense of being a person points to the type of being at the heart of things and provides a means of correspondence between them. This enables us to respond with what Martin Buber called an 'I-thou' relationship. It is surely a personal, divine realm that can speak to the embodied, dependent, social and mortal dimensions of human existence. Can an impersonal cosmos do that?

At stake is whether an impersonal universe have generated personal beings who are able to contemplate their own place within it. If not, how could it have "*ignored the rock from which it was hewn and the pit from which it was dug?*" (Isaiah 51v1). We can feel validated by a thou, not an it.

The problem is one of the very concept of God in relation to the experienced world. The 'experienced world' is usually discussed within debates about science and society or the problem of knowledge is usually seen as with respect to ultimate causes or design in the physical universe. The focus here is different. It is as the relation of God to the experienced world INSIDE. I argue here that there is 'best fit' between theism in the tradition of the Abrahamic religions, rooted in God as a personal being, and our own personhood. How a consciousness of valuable personhood, so vital for human functioning, could be generated by purely natural causes is inexplicable. We have, surely, to find a way of proceeding from the value-laden psychological realities as we experience them to the ground of experience that is ultimately real. What then is God's relation to our personhood?

A consciousness of valuable personhood or indeed spirituality (with which it is so integrally linked) that turns to its resonance for something outside itself cannot have its sufficient reason within the material interests and sense instincts of a purely natural existence. Fundamental to the enquiry here is the need for explanation of the individual and personal aspects of our existence. It is a sense of profound value (or its felt lack) that renders human personhood a unique centre of experience relevant to the cosmos. Either that or this is profound conceit. Nevertheless, should not a process which results in a dependence on a realm of value and spiritual values not be referred to a source which is itself spiritual and affirming of a personal dimension?

If not, it is puzzling that any purely natural processes should have resulted in personal beings. The dependence of human personhood on a realm of value points back to a deeper ground in the nature of things. A sense of connection with God could come about from our own experience of valuable personhood and that this therefore is an expected outcome of the way the universe has developed. The cosmos as we experience it individually is a realm in which fact and value are interwoven. It has to us in our daily round the feel of being teleologically structured.

The task of metaphysics was to go beyond the physical sciences and endeavour to find an explanation for the universe as a whole. Together with psychological insights, it has to take account of the progress of those 'natural sciences' (the disruption of which has been discussed in preceding chapters) and carry those into a final explanation and theory of everything that can explain them.[390]

There are, as is well understood in religious thought, different conceptions of the divine. Whether there is a single, experient subject expressed in a single will is a radically different conception to saying that there is God in the universe and nothing but God. In the Abrahamic religions, God transcends the world of things and is not identical with them. The pantheist refers to the identity of the self with the universe. The theist uses the language of communion and cooperation with God as experienced in worship and a spiritual way of looking at reality.

It makes a fundamental difference whether what we call God is an energy force or a personal Being. "*The pantheistic assertion is 'All is One', the theist transforms into the very different proposition, 'All depends on One'.*"[391]

The sense in which God is said to be personal shapes our view of the spiritual consciousness and religion. But it also has fundamental connection with our personhood. A personal relationship is very different from an impersonal relationship. Dialogue is possible between 'I-thou' but not between 'I-it'. Full relations are possible between persons but not between persons and things. Although one may commune with the universe, the Object of worship is a personal Being. A person differs fundamentally from 'a thing'. Something may be respected profoundly but not worshipped in a meaningful sense unless it is conceived as channelling personal force.

To the usual delineation of God as having omniscience, omnipresence and omnipotence, we might say that God is self-conscious. There is more to a personal Being than self-consciousness but there cannot surely be less. On this reading, God has the awareness of his own existence that we have of ours. To argue that God is a self-conscious and self-determining Being entails ascribing to him the essential characteristics of personality. A self-conscious Being who is personal strongly implies also ethical attributes. Ethical values cannot be real unless they are the expressions of personal wills. To speak of divine forgiveness is to speak of a personal act. Unless between persons, it is meaningless.

The old charge of anthropomorphism is a challenge here. Can our human conception of personality, with all the social and ethical aspects discussed in Chapter Five, be applied to a Being who so far transcends the conditions of our physical existence? The factors that shape our ideas of human personhood cannot surely be applied to a Divine Being? God cannot be just a magnified human. Are there not severe limitations which enter into the idea of God being personal in any real sense?

It can, however, be relevant if a distinction be made between personhood and the self. The latter is a construct, formed from a range of psychological and social ingredients. Our personhood is a something else surely. Moreover, it is a personhood that is so often compromised by irrationality and moral ambiguity; incoherence and inconsistency. To speak of the divine Being as 'supra-personal' is surely not incorrect if it applies to God who is self-determining and possessing a self-conscious Mind.

There are to be sure many examples of religions that do not have the element of a personal God. It is beyond the scope of this monograph to discuss how far they dispense with personal deity entirely, given the tendency towards statues and personal representations that is so prevalent.

In philosophy, there have been many currents that speak of God as the Absolute. Following Hegel, it became fairly common in speculative philosophy to think of a personal dimension being transcended and transformed into the impersonal character of the Absolute. An infinite being can seem to be incompatible with a sense of personality. The human self is bounded by restrictions that the transcendent Being of the world cannot be. God is not a developing Being subject to reflexive action and self-consciousness, always confronted by something external. Surely there cannot be a self-conscious

Will that is not constituted by a relation to something outside other than itself.[392]

The notion of all beings reduced to parts of the One Being makes the necessity for individual ethical practice illusory. Love or justice required of a particular person in a particular situation depends on an individual locus of action: a free-determining and self-reflective personhood in action. The reality of individual finite spirits has to be more than illusory. A personal being entails forming a mental representation of itself in distinction from other personal entities. For us and for the most part, that involves intersubjective recognition within a culture. Yet there remains the focus of immediate experience, the sense of being 'me'; the self-feeling by which we distinguish ourselves from others.

For God, it is surely different as philosophers of religion have endeavoured to explain. God is a necessary being, not contingent upon something external. Unlike a human person who needs the mediation of realities and persons, the divine person contains the conditions of existence within and is self-conditioned and self-conscious. In a perfect being, does dependence on external conditions exist to the same extent? It does not follow that the situation in a personhood formed within a spatial and temporal world bound by culture, would be valid for a perfect, non-contingent Being. Surely, God as a self-determined spiritual Being contains those changing states of consciousness that is implied through interaction with the world albeit within an abiding self. Human personhood with all its ambiguities need not define what personhood has to be.

A final thought pertains to psychoanalysis. The human finite self rarely penetrates itself to discover the full range of its own content. Much of human experience remains in the unconscious, beyond the reach of current mental life with its passions and interests. The self is often divided with the result of an incomplete fusion. Integration is usually the goal of psychotherapy but rarely achieved.

For our purposes here, it is important that the universe responding to the deepest needs of self-conscious persons is rooted in a teleological order which emanates from a self-conscious will. The fundamental desires of humanity—for value, love, meaning and spirituality—are such that none but a personal spirit can have. An impersonal spirit cannot surely validate those to anything like the same extent. *"The sole assurance that the highest aspirations of man are met, not frustrated, lies in the principle that the Ground of the World is a self-conscious and self-determining spirit"*.[393]

There is, on the contemporary scene a strong new emphasis on the ultimate reality taking the form of an impersonal spirit. Being open to a higher power might be labelled as a 'higher plan', 'fate' or 'destiny' rather than God. Yet if the ultimate being is non personal, we have an argument that can be made that individual ethical practice and meaning are illusory. If God is not personal, how can he validate our meanings? This is crucial. Because VLMS are mind-dependent but also structures, in many ways, of personality, only a personal God can validate them. Put another way, would an impersonal spiritual force care about VLMS?

The kind of classical theism proposed by Thomas Aquinas sought to demonstrate that the existence of God can be proved by arguments from the physical universe. His underlying principle was that of the principle of analogy which was then extrapolated to the existence of an ultimate power. The world is not self-sufficient. Its own structures signpost a higher reality. The very existence of beings that are more complex than others points by logical necessity to the existence of the highest of all beings. Such an ultimate being embraces essential traits of the lower.

Classical theism has not held the field without other challenges. One such example is that of process theology, associated with the name of Charles Hartshorne. God is supreme becoming in which there is a factor of supreme being . [394] This perspective drew on the philosophy of Alfred North Whitehead. [395]Process theology' suggests that God's being is dipolar. God is a loving reality; a necessary Being who is both loving and immutable. At the other pole, God involves himself in the changing states of humanity, adapting himself to the constant flux of the world. This was at odds with traditional theism. God is the ultimate origin of all things; his being must have an absolute character and cannot be relative to lesser beings. Central to classical Christian theology, however, is that such a being can allow for personal relationships with other beings and that they can have relationship with God. In Abrahamic faiths generally, God speaks and shows. For Christianity, Judaism and Islam, reference to the ethical values is the revelation of their unique personal God.

It is our contention here that the unique and irreplaceable value of every human life finds an echo in an ultimate reality that is personal; but that there is no response in an impersonal universe where energy is all there is. This is a silent deficit.

This view has been challenged by religious philosophy outside the Abrahamic faiths and the rise of contemporary forms of spirituality to replace Judaeo- Christian beliefs in many quarters. This is linked to the loss of faith in one of the central tenets of modernity: namely the Newtonian perspective seeing the world as a machine. Everything is reduced to sequences of conditioned responses arising from initial conditions. The challenge, however, is that *"the mechanistic world view and the value system associated with it have generated technologies, institutions and lifestyles that are profoundly unhealthy*". [396] Environmental degradation and the dominance of exploitative power are ruining the planet and damaging the human spirit. What that is being replaced by potentially is an awareness of the interrelatedness of all phenomena. Many voices are arguing for a new paradigm that transcends current conceptual boundaries and develop new ways of thinking. From chaos theory to systems thinking, new perspectives are emerging based on organism rather than machine.

The systems view of life is often seen as inherently spiritual in its deepest essence and consistent with many ideas in mystical traditions with their dynamic perspective on reality. "*The concepts of process, change and fluctuation, which play such a role in the systems view of living organisms, are emphasised in the Eastern mystical traditions, especially in Taoism*". [397] The mutual interdependence of reality is said to be linked to Chinese medicine and Buddhist approaches to life. The Tao of physics[398] was a strong marker to this way of seeing, as was the earlier work of Ilya Prigogine.[399] Eastern mysticism and contemporary scientific findings relate well: Eastern mysticism might also have the linguistic and philosophical tools required to undertake to some of the biggest scientific challenges we face. The tenets of Hinduism, Buddhism, and Taoism are mined in order to show their striking parallels with contemporary science.

In Confucianism, Zong San Mou proposes that the source of values is actually a universal moral entity that is both transcendent and immanent. The heavenly principle (tian dao) is above humanity and has all the characteristics of transcendence. There is mutual understanding and correspondence between human beings and heaven. It is in this sense that Confucius said heaven knows him. [400] The deepest centre of a person is a principle that transcends the finitude of human beings. In the construction of a collective social order beyond us Chinese people should work hard for their families and communities since they will continue to be members of their communities after death.

In the writings of Zi Chen Zhao, the main point is that there is no personal god in Chinese culture, which results in difficulty in pursuing the union of any heavenly principle with humanity. [401] Zi Chen Zhao did not stop at moral cultivation but argued that the lack of a personal god introduced difficulties in how we understand the manifestation of the union of heavenly principle with humanity. In Confucian belief, human beings stand in the same position as heaven and earth. There seems to be no need of a personal god in Confucianism and as in the Confucian classic Zhongyong, the person of entire sincerity 'can assist the transforming and nourishing powers of Heaven and Earth' (Zhongyong 23), and thus human beings take part in the nurturing operations of heaven and earth.[402] The lack of a personal god in Chinese religion is replaced by the Tian Dao (heavenly principle). Tian has three meanings: natural sky, representing a metaphysical principle, and the one who decides the fate of people. The term dao is mainly used by Daoists and Confucians is used to denote principle, way, and knowledge. Notwithstanding Confucius saying that people should not offend tian, Mengzi said Tian did not speak. Tian is impersonal, without subjectivity and an object to be understood by people. For Daoists, the heavenly principle is just a host of natural rules. They believe, 'Heaven and earth do not act from (the impulse of) any wish to be benevolent; they deal with all things as the dogs of grass are dealt with.'[403] Tian is not benevolent and hence is impersonal.

In religious systems such as Hinduism, Buddhism and Taoism, the world is conceived in terms of flow, movement and change: dynamic not static. *"Modern physics, too, has come to conceive of the universe as such as a web of relations and, like Eastern mysticism, has recognised that this web of is intrinsically dynamic".* [404]

This was well-received in many quarters. Fritjof Capra, in 'The Tao of Physics', seeks ... *"an integration of the mathematical world view of modern physics and the mystical visions of Buddha and Krishna. Where others have failed miserably in trying to unite these seemingly different world views, Capra, a high-energy theorist, has succeeded admirably."*[405]

Others were not so sure. *"At the heart of the matter is Mr. Capra's methodology—his use of what seem to me to be accidental similarities of language as if these were somehow evidence of deeply rooted connections."*[406]

This comes up on the contemporary scene with the swirling advances of artificial intelligence (AI). At the time of writing, there is deep concern that the machine learning which dominates AI has the potential to penetrate so many areas of our lives and do damage—from the potential destruction of jobs to the development of autonomous weapons systems that could violate the rules of war. *"There is also a more general fear that AI will begin to replace everyday interactions and that soon we will be living in a more dehumanised world".* [407]

There are to be sure many concerns about how humans could regulate the AI world. Whether these are ethical matters, resolvable by technical experts, or can AI be a force for good is one of them. Just because we can regulate does not mean that we should. Foremost amongst concerns is that of de-personalisation. Who is this 'it' before whom I become and 'I'? [408] De-personalisation has been a major concern in Western economic landscapes since the days of Marxian analysis of labour beginning to confront the labourer as an autonomous power, hostile and alien. [409] Writing of the remorseless factory system, he opined that "*it replaces labour by machines, but it casts some of the workers back into barbarous forms of labour and turns others into machines*". [410] Since then, de-personalisation has become a spectre, not just haunting Europe but anywhere that impersonal systems in public services reduce humans to objects of provision. Under assault from forces that erode and swamp it, the human dimension becomes increasingly important. What so many are looking for is kindness rather than being treated impersonally and becoming a mere abstract. [411]

It is an essential tenet of theology in the Judaeo-Christian tradition that God is Spirit, not matter. "*God is Spirit and they that worship him must worship him in spirit and truth*". [412] The material world depends for its existence on spirit, to which matter subserves. There is a spiritual presence in nature, claims Christian tradition, which can indeed be interpreted on the analogy of human personhood.

The spiritual backcloth to the universe has been treated as an inference; be it an inference from design, causation or the moral sensibility of things. As we have been exploring, the nature of the world is conducive to spiritual belief. Materialism and both the science and methods of natural philosophy reflect the machinery of the world. They relate to its properties, not the essence; physical relations, not spiritual and moral connections relating to the realm of value, love, meaning and spirituality. Matter (materiality) and indeed energy, is what moves in space and time. Consciousness and personhood utilise matter (grey matter and so on), but matter does not require either. Of what use is it? Put another way, what does consciousness and personhood add to matter?

Put this way, matter is the medium of the spirit; the medium of its realisation.[413] Yet the whole structure of the cosmos seems to be purposeful. Matter is fused with spirit. "*We attribute an absolute worth and dignity to spirit, simply because it possesses the power of purpose, purposeful thought, purposeful action, purposeful love. Purpose is our inevitable standard of value.*"[414] The character of the conclusion shapes the whole thing. Contrast between the cosmic immensity and the insignificance of humanity is challenged by the pointed significance of human beings in their lived experience. Personhood and purposeful value are integrally connected. Humankind has a particular ability to perceive both its own existence and a purposeful backcloth to it.

In Greek philosophy, Plato saw the world as the manifestation of divine ideas; forms that were more real than matter itself. Aristotle placed emphasis the other way round. Without material embodiment, divine ideas would be abstract and incomplete. "*For what else is nature*", asks Seneca, "*but God and Divine Reason, immanent in the world and its parts*". [415]

This is clear in Christian theology, which has laid stress both on transcendence and immanence; of which trinity and incarnation are correlates. "*The more profoundly we penetrate the laws on which the universe is founded and sustained, the more do we behold the glory of the Lord*" says Basil of Caesarea in his Hexaemeron.[416] Raise yourselves, he urges, by things visible to the invisible being.

Two ideas from Christian theology can help give an account of how God as a personal being might relate to our own personhood. The first is a notion of analogy of being; the second is 'participation'.

The analogy of being will be discussed in the next chapter. What is important to note here is to draw a contrast between metaphysical idealism and personal being. The divine realm is not merely 'spirit' or 'Absolute'. Whoever defends the notion of God as personality must show that this can equate to notions of 'the infinite' (which has had a firm place in Christian theology. [417] Yet an impersonal energy cannot relate to or validate the personhood on which we depend for our psychological existence.

Chapter Eleven

In Conversation
The Analogy of Being

A BRIEF EXPLORATION HERE of philosophical and theological conversation partners is a foray into questions of metaphysics and indeed anti-metaphysics relevant to the analogy of being.

As is well-known, the word 'metaphysics' does not occur in the writings of the one traditionally associated with it—Aristotle. It is a book 'next to and after the physics'.

In his book "*Spirit in the world*", the Catholic theologian Karl Rahner argues from human experience that there are grounds for belief in the classic arguments for God's existence.[418] This is rooted not only in the possibility of human knowledge of God but the very conditions of human receptivity to the transcendent. God is incomprehensible, never fully explained. Yet this Absolute Mystery has spoken and revealed God-self. Revelation does not travel new airwaves but frequencies that have already been constructed and which go out to everybody. We are already attuned.

Rahner's starting point is that of Kant. Beyond the fundamental structures of reason that Kant argued make it possible to know anything at all, there is BEING, that serves as a precondition. The human mind, Rahner affirms, is structurally oriented to a backdrop of being, Absolute Being as well as Absolute Mystery. This is an orientation towards God essentially. Although we can make an inference that the world of value, love, meaning and the spiritual is not adequately validated by materialism; and also that the mind is not adequately explained by materialism therefore there needs to be a deeper explanation of the mental field. Ultimately we can only know about the nature of that field as God as God reveals it to us.

IMMANUEL KANT

Kant had sought to establish the validity of knowledge in a way that did not depend on metaphysics. The medieval idea of thought as ontological was replaced by the subjective ego as the source of knowledge. His Critical Philosophy left little scope for the content of innate knowledge but the forms of knowledge were structured by innate categories imposed by the mind. Although all knowledge begins with experience, as he is keen to stress, that does not mean it is thereby grounded just in sensory impression. There are universal truths, he thinks, transcending sense data and coming prior to it. The content of knowledge, what we think *about*, might be based on senses, but it involves mental furniture that makes knowledge possible in the first place. Kant denied that the image of God and divine reason makes knowledge possible but also the empirical view that it is experience that makes mental conceptions possible (reading David Hume had roused him from dogmatic slumbers). Experience, he argued, is only made possible by our forms of thought. They come first—a priori.

In his inaugural dissertation at Konigsberg University in 1770, Kant's lecture refers to the forms of reason back to a *"certain law inborn in the mind for coordinating with one another the sensa arising from the presence of the object through which . . . impressions may take on a certain form according to stable and innate laws"*. [419] He is cautious about ascribing this innate knowledge to any kind of preformed awareness of the knowledge of the divine in which humans participate.

Kant's thinking had moved on by 1781 and the 'Critique of Pure Reason'. There, he no longer regarded fundamental conceptions of the mind a priori as determining things in themselves; only as forms of knowledge by which the mind interprets sense data. Such a priori conceptions he had previously understood as ways in which God as Creator and first cause of all finite and contingent substances combined them into one world. *"We like all other finite substances are dependent on one absolute substance whose unity makes the world one or maintains all finite substances in such relations that they can influence each other."*[420] By the time of the Critique, the objective world is viewed from the way we relate to it. The self has substituted for God as the unifying principle in knowledge. The emphasis is now not on how objects are combined into the unity of the world but how that world comes to be a unity for me. [421] If the world is one world for us, it is because it cannot exist for us or be known by us except in relation to the self.

Such an approach, however, raises serious questions. What Kant had been objecting to was the notion that God is purely objective and in contrast to the consciousness of the self. Yet in self-consciousness, there is not only consciousness of subject-object but consciousness of a unity that transcends it. The consciousness of self is inextricably linked to a universal focus. All knowledge implies that. It is one thing to recognise that objects are phenomenal (not things in themselves independent of consciousness), it is another to claim that ultimate reality consists of phenomena.

Kant objected to the notion of preformation of subjective dispositions of thought, implanted by the Creator from the first moment of our existence. Where were the limits to the categories of thought to which such a concept would be applied? [422] The world is one as we make it one.

Kant espouses a notion of a 'thing in itself'. Although we get on with life despite our transcendentally delimited knowledge where something 'in itself' is unknown. Lack of access to the absolute truth and validity of the world of experience constitute a knowledge that we can hardly dismiss though unable to answer with accuracy. The world is no longer mirrored in knowledge. This is anti-metaphysical.

The human mind thinks as it does surely because this is the way it has been constituted. A case can be made that the first principles of cognition are implanted. We have the sensibility we do in order to interpret our sense experience. Our mental furniture is innately part of who we are. This is what enables us to construct our categories of thought; it is what we think with and is near universal. The notion that we frame our experience with in - born categories is clearly very different from saying that all our ideas are the result of experience, which is the empiricist manifesto. Kant recognised that the world we perceive is only that because of our mental structure but surely that begs the question of why we all have the same mental structure. A unifying cause for all our mental structures is needed.

ANSELM

Anselm's ontological argument for the existence of God is well-known. It appears in the Meditation of this eleventh century Archbishop known as the Prosologion.

Less well-known is the Monologion, or more formally, *'A Monologue on the Reason for Faith' or, as some render it, 'An Example of Meditation on the Meaning of Faith.'* This was his first major theological work, *where* Anselm began to introduce his theology, rooted in logical exposition, instead of religious belief. It is to be carried out by the tools of natural theology rather than scripture. Unlike its better known Prosologion, Anselm's argued that the analysis of one's subjective understanding of moral goodness, one should find that some things are supremely good, or better, than others, which means that there must be something of superlative goodness—the Best. This best thing would need to be God according to the logic. The end of the book concerns God's relationship to moral goodness, arguing that God did not invent goodness, nor does he obey it, but rather, God is goodness personified, so that objective moral goodness is an extension of his nature. The terminus of his discussion is also the starting point: it is the conclusion to which everything points. *"There is something that is the best, the greatest, the highest, of all existing things".*[423]

Because the Monologion and Proslogion deal with the basic tenets in the Christian idea of reality, Anselm thinks he can construct his argument without making any specifically Christian assumptions. *"Now, take someone who either has never heard of, or does not believe in, and so does not know, this—this, or indeed any of the numerous other things which we necessarily believe about God and his creation. I think that he can, even if of average ability, convince himself, to a large extent, of the truth of these beliefs, simply by reason alone."*[424]

Anselmian metaphysics depends on premises such as that if two things have the same nature, then there is one common thing from which they have this nature and in virtue of which they exist. [425]

Completed in 1076, the Monologion is a meditation in which Anselm treats a number of issues to do with the Divine Essence, Trinity, Creation, and human destiny, all of which were based on Neoplatonic thought. Anselm tells us in his Preface that he had been asked to ground his investigations in the work on rational arguments rather than appeal to scriptural authority. In its purpose, the Monologion was both apologetic and religious, seeking to demonstrate the existence and attributes of God by an appeal to reason alone, not by church authority as favoured by earlier medieval thinkers. Anselm moves from the awareness of a multiplicity of good things to the recognition that they all share or participate more or less in that which is good ultimately.

Anselm's argument is more directly Platonic than subsequent or more contemporary approaches to a divine being. His doctrine of degrees of being is top down: from the divine nature to beings that have less being. A hedgehog has more 'being' than a piece of wood off a nearby tree. But it has less sense of being than a human. In turn, a human experience of being is greatly inferior to that of God. Anselm's concept of God is based on a single notion; that of a self-sufficient being that gives all things their being, their goodness and their excellence. *"There is a Nature which exists through itself, which is the highest of all existing things, and through which exists whatever is."* [426]

It is worth following this as it is relevant to our theme. If there is a highest value it gives a category by which we judge ourselves and our personal value is validated.

When it comes to goodness, the core argument proceeds as follows:

i) There are good things

ii) Some things are better than others; there are degrees of goodness

iii) The extent to which they participate in goodness reflects a scale against which we can measure that goodness

iv) Goodness is that by which all things are good

v) The ultimate goodness alone is good in itself

vi) This is better than if it relied on other things for its goodness

vii) Goodness is maximally good

viii) It is greater for it to exist by itself than deriving its existence from something else

ix) The maximal point on this scale is that which has independent existence

Few would be with Anselm in this kind of approach today. Similarly, the ontological argument in the subsequent Proslogion has few subscribers, despite it being rather hard to refute on logical grounds. The metaphysical framework of a gradually descending degree of being has been largely rejected in modern thought. The trend now is for 'bottom-up', as in degrees of complexity in the gathering together of the ingredients of sentience. Palpably, there are ascending degrees of sentience in living things, let alone the contrast between inorganic and organic matter. To argue that such a ladder of being reaches right up to the heavens and ultimate Being is another question, though it could not be dismissed a priori.

However, as regards the thesis of this monograph, the question arises. Can the leading idea of the Monologion be rehabilitated to charge its application to the value of personhood?

There are scales of value when it comes to personhood. Our dog may be much loved and have its own personality, but there is a depth, complexity and superabundance to each human personality that gives each person unique, infinite dignity. To think of what (metaphysically) may be of maximal value and supreme worth is an extension of this. There are degrees of personhood. This leads to the possibility that we can compare personhood and our self-actualisation against the knowledge of God as the ultimate person.

As discussed previously, how we understand ourselves as persons, what it means to be a person has been the subject of a vast horizon of discovery across the centuries, including the opening to interiority in Christianity.[427] It could be inseparable from 'what does it mean to be human?' were it not for important debates about the moral status of animals and the question of what sets us apart from other inhabitants (past and present) of our world. Philosophical ideas about the nature of human nature, a unified and stable self, the metaphysics of the soul and the connection between mind and body are all involved. Contemporary discussion has included such questions as whether all humans are persons and if we can lose personhood through cognitive impairment such as dementia or in situations of terminal illness. When do we acquire personhood—in the womb or in the journey of human development? Whether there is a single and unitary nature which all humans share has met with scepticism; often hostility. It has been much explored in cultural history and anthropology.

In the rapidly changing map of social transformations, the definition of what constitutes a person is at the beating heart of almost every contemporary debate- from abortion, human rights, euthanasia and capital punishment. If all we need to be a person is human DNA, then cells in our mouths are persons. However, when someone acts in an egregious way, moral consciousness is outraged. Inclusion in our moral community is a capacity to suffer. Personhood seems to be what must be possessed as a part of our moral community in which we participate, a being we can call a person or when society can recognise you as a person. Personhood is the subject of continuing debate both in philosophy and theology. Are Martians persons? Are intelligent animals such as pigs or dolphins persons and if so, how much sentience would be required in order to qualify?

In religious philosophy, the prevailing notion is that of a divine presence which either transcends the material order of things (as in the Abrahamic, monotheistic religions) or is coterminous with it (as it most modes of pantheism).

As Anselm argued:[428]

> 20. *The Supreme Being exists in every place and at all times.*
> 21. *[The Supreme Being] exists in no place at no time.*
> 22. *How [the Supreme Being] exists in every place at every time and in no place at no time.*
> 23. *How [the Supreme Being] can better be understood to exist everywhere than in every place.*

AUGUSTINE

Anselm wrote the Monologion in response to the requests of a believing community. This was a very different context from Augustine who wrote to refute a hostile audience. "*The following dissertation concerning the Trinity, as the reader ought to be informed, has been written in order to guard against the sophistries of those who disdain to begin with faith, and are deceived by a crude and perverse love of reason.*" [429] Faith is a reliable guide in our search for truth and wisdom: "*that what has not yet been made clear to our intellect, be nevertheless not loosened from the firmness of our faith.*"[430]

These considerations are sharply underlined in the Christian theology through the idea of the Trinity. Anselm cites Augustine's work 'On the Trinity' as an authority for what he is doing.

> *"Let him first look carefully at the books of On the Trinity by the aforementioned teacher, viz., Augustine, and then let him judge my work in the light of these books."* P2

Christian revelation does not begin with a general tract about God but the impact of a person. A case can be made that it is the valuable personhood of Christ, embracing the human situation, that is imparted to those that believe and that this is potent for the redemption of humanity.[431]

The term 'person' is a key word in trinitarian theology. In its classic formulation, the word 'persona' person' (persona) was adopted by Tertullian and his theological descendants in the Latin West as a common noun that applies to the Father, the Son and the Holy Spirit. The Latin word meant a mask worn by characters in a classical drama, hence the idea of a dramatis persona, a character in a drama. The theologian John Zizioulas argued that the concept of 'the person' is the only term that can be predicated of both the divine and human realm properly and without the risk of anthropomorphism. It can span both domains.[432] A central question that this raises is whether there can be argued to be traces of the divine being in human personhood which might justify the application of the term 'person' to both contexts? Participation in the divine is the context for articulating how we can even speak of God in human language.

Karl Barth argued that this vestigium trinitatis goes back to the thinking of Augustine where "an analogue of the Trinity" is in some creaturely reality distinct from God which nevertheless manifests a similarity to the divine being.[433] It should be noted that Barth was concerned that discerning vestiges of God in the created order opened up a second root of doctrinal understanding about God in addition to revelation and which could be gleaned independently. The idea of correspondence or analogy can then be caught between two axioms that seem mutually exclusive. On the one hand God is fully incommensurable with the creation and yet genuine revelation is possible in human terms about the divine purpose, word and emotions. For Barth, there is not a 'correspondence' or 'similarity' of being between God and humankind but in affirming that, he is at pains to stress divine revelation. There is a contrast between sovereignty and grace on the part of God and need on the part of humankind.[434] Analogous correspondence is only possible because of divine revelation.

This is more than a question of philosophical language. It is about triune personhood in relation to human personhood and whether the latter finds the ground for its existence in the former—not just how we speak of it. The weight of theological tradition is that the 'good news' is founded on God taking to himself the same humanity that cannot approach him by its own efforts.[435] There is no sense in which Christian faith has three objects;

rather a single 'Thou' *"who meets man's I and unites himself to this I as the indissoluble Subject and therein reveals himself to him as his God".*[436]

The best way to think about this, is probably to speak of communal participation in which there is a dynamic, personal co-presence, drawing and meeting; a vicarious presenting of the human person to the Father and the Father to the human person in and through Christ by his Spirit. This communion becomes intrinsic to the extent that believers are 'in Christ' and he in us.[437]

Participation—entering into the life of the divine- has had a long running in philosophical theology of all stripes. There has been a debate in the Christian tradition about how far the atoning death of Christ is about substitution or participation- or both! Jesus is inserted into the human situation as the sin-bearer 'instead of us'. As 20th century writers emphasised, in Paul's thought there are two sets of terms that speak of the effect of the cross of Christ. One is about <u>participation</u> (from one state to another); the other is <u>judicial</u> (emphasising guilt that is then compensated for). With the first, the focus is on being 'in Christ' such that being in His position through mutual identification enables us to switch our state. With the second, 'Christ dying for us' does the heavy lifting and we have forgiveness. These are different lenses, not contradictory.[438]

'Divinisation' is not part of Christian theology. The idea of participation, of being included 'in Christ' is a not, however, one of absorption as in an Eastern religion, but of being a person within a greater personhood since that is the God-given potential of humankind. This leads naturally into the notion of union with God lying at the heart of redemptive destiny and some would argue this is where the New Testament places emphasis. [439] Similarly, Macaskill exploring key implications for the Christian moral vision of the New Testament idea of participatory union as they unfold in Paul's Letters.[440]

There are schools of thought that describe how grace and nature, creation and deification, nature and supernature are only different vantages on a single transcendent reality. In Christian theology there has been a 'two-tier' approach whereby human nature has no claim on grace. Some would argue that the divide between nature and grace nevertheless allows for *"a structural aptitude in us for grace that is nevertheless, in no sense an inchoate possession of grace or an intrinsic disposition towards a supernatural end".* [441] Whatever is not alien to a finite nature is an intrinsic possibility of that nature.

On this view, divinity is an inherent possibility of humanity. As Bentley Hart observes of the biblical story, God could make Sarah bear a child well past her fertile years without imposing a state foreign to her womanhood. It was a flowering of what was there. Humanity has a divinely given vocation to union with God; deification. By contrast, the Reformation emphasised a sharp distinction between the gift of creation (that became terribly marred through sin) and the supernatural realm of grace. We cannot get to God through the natural order of things. Grace must come from outside.

All this is a way of hypothesising hat the final horizon of a sense of value that humans experience on a good day could be seen to have its final cause in deity. The reality of this final cause is a way of explaining the reality of the value that humans seem to require in their lives.

Is valuing the human dimension religious experience or normal experience? I have argued in this book that the need to be of high worth is fundamental to everyday psychological experience; not to be marginalised in some department of being or philosophy marked as 'religious'.

The argument from religious experience remains potent. In geometry, seeing the truth of a conclusion comes back to seeing the truth of some premise or starting point. In theology, it is the believing of some conclusion that leads us back to the believing of some promise or premise. This faith will be retrospectively verified by experience. Swinburne claims that religious experience argument succeeds only as part of an overall probability type approach. Swinburne makes the existence of a personal God with infinite capacities a simpler explanation of the universe than any rival hypothesis.[442]

THOMAS AQUINAS

Correspondence and the analogy of being was a pivotal idea in the philosophical theology of Thomas Aquinas. Analogy was taken to be foundation for the causal demonstration of divine existence but also the doctrine of participation. From an earlier work, *De Veritate*, Aquinas invoked the notion of analogy in exploring the truth of propositions.[443] Proper proportionality was essential to any analogy of the creature to God. The being of the creature is not God. Analogy is transferred. "*It is on the basis of the being of creatures that the truth of the proposition that God exists is demonstrated*".[444] Being is predicated of the created being which is the basis of the truth of divine reality. Relation to God as createdness assumes the being of the creature.

Aquinas explored this with regard to language. Univocal terms, for example, pertain where a term has only one meaning, one concept and one definition. Equivocal terms have more than one meaning and more than one definition. With analogous terms, the linguistic situation is different: they convey similar characteristics that exist between two concepts. My dinner was good but so was my journey. There is no common constituent but 'proportionately' there is a similarity between what both ought to be. Theologians, however, were concerned with language about God. How can we speak about a transcendent, totally simple spiritual being without altering the sense of the words we use? Analogical terms seemed to be especially relevant to metaphysics and theology and much discussed in commentaries on Aristotle's logic. This is the analogy of being pressed into service in metaphysical conceptual analysis: the notion that reality is divided horizontally into different realities of substances and accidents (Socrates v the beardedness of Socrates) but also vertically into the very different realities of God and created beings. These realities are analogically related.[445] How far the created realm is knowable only through revelation has been much debated.[446] While pagan and other natural religions see God as the most powerful part of the world, Christianity understands God to be separate, not added to in any way by the act of creating the world. This understanding of God and the world lies behind the belief in Creation. That would negate Aquinas on this, for whom it is naturally demonstrable but also Aristotle who Aquinas believed supported his argument.

All these considerations indicate the difficulties in making some kind of correspondence between human personhood and divine personhood. The analogy of proportionality entails common characteristics that belong truly to each participant and all proportionate to their respective being. "*Whatever perfection is analogically common to two or more beings is intrinsically possessed by each, not, however, by any two in the same way or mode, but by each in proportion to its being*".[447]

What would it mean to say that there is a similarity between divine personhood and ours?

In that the created being exists, it is related to God as its cause. There are good metaphysical arguments for the analogy of being that ascend from the very notion of being to the conclusion that God exists. [448] The question is whether these arguments could ever belong in physics. Metaphysics began with Aristotle as a discourse on the nature of being but not specifically in relation to God. The focus of metaphysics was the being common to substance and categories of subjects (the redness of a rose). It was a central concern of philosophy to delineate an ontological scheme that classified being in general into different types and forms of predication that describe subjects. [449]

In the hands of Aquinas, the existence of God is demonstrated through distinguishing essence and existence in respect of every other being. God is a necessary being; not requiring the addition of act or potency (potentia). Being is analogical for other multiple types excepting for God, whose essential nature is in full accordance with the divine will. God is wholly without potential, the proportion which accounts for limitations that constrain everything else. There is, in other words, correspondence. Created effects and beings, participate in the divine causality. [450] Any reality that is pure act, not limited by any potential will infinitely surpass all created beings in its perfection in being (and truth and goodness). [451] In God, there is no proportion to created beings; the correspondence is in the other direction. The perfection of being infinitely exceeds any proportion to created beings. God is not really related to other beings in the sense of being contingent upon them: they are wholly dependent on God. The meaning and being of perfection in God is without any limit. *"Things that are not their being but receive their being from without, depend on the gift of being from the One who alone and fully IS."*[452]

The position is complicated by the reality that the exposition of Aquinas by the 15th century Thomasian philosopher Cardinal Cajetan has been shown to be both flawed and inadequate. [453] Aquinas is clear, however, that there is a secondary and limited proportionate analogy of being between humans and the divine as long as the direction of correspondence is clear. All other created beings participate in the divine as gift; as participating beings derived from the un-participated. In this way, it is proper to speak of human personhood resembling divine personhood. The perfection of the divine being is not identical to the being of human persons but there is a likeness. We can affirm that the perfection of being in God is not the perfection of being in people but the very name of God—"I am that I am" (Exodus 3v14) is such that the full perfection of being is more properly affirmed of God than anyone else. This is not the same as resemblance between two things that just differ in scale, such as when two quantities are compared with each other. *"Nevertheless, in the sense in which the term proportion is transferred to signify any relationship of one thing to another (as we say there is a likeness of proportions in this instance: the pilot is to his ship as the ruler to the commonwealth), nothing prevents us saying that there is a proportion of man to God, since man stands in a certain relationship to Him inasmuch as he made by God and subject to Him."*[454]

Plato sought to acknowledge an immaterial source of reality. Yet that was a long way from the Christian position. No place was accorded for a personal Creator and there was no account of how ultimate forms came into being; rather a timeless process without purpose, beginning or end. [455] Aristotle did not consider that the unmoved mover would have any interest in his creatures.

The approach taken in this book points us towards classical theism. A conscious, creative power that is fundamentally 'other' and yet fulfils the position that such a stance ascribes—amongst these being perfect source of all value and the goodness towards which humans aspire and strive. [456] There is though a real metaphysical question in God being the source of value and meaning in human life.

What does it mean for God to create value and give commands that are worthy of our obedience, it must be that they are good in themselves. But how then can God's will be the source of value?

As Bertrand Russell argued, *"if you are going to say. . . . . .that God is good, you must then say that right and wrong have some meaning which is independent of God's fiat. . . logically anterior to God."* [457]

The response from Aquinas was that goodness is inseparable is God's nature. Aquinas' notions of God's personhood and how he can be the source of our value, defied Euthyphro's dilemma as he simply is goodness rather than valuing us by an external measure of value. God does not issue arbitrary commands: they reflect God's essential nature as being wholly and perfectly good. *"For God alone, essence is his being. . . . . .and so he alone is good through his essence."*[458]

For Aquinas then, God is goodness itself. Goodness and value are ascribed to God because of his very nature. *"There is for the theist a domain of eternal value and reason, a domain that impinges on our empirical world, making us respond to something beyond the mere sequence of brute facts. We human creatures. . . . are responsive to reason and value, and in being so responsive we participate, however, dimly in the divine nature".* [459]

He was clear about the importance of the imago dei, humans made in the image of God. *"Since human beings are said to be in the image of God in virtue of their having a nature that includes an intellect, such a nature is most in the image of God in virtue of being most able to imitate God."*[460]

We resemble God in being able to reflect on our being and understand our world and even God! *"Only in rational creatures is there found a likeness of God which counts as an image. . .as far as a likeness of the divine nature is concerned, rational creatures seem somehow to attain a representation of [that] type in virtue of imitating God not only in this, that he is and lives, but especially in this, that he understands."*[461]

Chapter Twelve

The Seeing God

"The true position of mankind as no mere atom of the infinite but a finite reproduction of his maker is likely to stand and will stand, unshaken." [462]

"Who are you?
A number.
Your name?
Gone. Blown away. Into the sky. Look up there-the sky is black, black with names" [463].

"For God, who said, 'Let light shine out of darkness,' made his light shine in our hearts to give us the light of the knowledge of God's glory displayed in the face of Christ." —2 Corinthians 4v6 (NIV)

THE QUESTION WE HAVE been pondering is this. What can give rise to and answer to our personhood?

Martin Buber's protest against de-personalisation struck a chord. Via the door of empathy, the emotional indifference of an I-It relationship has a very different feel than the connection made with an 'I-Thou' mode. [464] The boundary between them though is fluid. Even in close relationships, we slip into the 'I-It' mode. The 'Thou' can become an 'It' to me. But is this true of the cosmos, which could be impersonal or personal, dependent on the way it is viewed?

Through TV and cinema, visual culture is all pervasive. We have seen though how acts of seeing are important in some key settings. In quantum physics, objects become an actuality upon their observation. The observing of one entity can instantly influence the behaviour of another even if the other entity is distant and no physical force connects the two. In social and inter-personal life, recognition becomes salient, converting invisibility into status (though moral status had been there all along). In neurobiology, the gaze of the caregiver is crucial for the wiring up of infant brains. Psychotherapy too is a project in which inter-personal visual bonds are vital to hold two subjectivities in depth exchange. One personhood is validating the other. This is not just about eye contact but a mental representation in which the image of the other performs heavy duty labour.

Arising from client work, here is someone who needs to be validated and have their value confirmed. It did not happen as it should: through the gaze of parents to give their child worth. Affirmation of identity and worth comes through attunement. In this case it is a therapist who begins the healing journey- crossing over into someone else's frame of reference brings value and worth. [465]

We have noted how so many notions of what it means to be truly personal are a being in relation to others. Therapy seems to work because of the attunement inherent in our essentially social brains. As Cozolino writes, *"the most important information in the world comes to us from the faces of others. Eye gaze, pupil dilation, blushing and facial expression link us to the hearts and minds of other people"*. Moving from a single skill understanding to an inter-subjective context of two minds is vital. Most forms of human suffering are the result of breakdowns in human synchrony. [466]

The development of value as a psychological phenomenon is so characteristic of what it means to be human that it requires explanation on any theory of the universe. This cannot be solved by a purely naturalistic theory of reality. In addition, it presents a serious challenge to a view of things where the cosmic underlying principle is impersonal. Impersonal things can validate us only up to a point.

Post-Freudian theories of the unconscious mind point to the structure of the psyche as internalised patterns of interaction. We have moved away from linear causality and the determinism of discrete atoms to reciprocal interactions amidst a larger pattern of experiences. This picture reflects the foundations of material reality seen, not in terms of discrete particles but relational exchanges.[467]

It seems to be part of our operating system. Valuable personhood is etched into our very being, in the essence of ourselves that is so often immune from critical influences that impose limits. 21st century science can no longer dwell in its silo, in the objectivity and rationality that pervades its method. How do we disassociate our thoughts about the world from trying to make sense of ultimate purpose and value as people? As much as anyone else, scientists live with a gap.

To address this gap, here is an original proposal for a positive philosophical theology for what will be termed, 'an approach from value'. It endeavours to lay out an approach to ultimate questions derived from the value and worth that humans need in order to thrive. Large numbers of books and articles show that people in a valuing environment and can internalise that are more likely to do well. With it we flourish. Without it we wither. These concerns can be traced through multi-disciplinary domains.

There is a question arising from such an extensive literature. Grounded in such examples of human experience, what is it about us that we are strongly motivated to pursue high worth; that something happens when absent? If there is no answering echo between our own yearning to be of value and the structure of material reality, there is no place for ultimate validation and we are truly alone.

The book now probes what ultimate realities are suggested by the drive towards what is being termed 'valuable personhood'. Are there steps <u>from</u> the ways in which personhood needs affirming through recognition and practice <u>to</u> a universe in which our personhood is validated?

We have considered pathways by which valuable personhood' leads to a theory of everything in which that personhood is endorsed and valued. Does that take us to a personal God? Consider alternatives. Does an impersonal universe shaped by objective laws of physics have any space for our subjectivity? Does an approach such as panpsychism yield personhood and not just consciousness?

Even if we accept, however, the proposition that human beings need to be valued at some level in order to flourish, there are some weighty objections to making this a core and key to cosmic reality. We will considered these objections.

It is now time to lay out our proposition and what kind of account this might give that illuminates the ultimate reality to which our valuable personhood responds?

An account of reality that goes beyond the mechanistic approach within scientific naturalism needs to show how our human experiences as self-conscious beings involve aspects unrecognised by physical sciences that are not illusory but definite factors requiring explanation. We have noted the importance of fields in physics. A holistic philosophy of nature is required that goes beyond 19th century physics to that of fields that organise entities such as mind and consciousness.

We have at least two choices. One is to hypothesise the data of our self-consciousness and indispensable sense of personal worth as an emanation from the psychology of human culture; of interest to ourselves but posing no fundamental questions for the way the universe is set up. The other is to explore such data as an evocation of an ultimate reality; indeed an imprint of it. On the latter reading, there is a personal realm of reality that endows humans with reflexive capability to inhabit our self self-consciously and to imbue ourselves with high value.

The hypothesis put forward in this book is that, behind material reality, there is a person-centred dimension that has measurable effects. This 'field of the personal' mandates our very being but also legitimates our personhood. It is an extension writ large of the observer effect in physics but it also shows why humans seem to require external validation. Metaphysically, this goes beyond idealism per se or a cosmos suffused with Mind as the most fundamental form of reality: the universe existing as an appearance or an expression of mental formulation as in Plato, compared to which the cosmos is somehow unreal (also Kant or Hegel) Our formulation here is that of person to person interaction.

These effects can be tested empirically. They will show up:

i) in the quest for spirituality and the transcendent within humans, who are spiritual beings, oriented towards what is beyond themselves and driven incessantly to find patterns of meaning and forms of explanation;

ii) in the quest for high value and worth as a psycho-social milieu in which to thrive; something that seems to go 'deeper' than the legacy of attachment systems in mammals since it can be mobilised in the absence of attachments;

iii) in the consciousness and beyond that, self-consciousness of human observers.

OUR INFERENCE

It is of course theoretically possible on a developmental theory of the universe to suggest that we do not have to offer correspondence with the early conditions of life and matter. Rather we deal with emergence and a level of complexity and organisation several stages further on. The proposal here, however, is that the only way of accounting for the realm of value, love, meaning and spirituality by which supplies the emotional content of our consciousness is that there is a deep field of reality to which it responds in some way. This goes beyond consciousness as a mental event which may be connecting with some sense of an ultimate Mind. What needs to be accounted for is that human significance is not only a philosophical and existential enquiry but a vital inner milieu.

Information theory would seem to be a fundamental concept in thinking about this. Every system has some element of information as part of its fundamental operation. Classical Information Theory is the mathematical theory of acquisition, storage, transmission and processing of information. Arising from this, Quantum Information Theory (QIT) lies at the intersection of Mathematics, Physics and Computer Science. [468] An integrated information theory may account for the relationship between consciousness and the brain, or at least some elements of it. [469] It starts from essential properties of phenomenal experience which leads to requirements for the physical substrate of consciousness.

How shall we give an account of a mentality behind everything? Something needs to account for:

a) What gives rise to and answers to our own personhood that seeks to be valuable?

b) A range of questions such as the sensitivity of quantum mechanics to observation

c) the strong role that 'information' appears to have in the scheme of things, especially non-physical systems, that could point to mentality as a shaping principle.

d) the anthropic principle—and most likely the strong version—in which remarkable sets of parameters seem to have been fulfilled for conscious observers to develop.

e) linked with this, the astonishing rise of eukaryotic cells and photosynthesis based on oxygen that transformed the potential for life on planets such as ours towards generating life forms and eventually rational creatures such as ourselves. *"There is no physical mechanism (either inside organisms or outside of them) that detects which mutations would be beneficial".*[470]

- f) the perhaps even more astonishing emergence of consciousness in the resultant life forms whereby they become aware of their surroundings and turn into conscious observers.

- g) Beyond that the generation of self-consciousness in which humans can ask questions about themselves and their place in the scheme of things; a self-consciousness that seems to draw on some sense of value and worth in order to prosper with significance, requiring meaning.

A theory of a cosmic presence of mentality could go some way towards explaining how the developmental process is guided (b-e above). There is an Intelligence behind everything. But engaging with self-consciousness and capacity for reflexivity whereby observers observe themselves and ask profound questions about their existence and worth signifies a deeper layer of reality. The deep field is that of a Mind and Spirit; a personal cosmos with whom our personhood connects.

Though not the focus of this book, the 'field of the personal' as backcloth to cosmic reality might tell us why a strong version of the anthropic principle is valid for development of human observers.[471]

Let us propose then that there is a cosmic mental field: a field which could have characteristics of being the template for myriad acts of observation across the world at any one time. It would be:

1. Non-physical—it is non-corporeal; mind rather than matter. It is not subject to physical laws of time and space but permeates it all as in another dimension.

2. Non-localised.

3. A trigger for consciousness in any beings that have the requisite capability.

4. A field that supplies a capacity for I-thou encounters amongst humans because it is personal

A means of exploring this is through the gaze where in-person encounters take place. There are various philosophical moves available here, including the metaphysics of idealism such as propounded by Bishop Berkeley.[472] It is in his 'Treatise concerning the Principles of Human Knowledge' that he puts forward the astonishing claim that there is no external world, that material reality is a collection of ideas. Importantly, it is God who produces ideas or sensations in our minds.[473] Berkeley's starting point is the assertion that existence is the state of being perceived by a perceiver. "To say that something exists is to say that it is perceived by a perceiver" (Esse is percipi)."[474] These ideas were written in contradistinction with his contemporary John Locke about the nature of human perception. As did all the Empiricist philosophers, Locke and Berkeley concurred that we are having experiences, regardless of whether material objects exist, Berkeley's position was that the external world, which generates the ideas within the mind, is composed solely of ideas.[475]

Our position here is somewhat different. The external world exists. It is constructed from the materials of our experience but it is nevertheless a tangible reality. The 'real world' is generated by Cosmic Mind but that ultimate mentality is personal. It is this that has generated and responds to human personhood. We now proceed to headline this phenomenologically from human experiences as noted in psychotherapy but also theologically.

For this, we turn to the locus for recognition and acts of seeing; namely the face. It is the face that presents an outward image of a person and subjectivity by which human subjects make themselves known. It is the face that structures human experience and our way of being in the world. The face plays a central role in inter-personal relations. As Levinas observes, the face is "*in and of itself visitation and transcendence.*" In other words, the face comes into our communal world from a place beyond itself yet it remains beyond it, just out of reach. [476]

The face is a medium of meaning. It serves as an intermediary between the self and other selves. As Grice shows, the face can disclose a range of meanings which go beyond 'natural signs'. [477]The capacity to 'mean' something by facial expression is key to human societies. The 'speaker's meaning' is a statement of intent that another should grasp the content of my action.

THE GAZE

It is neuroscience that discloses the remarkable way that the self-organisation of the human brain takes place in the context of another brain—that of the primary care-giver. [478] This is hugely affected by affect. Allan Schore proposes that the mother's gaze is by far the most potent stimulus in the infant's environment. It is the child's intense interest in her face, especially her eyes, that leads the infant to track this. Mutual gaze interaction is set up, dependent upon the capacity of the mother to be psycho-biologically attuned to the child's internal resting state. There is a matching of both partner's interaction to the point of regulating the stimulus and arousal of the child's brain states. [479]

Where do we go with this relevant to our concerns here? We can invoke the divine gaze as formative in a theory of how deep might call to deep and person to person interaction becomes possible. It is perhaps this 'seeing' of us that imparts the light of being as the cosmic consciousness represented in a divine personal being looks on us with enlightenment.

> *"For you created my inmost being; you knit me together in my mother's womb. . . ..*
> *Your eyes saw my unformed body; all the days ordained for me were written in your book*
>   *before one of them came to be."* (Psalm 139v13–16)

In that key text, v16 is especially interesting: "*Your eyes saw my unformed substance*" (NRSV).

If a newborn baby has no soul (even an undeveloped one), then it is not really a full human being. The soul is not something that we can detect scientifically given its focus on empirical data. Yet there is no other genetic match to those cells. It is a new genetic entity, and in that sense is a unique, new being.

The extent to which human personhood comes to be or is given does not depend on whether we use the language of 'soul' or 'spirit'. The status of 'personhood' or 'consciousness' is widely used in an ontology of human persons for social sciences without deploying such words. In "What is a Person?", Smith spells out a new model for social theory that does justice to the best of our humanistic visions of people, life, and society. Drawing on critical realism and personalism, he defines a person as a conscious, reflective, embodied, self-transcending centre of subjective experience, durable identity, moral commitment, and social communication who—as the efficient cause of his or her own responsible actions and interactions - exercises complex capacities for agency and intersubjectivity in order to develop and sustain his or her own communicable self in loving relationships with other personal selves and the nonpersonal world. [480]

But how a personal being comes to be has a different ontological status from that of its subsequent development as a social being. 'Human being' is separable from 'human becoming'. We might then theorise as follows: the divine gaze is what imparts being to us; not just human status as requiring dignity and protection but its very existence. The social gaze is what can legitimately be claimed to wire us as socialised beings who are not invisible but active participants. Going back further, it is the maternal gaze (or that of principal caregiver) who has a major role in imparting the software for interpersonal life. But this to work on and work with what is there latently, within the human DNA.

We have seen how observation and gaze are not dispassionate, uninvolved acts when it comes to the wiring of infants. The gaze of the caregiver is not just looking and noticing, it is pregnant. Active looking is combined with speech acts. This is also true of social and not just inter-personal recognition where many labour under the burden of invisibility. It is also true of quantum physics.

We have noted John Wheeler's comment that the old word 'observer' simply has to be crossed off and must put in the new word 'participator'. [481] *"......this observer who was brought into existence by the universe has, by his act of observation, a part in bringing that universe itself into being".* [482] In the Copenhagen view of quantum reality, the act of measurement played a decisive role. As Heisenberg had articulated it, *"everything observed is a selection from a plenitude of possibilities".* [483] Only what is finally observed is real. The position of an electron can be measured or its velocity but not both. It is not given by a number but a matrix disclosing probabilities of location and motion and transitions. It is not just position and momentum. Energy and time are also complimentary. If you know where something is, you know nothing about its energy. All this makes the observer part of the system. The choices you make about what you measure determines the results you get. The theory is empty without an observer. If there is no observer external to the system, no predictions can be made. The concept of measurement is central. But it leaves us without any idea of what the overall system is. *"All of this does not imply that you can choose your own reality. Firstly, you can choose what questions you ask, but the answers are given by the world. And even in a relational world, when two observers communicate, their realities are entangled. In this way a shared reality can emerge."*[484]

As neurologist Sir John Eccles observed, *"I maintain that the human mystery is incredibly demeaned by reductionism with its claim in promissory materialism to account for all the spiritual world in terms of patterns of neural activity. This belief must be regarded as a superstition. . . . . . we are spiritual beings in a spiritual world as well as material beings with brains and bodies existing in a material world".*[485]

Clearly this is a non-physical explanation of qualia—experiential aspects of our mental lives that can be accessed by introspection. A full grasp of another mind and understanding of another's personal consciousness is not possible. As Wallace observes in 'The Taboo of Subjectivity', the direct evidence we have of consciousness is of first-person reports. [486] Although brains and consciousness are obviously entwined, there is no physical mechanism that accounts for their relationship. Albert Bandura observed that making a map of neural circuits underlying Martin Luther King's famous 'I have a dream' speech would give no clues as to how it came to be created or indeed the social influence it produced. [487] Humankind has a spiritual nature.

Discussion of the role of the mysterious human consciousness within the creation has always been fundamental to Christian theology. To say that mentality lies at the heart of things and cannot be reduced to non-mental and purely physical forces is nothing new. Yet there is no single view of how God relates to all that is not God or how personhood could possibly be a feature of the cosmos.

WHAT ABOUT THOSE WHO HAVE NO SENSE OF VALUE?

A question that raises itself in giving an account of the formation of a sense of value and whether the pathways concerned have anything to do with divine impartation is about those who have had poor attachments. If the foundation for a valuable self comes from secure attachments, what about those who have little sense of value due to disorganised attachments or institutional neglect?

Attachment theory has become the dominant theoretical model of development and the most powerful source of hypotheses about the infant mental health. [488] A secure bond forms the infant and mother which is then internalised into an enduring capacity to regulate and generate emotional security. [489] This affects subsequent ability to cope with stress. [490] Sadly, there are all too many examples of infants who experience relational trauma due to developmental instability, neglect or abuse. This can result in dysfunction, disruption to emotional processing and behaviours associated with Type D (disorganised attachments). Dissociation (in effect, brain freezing to numb the pain) is common. [491] Maltreatment in infants—especially traumatised early relationships—"*is associated with adverse influences on brain development*". [492] an internal working model of the attachment relationship is stored in the brain. Their sense of value is represented through this.

There has been much interest in brain scans of orphans, neglected in virtual absence of care and loving interaction in State-run institutions in Romania during the communist regime of Nicolae Ceausescu. In the 1990s, horrific images flooded the news of such children in poor. Following the Romanian Revolution of 1989 many of these children were adopted, some by British families. This was a particularly severe but time-limited form of institutional deprivation in early life experienced by children who were subsequently adopted into nurturing families. What stood out in a long-term study of 165 Romanian orphans was the lower total brain especially in prefrontal, inferior frontal, and inferior temporal areas. They grew up with brains 8.6% smaller than other adoptees. The time spent in institutions before adoption into families in the UK varied between 3 and 41 months with each additional month of deprivation associated with a 0.27% reduction in total brain volume. *Their 'white matter'—the part of the brain which helps neurons communicate—was significantly damaged by their ordeal leading to poor language skills and decreased mental ability.* Early childhood deprivation affected adult brain structure, despite environmental enrichment in intervening years.[493] Despite being brought up by caring new families, emotional and social problems were commonplace. Yet one in five remains unaffected by neglect they experienced. Remarkably, a 12-year study by Harvard University and Boston Children's Hospital in the US found those children who found loving foster homes were able to regrow missing connections and restore lost function.[494]

Most emotionally neglected or traumatised children do not turn into violent criminals or socio-paths. Usually if these children have had some positive relationships- for example with a grandparent or cherished teacher—they will manage to function, even prosper. However, those not so lucky will most likely suffer a sense of emptiness and loneliness because they are unable to connect with others. Others connect but often through relationships that are destructive or disturbed.[495] Even a single benign, timely and attuned relationship will be able to alter a trajectory away from violence. What is needed are the loving eyes of someone who will affirm and believe.

Here is a true-life narrative of and remarkable life of a young man who defied the odds and found his voice amidst adversity. From a tumultuous childhood in the foster care system to becoming a respected journalist and advocate, Ashley John-Baptiste's story is one of resilience, determination, and hope. Early years were marked by constant upheaval and uncertainty as he navigated through multiple foster homes. What turned the tide is someone who believed in him who encouraged him down the path of education. It led to high level qualifications. Through sheer grit and perseverance, he excelled academically, defying stereotypes associated with foster children. Transitioning into adulthood he faced a daunting task of finding stability and forging his path in the world.[496]

A conclusion that suggests itself is that the potential for a sense of worth goes deeper than presence or absence of the nurturing experiences in early emotional history. There is that which subsequent experiences of good relationships recruits. Neuroplasticity effects repair but it builds on something.

THE MIRROR AND THE LIGHT

We are considering what can account for data about personhood. It could come down to the cosmos being brute fact and there is no deeper arena of meaning. Things are as they are without a purposing Mind.

It may be also that the cosmos is constituted by energy as some forms of contemporary mindfulness or that older Daoism would corroborate. This does not, however, yield any place for our personhood.

Alternatively, there is a deeper field of cosmic consciousness (the panpsychism route). This is not the same as arguing in terms of metaphysical idealism that the only things that exist are immaterial. Panpsychism does not explain how the precision engineering of the universe came to be nor yields testable science unless it is linked to the idea of divine creation as Leidenhag proposes.[497]

Or we can propose correspondence with our personhood. The deep field is held by an ultimate Observer who sees and knows and whose omniscience undergirds everything. Such omniscience provides the template for local acts of observation as well as ways in which human social experience draws on acts of seeing and recognition. It is what has enabled the potential for wiring in the brain.

The ultimate Observer is personal, though we are using the idea of a person analogically. God is not a person like us clearly but as discussed with reference to the analogy of being, there are grounds from our own personhood to extrapolate in the direction of God having personal aspects on a cosmic scale

This deeper field entails that behind all that we see is a purposing Mind and ultimate Subject. It is a stance of philosophical idealism that affirms the primacy of Mind before matter. It is Mind that has given rise to our matter, to other minds and other subjects.[498] There is a long tradition in philosophy that discusses whether Mind is behind everything but doubts ultimate reality is actually knowable.

The face of God' is an anthropomorphism for a representation of the ultimate personhood. For theists, God does not need the sense organs of our perception with which to see things. Newton saw the immediacy of divine perception in terms of 'God's sensorium'. When people saw things, he thought, the images are conveyed to a sort of internal cinema, a sensorium. We only see such images of things but God sees directly what we see only indirectly.[499]

The divine gaze is what summons us into being in the first place. It is that which switches on our personhood and gives us being. The precise moment when that could be said to happen is less important (and difficult to determine) than that it happens. If personal being is logically prior to the flickering of movement and responsiveness that mark the dawn of consciousness, then the formation of embryonic brains is secondary. The important point is that valuable personhood arises because of the action of God in taking notice of (and therefore summoning) another human life.

It is noticeable that the creation story in Genesis One speaks of a two-fold action of God. "God said" and "God saw". The creative act (reserved exclusively to God by the Hebrew word 'bara') is enhanced by the use of statements such as 'God made', 'God created'.

It is light that enables the perceiving for humans at least. (It would be grotesque to discuss whether the divine being can see in the dark!) But light enables vision. To invoke Johannine vocabulary in the New Testament, it is the life that is the light of humankind. (John 1v3–4).

And God said, 'let there be light: and there was light. And God saw the light, that it was good." -v3–4 The spoken word is constitutive and creative. It summons. But performativity cannot be restricted to the speech-act. The act of divine gaze is no less part of the creative process. What function does the act of seeing play? God does not take the part of an on-looker, even of his own work, surveying what has been made. The divine gaze does something, imparting a seal of validation and approval. It is emphasised repeatedly in this account of creation as if to complete at each stage what has come into existence. 'God saw that it was good (or beautiful)'. Of the creation of humankind in v26–27, we do not read this same formula. It is left to v31 to sum up the created order as a whole, of which the formation of humankind was both capstone and destination. *"God saw everything that he had made, and behold it was very good"* (1v31).

These ideas can inform the bigger picture in theological philosophy. Divine vision confers. It is performative. It brings things into being. It confers both existence and status. A local system is susceptible to a local observer. The overall system requires an ultimate observer.

It is relevant to our discussion of the mental field indicating a personal God that in the Judaeo-Christian scriptures vision and seeing is more than merely taking notice in an external, cognitive way.

"His eyes behold, his gaze examines humankind" (Psalm 11v4—Hebrew chazah, 'to view'..' to see').

Other words are used to denote varying degrees of divine perception from looking and viewing to fastening attention, observe fully and to behold attentively with intent. When God is said to 'see', this is no quick glance but full attention is given in studied perception—to 'really see' we might say.

The servant girl Hagar, fleeing from oppressive circumstances and the harsh treatment of Sarai is the first person in the Bible to name the One she encounters: *"you are El-roi"* (the God of seeing). [500] The creative promise Hagar is given by the God of seeing is deeply instructive because of what follows (Hagar's son Ishmael becomes the father of nations, venerated in Islam, and the opening chapters of Exodus sees Egyptians—land of Hagar's origin—persecuting Hebrews as she was once persecuted). This statement in Genesis is deeply instructive. Hagar is escaping the hostility of Abraham's wife Sarai. Then comes an encounter with God; One who knows and sees her fully. In that encounter, she affirms that God somehow knows all about her and sees who she is. It is in the gaze, in the act of seeing and knowing that human identity is formed and cradled.

Yet there is more. With the creation of humankind there is both conference and deliberative intent to create something resembling the creator; an entity that can bear the personal imprint of God. The formation of humankind is expressly in the image of God. [501]Much debate has occurred across the centuries as to the content of the imago dei and what aspects of humanity hold some sort of resemblance to God. Image of God" seems to denote the metaphysical expression, associated uniquely to humans, which signifies the symbolical connection between God and humanity. Thus, humans reflect God's divine nature in their ability to achieve a particular and unique set of characteristics with which they have been endowed. These unique qualities make humans different than all other creatures: conscience, rational understanding, creative freedom and the potential for self-transcendence to look at oneself in acts of gaze. It speaks of the value that is placed upon the particular type of being and consciousness that has been formed. This special creation was "in our image". This goes beyond the notion of statues and mini-replicas. Humans are made in the mirror.[502]

The gods of religions that have filled history were seen by humankind sensing that they were looking at us. The cosmos looked back even as they were looked upon, scrutinising action and thought.

When we look into a mirror, we see ourselves looking back at us. The mirror takes our image and returns it for an act of validation. The idea surely in Genesis 1v26–27 is that God sees us -and sees divinity looking back. The knowledge of God and self-awareness are thus bound together. The divine gaze would seem to be central to the constitution of humankind. Humans are recognised in their being and their personhood reflects this. The decision to make humans in God's image instead of the image of the other creatures surely demonstrates our value in the divine gaze. God is not an interested spectator. He creates humankind in the imago dei to look up and reflect the image back. The bearer of a spiritual nature and self-conscious image (by which it can behold itself) looks back. This is surely the birth of self. As Dietrich Bonhoeffer observes in his 1932-3 lectures 'Creation and Fall', how can God see, recognise and discover himself in his work: obviously only if the thing created by him resembles him; *"he is in the image of God in which the free Creator sees himself reflected."*[503]

As Brueggemann points out, this statement is a surprising counter-assertion against every attempt to image God in the contemporary culture. *"There is only one way in which God is imaged in the world and only one: humanness. This is the only creature, the only part of creation, which discloses to us something about the reality of God. . . .God is not imaged in anything fixed but in the freedom of human persons to be loving and faithful"*. [504]Two words are used here: 'image' and 'likeness' (Hebrew 'selem' and 'd'mut'). One tends to denote a concrete—'let us make man <u>as</u> our image, <u>as</u> our likeness' (Genesis 1v26). Humanity *"belongs to the visible world, as befits an image. But. . .we are defined in relationship to God. . . . .the created representation of his Creator"*[505] The very idea of 'image' suggests the radical nature of our dependence, *"blessed, not because of good actions but by participation in God".* [506]

In an analysis of the use of selem and d'mut, it is clear that the former term generally refers to a statue, a figure or a replica made of metal or painted stone. [507] In Genesis 5v3, selem refers to a human, Seth, created in the image and also likeness (d'mut) of his father Adam. Human flesh here is a representation, likeness or a copy of an original. [508] D'mut derives from the verb 'to resemble, be like' and expresses similarity, likeness or correspondence. [509] It has royal connotations and it is the king who is in the divine image principally but the idea extends to humanity in a quasi- regent status.

Karl Barth in his exposition, noting the historical background of interpretation, insists that the talk of imago dei in Genesis is always associated with "I-thou' with reference to differentiation between male and female. [510]It is not only 'I' within deity but 'I-thou'. *"This God can see, recognise and discover himself in man; and for his part the man who corresponds to Him can know God and be the seeing eye at which all creation aims. . . . .".* [511] Barth notes that very little is said directly about the divine likeness in the rest of the Old Testament. He does point out that there is an analogy of being: *"God has created him on this correspondence as a reflection of himself. Man is the image of God".*[512]

As Marc Cortez shows, Barth clearly believes that ontology has decisive importance for understanding the human person. [513] Barth presented an account of human ontology that is grounded in Christology, pneumatology and the covenantal relationship between God and human persons.[514] He denies that any 'purely' phenomenological depiction of humanity is adequate for establishing a firm foundation upon which to develop an understanding of human ontology." *In keeping with his well-known dislike of abstractions in theology, Barth maintains that theological anthropology must begin with the 'concrete reality' of Jesus Christ."*[515]

There are two elements: image (zelem), reflection or representation, and likeness (demuth). Many older writers thought that the word 'image' referred to the body; by its beauty and erectness being an expression of the divine. The idea of 'likeness' referred to our intellectual and moral nature. Augustine categorised 'image' as the rational element and 'likeness' referred to moral faculties. Scholastic theologians tended to follow this line of interpretation. Luther distinguished between 'image' and 'likeness'. It was moral mirror. The image was lost in the fall and recovered through redemption. [516] This was a narrow view of the imago dei based on holiness rather than the broader notion of Aquinas regarding the deployment of human intellect and understanding more generally. Reformed theologians followed Calvin in taking the middle ground between seeing the imago consist in rationality or in moral conformity. [517] Both are included.[518] Reason, conscience and will are bound up with our intellectual and moral nature as is our capacity to know God, the foundation of our spiritual nature. "*If we were not like God, we could not know him.*" [519]

Made in the mirror means that humanity possesses three Cs:-
Consciousness - Creativity—Conscience

Whatever else the imago dei represents, the claim is "*that God intended to create creatures of a certain kind—rational creatures with a moral sense and the capacity to know and love him- and then acted in such a way as to accomplish this intention*".[520]

This is antithetical to any notion of unguided evolution such as biologist George Gaylord Simpson states: "*man is the result of a purposeless and natural process which did not have him in mind*".[521]

We are defined in relationship to God, the created representation. The creation of human beings in the image of God is not saying something has been added to the created person but is explaining what the person is. Their very existence lives in relationship with God. Relationship with God is not something added to human existence. We are not isolated entities. The image of God does not mean that we look at ourselves as if in solitary confinement. We are hard-wired for connection.

Humans are intrinsically related; it is not just in gender differentiation that we are joined at the hip. Personhood is relational. In a mirror, we see our own image. In looking at us, God sees something of himself, some recognition that leaps up albeit in muted response. The image calls back to the image maker in dialogue. In our horizontal relationships, there is a social refraction of our vertical connection with God. The imago dei is about the value and worth of humanity. If God sees his own reflection looking back and calling back, that speaks volumes about how valuable we truly are. The image ought not to be defaced. It is a declaration of the value of personhood but it is more than that. It is a sharing of the divine worth. Do not touch a painting or rubbish a treasured photo of someone. It represents them. A tramp is as valuable as Michelangelo since God would have it so.

God gives a vote of confidence in something he has made that resembles him in part. Humanity is a microcosm of God, gifted with the capacity to respond. Mad King George could shake hands with an oak tree but it could not answer back. Humans might commune with nature but not the deep level recognition that comes with being of like-mind. It is the recognition through which a parent and child can connect. It is the recognition through which some people can remind us a little bit of God.

The act of recognition is constitutive and sets the developmental trajectory of multiple acts of recognition in both interpersonal and social life. It becomes enabling.

There is much here beyond the scope of this volume. A biblical scrutiny could include reflection on such instances as the man born blind 'but now I see' (John 9v25) or Saul of Tarsus who was blinded temporarily (Acts 9v8–9). On the Damascus Road, Paul's brain is re-wired as it were though he cannot see until he looks out on the world with new eyes. Spiritual vision entails looking back on the Creator who looks on humankind and who imparted personal being to us.

Theologically, there is a Christological dimension to this that is very far from being an add-on. Even in epiphanies, there are few references in biblical literature to humans seeing the face of God. It is not a two-way exchange. But the situation changes when it comes to the face of Christ. Acts of seeing take place regularly. People look upon Jesus and Jesus looks meaningfully on people.

In the Johannine literature, acts of seeing have an important role. "*We beheld his glory. . .behold the Lamb of God.*"[522] This is more than a cursory glance; more a steadfast looking with steadfast intent.

"*That which was from the beginning, which we have heard, which we have seen with our eyes, which we have looked at and our hands have touched—this we proclaim concerning the Word of life. 2 The life appeared; we have seen it and testify to it, and we proclaim to you the eternal life, which was with the Father and has appeared to us. 3 We proclaim to you what we have seen and heard, so that you also may have fellowship with us.*" [523]

However, let us remind ourselves.

What has to be accounted for is our sense of personhood and how that fits in with a cosmos that is at best neutral? A better approach than the metaphor of wifi universe is 'the seeing God'. Rather than a soulless device being switched on, how a human psyche comes to a sense of value is the issue here.

Such is the frame of the time-bound life. Time without change is improbable: mortality inescapable. It exists outside the mind. Time had a beginning. This all-pervasive condition of life enables us to stand outside of ourselves and compare past, present and future with heavy regret or bright-eyed anticipation. What a puzzle. As Augustine pondered, when things become past, where do they go?

We tell a master story of origins that neither exhausts nor excludes other ways of seeing but need not live in the binary. With the physics of both very large and very small, science has responded magnificently to the inscrutable. Yet we need a sacred realm where science and tools are but tools and do not exhaust the wonder of endless night or the unfathomable depths within.

Irenaeus, second-century theologian and Bishop of Lyons, wrote words that are routinely hijacked by CEO's in management self-help, "the glory of God is a human being fully alive!" The glory of God is humanity 'alive'. Actually he said no such thing. *"Life in man is the glory of God; the life of man is the vision of God"*, is what he wrote. [524] This is the beatific vision; seeing God as the essence of human life rather than a humanist vision devoid of divinity.

The conclusion that all these considerations lead us to is that there is a dimension of reality that our minds connect with, knowingly or not. Mind and brain are not identical.

There is a great deal going on intra-psychically - realization of a 'me' corresponds with an invitation for 'I' to become like the object of sight. We become like what we behold. [525] Nevertheless, personhood and subjectivity are relational in orientation. Humans are quintessentially relational, not purely cognitive. There is me, there is you and there is the space between. This space distanciation in social science has theological resonance, relating to what Underhill called the 'Trinitarian definition of Reality' where subject and object are incomplete and not fully informed apart from the relation—the interpersonal space—between the believer and God.[526]

We are not the product of blind forces of random natural selection. Humankind is part of a creation that is pure gift. All that exists is not God but has its source in God as contingent. Matter is contingent. From a substrate of potentiality it arises. Matter has malleability and needs form. Made from nothing—creation ex nihilo comes from nothing but God moving towards God to complete its journey to being and existence.

The human condition is marked by fragility, by dependence and contingency. The exigencies of personhood implies that we are becoming, not possessed of a fixed unchanging human nature. They presume a subject that changes. De-personalisation is characterised by faceless people stripping faces of subjects that are objectified into invisibility. Such is the condition of life here.

Behind the cosmos is a friendly face that often seems masked by the very creation it gives rise to. Vere tu es Deus absconditus—"*Truly, you are a God who hidest thyself.*" In commenting on this verse from Isaiah 45:15, Luther forges a broad theological perspective. A lamentation from Psalm 13 is expressed like this. "*How long, Lord? Will you forget me forever? How long will you hide your face from me?*" (v1- NIV). Yet that is not the last word.

Paul refers in the Corinthian correspondence to the lure of the future. "*And we all, who with unveiled faces contemplate the Lord's glory, are being transformed into his image with ever-increasing glory, which comes from the Lord, who is the Spirit.*" (2 Corinthians 3v18). He goes on to speak of where the dazzling glory is to be found. "*For it is the God who commanded light to shine out of darkness, who has shone in our hearts to give the light of the knowledge of the glory of God in the face of Jesus Christ.*" (4v6). The face that structures the human lifeworld is interposed between embodied flesh and the light of spirit and soul that is the lamp within. It is the emblem of personhood.

Let the once-blinded man have the last word here: "*For now we see only a reflection as in a mirror; then we shall see face to face. Now I know in part; then I shall know fully, even as I am fully known. And now these three remain: faith, hope and love. But the greatest of these is love.*" [527]

Critique
Difficulties with This Proposal

"What or where is the unified centre of sentience that comes into and goes out of existence, that changes over time but remains the same entity, and that has a supreme moral worth?" [528]

"Man no longer has need for 'Spirit'. It is enough for him to be Neuronal Man"[529]

"Post-modern people are looking for experiences that give them a sense of value"[530]

"We are by-products of a process that is entirely indifferent to our well-being, machines developed by our genetic material and adapted by natural selection to the task of propagation" [531]

WE TURN NOW TO problems with the approach we have been developing thus far.

This is an approach to ultimate reality from value, specifically the value of personhood. This is positioned between two worlds- the cosmos but also, the human indispensability of being valuable, of being significant. The question is how these are brought together.

It is the philosophy of scientific materialism, in which nature by itself is that by which everything is generated, that is sharply at question here. Every attempt to argue these issues has difficulties. The philosophy of scientific naturalism is profoundly monistic; everything exists from only one substance. It can be undermined by any evidence against it. A critical examination of empirical evidence might argue against the whole assumption. How could we find out if these assumptions are incorrect? All events have a material, physical cause: an object will always act in accordance with forces of nature.

Our argument has been that there are aspects of our existence that this philosophy cannot explain. It cannot do justice to the inner cry and sigh of those who do scientific work or indeed live out the human project in all its forms and ponder the realm of value, love and meaning. As probed in earlier chapters, we need someone or something to validate us, to have regard to our existence. Our being is called into being by acts of recognition. An argument can be made that it is this aspect of our identity that points us in the direction of theism. Our identity as a person requires that something beyond ourselves validates us, sees us and knows us- thus redeeming us from cosmic loneliness.

This is rooted in the very human search for re-assurance and recognition that characterises our lives. Does my sense of value and worth relate to anything 'out there' that affirms me and corresponds to me? We have probed whether an impersonal universe can ever do that and give validation to ourselves and what we hold most dear. If a neutral structure of material reality is all there is, then we as conscious observers who sigh for significance have risen far above the source.

We can posit various responses this, however, that will sharply question such a direction of travel. Here are some objections:

A RESPONSE FROM INTERPRETIVISM

One response might be that a sense of personal value, though psychologically necessary, is what we humans have evolved simply to get through. It is how we handle the neuroses of everyday living in this world that sometimes, would be so hard to bear otherwise.

Time and chance frame this vast arena in which our lives are set—inimical to human interests, or so it feels. Events happen. They just happen. Existence unfolds within a river of time; random, baffling and pointless, or so it seems. What time is, what chance is remains the stuff of life and mystery. Things come out of nowhere and knock you down, like a car running amok on a busy high street.

The sheer contingency of life appears to run counter to any sense of humanity having awesome value. Time brings decay though also renewal. To some, ageing comes at different rates; to all, disease and death (struck randomly by one; slain universally by the other). Without God as the meaning maker in chief, to claim significance for humans is to hear a mocking laugh. To advance a stance of high value is to run straight into the smirk of a sphere where anything can happen. Unpredictability is predictable. Yet the laws of physics, how everything works, set things on a clear path; the stars in their courses inhabit their motion along fixed trajectory.

Schopenhauer referred to the "bottomless abyss of its heart," and that no worldly satisfaction could fill its infinite cravings. [532] People generally regard feelings of emptiness and loneliness as distinct from themselves and cling to the illusion that their inner void could be eradicated, avoided, or filled. They can spend their lives trying to do so, perpetuating endless internal conflict. Twelve-Step Programs are founded on the premise that cravings and inner emptiness cannot be filled through addictive be-haviour, and that relief is spiritual. Bill Wilson, the founder of Alcoholics Anonymous wrote to psychoanalyst Carl Jung who replied explaining that alcoholism was a spiritual problem⊠"a spiritual thirst of our being for wholeness, expressed in medieval language: the union with God," which he believed to be the answer.[533]

"The majority of patients are bedevilled by a lack of meaning in their lives", declared Professor of Psychiatry Irvin Yalom. [534] Our profound need as human beings is to inhabit a coherent, meaningful universe. 'Why am I here? Where am I headed?' are fundamental questions to human existence and lie at the heart of existential therapies.

For now, it is worth noting that the void and a sense of emptiness seems never far away; the sense that something is missing. This has been the focus of both philosophy and the major religions. *"To live, conscious of the inevitability of suffering, weakness, age and death, is impossible"* added Siddartha Gautama, the Buddha. *"We must free ourselves from life, from all possibility of life".* [535]

Emptiness is an inescapable reality of existential life for many humans. It is the dread black hole over which the self is suspended. Theologian Paul Tillich believes that existential anxiety is at the root of it all. "*Neurosis is the way of avoiding non-being by avoiding being.*" [536]

It is therefore possible that talk of value and meaning is illusory and an inevitable result of self-conscious humans living in the interpreted world.[537]

It is to embrace that which is and is not; to embrace the reality of a real world that is real to some but not others. In the relativity of perspective, things look different according to your vantage point, there are few hard and fast facts and where you stand is shaped by where you sit. It is to embrace a timeless zone where history and psychology blend and bleed into one another as we contemplate human actions and human actors. As we read the narratives of past lives or the history of nation and movements, we need to read the past not in terms of the cultural meanings we wrap around actions but to ask about the cultural meanings for those concerned at the time.

The human unconscious is of this order, of what is real and unreal. Conflicts and yearnings are shadows, subterranean forces that need to emerge into the light of conscious day to be interpreted. Even then, what rules would apply? The drive to find meaning for our lives is very powerful. "*Meanings are made within contexts not only of private thought and event but within the contexts of dialogues with those significant others who teach us, confirm us, challenge us and contradict us.*" [538]

According to Martin Heidegger in his 'Being and Time'[539], the hermeneutic 'how' refers to how we interpret our lives and our 'being with' one another in the world. "*Interpretation is not an isolated act, one thing among many that we do; it is what we do, what we are, the pivot, the crux of our being*". [540] This lead was followed by philosophers such as Hans-Georg Gadamer, Jacques Derrida, Richard Rorty and Gianni Vattimo who take us into the thicket of post-modern interpretation.

The interpreter deals in the currency of meanings. The interpreter does not just take the words used and translate them into the language of another. Rather, the communication is one of taking the meanings that are inherent in things that are said and lodging them as accurately as possible within the heads of hearers.

This is important across human endeavours. The historian's art is one of discerning what actions and processes meant to the participants of the day, not to bring today's cultural meanings and wrap them around events that took place in the past. Rather than putting the people of the past in our shoes and judging them by contemporary standards, it is the other way round. What meanings were relevant at the time? Instead of endeavouring to classify the experiences of people who have lived before from the outside, the contemporary historian is much less of a curator or collector but an imaginary. Considerable imaginative effort goes in to re-creating how things seemed to the participants at the time. Respect for what they thought and felt sits alongside a new respect for the subjective experience of those who walked the world before. [541]

This change of register is noticeable too in the sociologist's art, which includes trying to discern what perspectives shape human action, in what way they reflect the markers of identity, how people would describe themselves and what is most important about them. Where you sit determines what you say. To be sure there are differing views of the world within the very idea of trying to describe social reality. Can what is going on be discovered by counting and qualitative methodology? Or do we use the interpretive model and seek to gain in-depth insights as a clearer window on the world?

The anthropologist's art, and indeed that of the linguist, is to understand meaning of the action and the voice and the culture that gives rise to them.

The leadership art is to hold the meanings of life and purpose for a while and interpret the narratives of our contemporary existence. [542]

The politician's art is to assess the scope for action within the web of power relationships and human interests that crowd the public square.[543]

The therapist's art is to try to understand what is important to distressed souls in front of them; what comes up in different circumstances, what existential meanings they bring to that distress and why.

To enter the human life-world is to enter a messy zone where each consciousness constructs reality. Humans are compulsive meaning-makers; incessant hermeneutics is the stuff of life. [544] Hermeneutics - the theory of interpretation—can be applied to the notion that there are no pure facts. Comprehension of anything requires having a particular stance; an interpretation without which nothing would be understood. The nature of truth itself is, for the most part, acquired through interpretation. In any knowledge, in any project, we begin with interpretable 'facts'. This is also true of science in which interpretive skill is vital.

This does not mean everything is interpretation and there are no truths such as of mathematics. But it does reinforce the interpretive view of things. Can we extrapolate this, however, to say that our sense of value and meaning is what we humans have to do in order to get through? That could mean it is but illusory. Change is, however, always possible. Neuroplasticity is a reality. [545]

Our contemporary situation is rife with rumours that there is no great distance between the human non-human, the natural and the artificial (intelligence) humanity and our machines. Every human culture is an interpretation. Universalist claims are deeply suspect. Being human can denote so many things. Virtual reality has broken down the borders between 'truth' and 'fiction'. We seem to be confined to a 'post truth' existence.

And yet we also know something daring. Our formal positions are betrayed by secret knowledge; knowledge that we count, we matter. Whatever the way we might view the external world with its confusion of landscapes, we know something inescapable that registers dismay whenever denied. It can be seen as a psychological construct arising from self-consciousness; a hidden knowledge of our own moral worth against which protest is a sure sign of our humanity.

A RESPONSE FROM PSYCHOANALYSIS

"The trouble with my generation is that we all think we're geniuses. Making something isn't good enough and neither is selling something or teaching something or even just doing something. We have to be something. It's our unalienable right as citizens of the 21st century." [546]

The counterargument from psychoanalysis might be that the human quest for value is an expression of narcissism. It might be that our sense of being valuable is but self-importance and fundamentally self-absorbed. It is what we do to get through. Presumably cats are interesting to themselves and each other; so it is with humans- even more so with our highly developed powers of pondering.

It is possible that the human drive towards feeling valuable is self-obsession in the form of narcissism. On this reading, valuable personhood says nothing about metaphysical realities and everything about our pretensions, our need to derive security and the illusion that we count against the backcloth of an impersonal universe that otherwise gives us an unfriendly face. After all, Western society seems to be faced with a narcissistic selfie epidemic. The word can include everything from excessive interest in or admiration of oneself and one's physical appearance to

As Freud and others wrote, however, narcissism is complicated. He wrote a whole paper, '*On Narcissism: An Introduction (1914)*,' [547] to exploring its psychodynamics and its relation to libido. In earliest experiences, the child is highly egocentric, at the centre of the world because almost all of his needs and desires are being fulfilled by his mother. With maturation, things cannot always go the way the child wants; not everything is for him or her. Such realisation marks the decline of self-centeredness. Libidinal energy will be directed towards outward objects, not just the self. If this is unreciprocated, the libido focusses on itself.

Depending on definitions, a degree of self-love can give us self-respect. A healthy sense of narcissism can help cope with life and manage relationships. There is, however, a problem with seeing the existential reaction against insignificance and indignity in terms of self-love. Valuable personhood is not self-directed. It thrives in a relational context. When narcissism is the criteria of life, selfish disregard and often violence result. Selfishness, involving a sense of entitlement, a lack of empathy, and a need for admiration ensue. Value arises from inter-stellar spaces between people. It is not individualised. The notion of community rests on the importance of 'persons-in-relationship' and of shared values. People are drawn together. They express their relatedness by focussing on things they have in common. Our identity is defined relationally. This does not disintegrate the notion of the unique person. We are not dissolved.

Brain research supports the assertions of such developmental theorists as Winnicott, Bowlby, and Stern who studied the early origins of the unconscious: early experience is imprinted at non-conscious, nonverbal, bodily based levels, and before the conscious verbal mind operates. As Shore argues, to grasp human, overt conscious behaviour, we must first understand the brain systems that operate beneath conscious awareness. An interdisciplinary perspective has shed light on what had previously been off limits. The study of circuitry regulating emotions has now become well established in all scientific and clinical disciplines, including clinical psychology. Neuroplasticity is known and justly celebrated as a healing force. [548] Knowledge of how early attachments are patterned into the brain can inform the way in which therapists work with their patients. [549]

What is missing so far is a consistent and comprehensive theory of Mind arising from this work. What is worth stressing is that just because nothing happens without a brain does not mean that this is all that is going on. [550]This is perhaps why there is fresh interest and indeed a conversation between cognitive neurosciences and psychoanalysis. There is now a fruitful dialogue between brain science and psychoanalysis. For example, the International Neuro-psychoanalysis Society is an academic group dedicated to exploring the connections between brain science and the map of mind that the psychoanalytic theorists articulated a century ago. Its project is the neurobiological underpinnings of how we act, think, and feel. The suggestion is that as we begin to link brain activity with a psychoanalytic model of the mind at the deepest levels, a truly dynamic understanding can emerge.

Yet we really do need to be of value for psychological flourishing. "*I am a homeless man...my life can be thrown away just as easily. I've been kicked, ignored and stuck in the gutter for years. People don't see me as a person—just a piece of rubbish on the pavement to be stepped over.*"[551]

A deep sense of worthlessness cripples human life. "*I don't feel ok about myself.....I believe I'm not worth very much... not a good person.......Don't talk to me about being told I don't count for anything. I've lived with that for 40 years!*" [552] Something has been impaired at a profound level when we agree with our critics. "*When I am low, the old internal dialogue kicks in. All that self-talk, all those negative voices telling you that you are not worth much or even rubbish!*" [553]

This matters profoundly in human life. The question is whether what we are describing is a Western luxury and how far in a different social setting, people construct their sense of self differently.

A RESPONSE FROM COLLECTIVISM

This response is to argue that all this is individualism and probably recent at that. The social self has much more of a running in non-Western societies characterised by individualism. It may be that seeing the self as valuable is a comparatively recent construct.

Zeldin argues that one of the most important promises of democracy is that it will provide respect for everybody. But mutual respect in Athens only worked because Athens depended on an Empire, slaves and women to keep their wonderful philosophical discussions going.[554] Minorities aside, it was inclusive, unifying disparate groups such as wealthy cavalrymen, hoplites and poor sailors in a shared experience glamorising the notion of everyman as Achilles.[555]

In his book of 1820 to put the University at Berlin on the map, Georg Hegel's '*Philosophy of Right*' sought to confirm the direction of the Prussian reformers to bring about a more dynamic and liberal society. [556] People are, he suggested, coming to think about themselves in a new way, as those who give meaning to their lives and are conscious of themselves as autonomous individuals.

Reflection on the social principles of the democratic state[557] goes back at least to Aristotle. As Mortimer Adler commented, "*all human beings are equal as human. Being equal as human they are equal in the rights that arise from needs inherent in their common human nature.*"[558] The Stoics too discussed the importance of a common humanity which enables us to offer recognition. Diogenes refused to be defined simply by his local origins and group memberships, rather in terms of more universal aspirations and concerns. "*When anyone asked him where he came from, he said, 'I am a citizen of the world.'*"*(Diogenes Laertius)* [559] The Stoics developed his image of the kosmopolites, or world citizen, arguing in effect that each of us dwells in two worlds, the local and the global. Stoics said the latter community is "*most fundamentally, the source of moral and social obligations.*"[560]

From the US Declaration of Independence to the UN Declaration of Human Rights, modernity has witnessed the development of the ethic of humanity, a powerful countervailing tendency to differentiation or tolerance of atrocity. The idea that the ordinary person has potential for meaning as much as a King has been vital to political debates about both democracy and equality since the 17th century. "*The poorest he hath a life to live, as the greatest he*," proclaimed Colonel Thomas Rainborrow in the Putney Debates following the English civil war. Today's single most important political principle comes down to us from these debates.[561] People matter. There is not a hierarchy of value but an equality of value. A case can be made for saying that this arose from the emphasis in the Reformation on individualism. Whether that historical case can be pressed, it is clear that in modernity, the search has been for the unifying or the unitary, for the same, for the transcendent in the Kantian sense of the universal. Kantian ethics has sought a categorical imperative, seeing laws as laws for everyone. The Enlightenment went on to develop the idea of humanity, an acknowledgment that in some sense, all people are the same and that cultural differences are external. Historically, the sanctity of life was slow in coming. Behind the foundation of the Red Cross by Henry Dunant in the 19th century and caring for the wounded in war lay a moral sense of the value of each life.[562]

Modernity generated not only universals, however, it also generated an awareness of difference and, in time, enormous anxiety about civil and legal rights as well as those being exercised in the political sphere. It was following the unmasking of racism after the Second World War that there came an exponential growth in human rights discourse. Legislation was accompanied by a considerable literature, little of which was the subject of the sociological imagination. The United Nations could not for long espouse human rights discourse in a post-2nd World War without a growing clamour for recognition of black Americans and also women. The heady days of the 1960's and 70's brought about sweeping social change ranging from civil rights and legislation about discrimination through to a new world of equal opportunities for all.

The question of how native peoples in the Americas should be treated was linked to what sort of people they were. Were they true humans? Were they made in God's image. The debate raged for much of the 15th and 16th century. Ferdinand and Isabella issued a decree saying that " a certain people called Cannibals' and 'any, whether called cannibals or not, who were not docile' could not be enslaved.[563]

The Charter of the Royal Africa Company, which orchestrated the English slave trade, defined slaves as 'commodities'. A series of codes constructed for English, Spanish and French colonies saw slaves as 'chattels'- literally, a thing, not a person. Later, the Dissenters in the anti-slavery movement advocated abolition because every slave was "a man and brother"[564]

The auto-biography of the former slave girl Mary Prince is illuminating. Enslaved in the late 18th century and taken far from home, she lamented how those who took her had neither conception or recognition of the feelings of those they captured. "My heart tells me it is otherwise", she wrote. [565]

We are still haunted by these battles today as we talk about race and gender. In the late 19th century and early 20th century, the Deep South in America witnessed ordinary men and women transformed by hate and fear into murderers and torturers. In an attempt to restrain the perceived savagery an depravity of black men, white violence erupted against a new generation of black people, born in freedom and unschooled by social etiquette. It was the age of Jim Crow laws, denial of a political voice and economic emasculation in rigid patterns by which tenancy was restricted.

As a Memphis newspaper insisted, this generation of Negroes had *"lost in large measure the traditional and wholesome awe of the white race which kept the Negroes in subjection. . . .There is no longer restraint upon the brute passion of the Negro".*[566] Two or three black southerners were publicly lynched or burnt at the stake each week in private 'nigger hunts'. It was de-humanisation.

"Back in those days, to kill a Negro wasn't nothing. It was like killing a chicken or killing a snake. The whites would say, 'Niggers jest supposed to die, ain't no damn good anyway- so jest go and kill' em'". [567] Black life was cheap. Southerners had come to think of black men and women as being inherently inferior, less than human, little more than animals. *"The people of the South don't think any more of killing the black fellows than you would think of killing a flea. . . .and if I was to live a 1,000 years, that would be my opinion and the every other Southern man".* A former Governor of Georgia found the same disregard of human life when it came to black people. *"I was amazed to find scores and hundreds of men who believed the Negro to be a brute, without responsibility to God, and his slaughter nothing more than the killing of a dog".* [568]

It has not just been about white killing of black people. The killing in Rwanda started in April 6th 1994 when the President, a Hutu, was assassinated in an attack on his aircraft. Hutu militias and the army turned on members of the other main ethnic group, the Tutsis. About 800,000 Rwandans, mainly Tutsis were massacred over the next 3 months. A Hutu radio station called for these atrocities by referring to Tutsis as 'cockroaches'[569] or 'rats'. *"To kill big rats, you have to kill little rats".*[570]

As is intensely salient on the contemporary landscape, anti-semitism has a long history. Statements of the 5th century Church leader John Chrysostom reflected sentiments of the day regarding the Jews. *"Jews sacrifice children to Satan...They are worse than wild beasts.*[571] Shylock's eloquence in denouncing the injustice of his treatment remains remarkably telling as he gives voice to the scapegoating of those who are culturally different.[572] The moral and ethical questions Shakespeare raised were not for his own time only.[573]

"Hath not a Jew eyes Hath not a Jew hands, organs, dimensions, senses, affections, passions? fed with the same food, hurt with the same weapons, subject to the same diseases, healed by the same means, warmed and cooled by the same winter and summer as a Christian is? If you prick us, do we not bleed? If you tickle us, do we not laugh? If you poison us do we not die? And if you wrong us, shall we not revenge?" (Act 3 Scene 1)

Outrage against the Holocaust has been key to this development. There are to be sure many narratives operating in such a complex world-historical phenomenon as the Holocaust. [574] The centrality of Auschwitz as the icon of evil prevents us seeing other aspects of mass-murder. There were wider circles of perpetrators than the Nazis. [575] Yet the Holocaust is a continuing and terrifying warning against de-valuing human life. As Primo Levi, an Italian writer who survived Auschwitz said, *"My name is 174517. We will carry the tattoos on our left arm until we die."* [576]

Hans Kung asked, *"why should people be friendly, compassionate and even ready to help instead of being heedless and brutal; why should a young man renounce the use of force and in principle opt for non-violence? Why should a business or bank behave with absolute correctness even when there are no controls? Why should human beings never be the object of commercialisation and industrialisation (the embryo as a marketable article and an object of trade)?"* But then Kung poses questions addressed to the great collectives, as he puts it. *"Why should one people show tolerance, respect and even appreciation to one another?"* Why should one race show these to another? Why should one religion show these to another?"[577]

Kung's answer is that *"human beings must become more than they are; they must become more human! What is good for human beings is what preserves and furthers their humanity and makes it succeed... human beings must exhaust their human potential in an unprecedented way to produce the most human society possible and in an intact environment."*[578]

The problem is, with regard to collectivist culture, 'can you find an 'I' in a 'we'? The move from Western forms of modernity to what has been the case in traditional societies for centuries is to do with relation shifts—taking lead from the group rather than family.

Against this background, the notion that we can gain access to a pristine human core is deeply problematical. Humans are culturally embedded and different cultures emphasise different aspects of what it might mean to be human. Nevertheless, as Nussbaum signals, the notion of a common humanity does rest empirically on what we know of human flourishing.[579] Cultures are embedded in universally shared features of human experience. A landmark Report on multiculturalism observed that, *"to be human is to belong both to a common species and to a distinct culture and the one only because of the other."*[580] The cries for human recognition are ultimately based on core and common humanity. The very quest for emancipation conceals a protest, that we are worth more than this, that we have a claim to be treated with justice and equity. I am arguing that this very claim and protest is ultimately rooted in innate human worth.

Enlightenment thinkers had not assumed people were alike; rather that differences defined their *particularity*, not their humanity. All this was to change as modernity progressed. Social theory readily embraced the emphasis on diversity and multiculturalism. It accorded with the mood of late (or post) modernity that denied vantage points and authority to fixed positions and traditional perspectives. The challenge before us is that, given the on-going struggle against human devaluation in the contemporary scene, how we can affirm human value and dignity as a theoretical and practical necessity. This is not a modern pre-occupation. Yet as Habermas observed,

"I do not believe that we as Europeans can seriously understand concepts like morality and ethics, person and individuality, freedom and emancipation. . . .without appropriating for ourselves the substance of a salvation-historical thought which originates in Judaism and Christianity"[581]

Concerns here take as far beyond the scope of this essay. It can seem as if much conflict in the world today is about religion. In practice, the conflict has other causes and religion is only one ingredient in a clash between different cultures asserting themselves. Yet there can be universal condemnation of genocide. *The 'White House' was the single storey building in which the worse crimes of the Bosnian Serb's Omarska concentration camp took place as Europe's deadliest conflict in almost 50 years caught fire during the summer of 1992. Hundreds of Muslims and Croats were tortured and slaughtered there by Bosnian Serb guards.*[582]

There has to be a core sense of the human person that can assert this is unacceptable, if only on grounds of membership of a common species notwithstanding the very great wrongs of the past. As Hans Kung argues, *"should it not be possible to formulate, with reference to the common humanity of all men and women, a universally ethical, truly ecumenical basic criterion which is based on the humanum, that which is truly human, and specifically on human dignity?"* [583] True humanity is the pre-supposition of true religion. The humanum, respect for human dignity and basic values is a minimal requirement for any religion. What is truly human, what has human dignity, can with justification, appeal to the divine. Kung wrote a report for a colloquium in February 1989 which was addressed by the Director-General of UNESCO. UNESCO had a programme, 'Education in Human Rights'. It was clear that the idea of humanity was not seen as an invention of the West. The Jewish representative spoke of how Judaism has a classical religious basis for affirming a universal ethical dimension. The Muslim representative spoke of the Qur'an as the 'ideal codex of human rights', referring to an official Muslim declaration on the subject the year before. The Hinus representative spoke of a close connection between morality and religious feeling. The Buddhist representative argued that recognition of the cosmic dimensions of human beings in Buddhism did not exclude specific human significance. The Confucian representative spoke of how 'the humanum has always been the central concern of Confucianism'. [584]

The very universalism of human rights has also been subject to penetrating critique as serving a western agenda that represses cultural diversity. Munro is right to point out that *"the current tendency is to reject universalism and, in line with a greater respect for the linguistic integrity of specific practices, go the other way, preferring the emic to the etic, local distinctions to global abstractions."*[585] Hence the relation between human rights and the right to cultural difference is *"one of the greatest antinomies of our time"*.[586] One perspective on this is that of Cornelius Castoriadis, who argues that *"we Westerners claim we are one culture amongst others. . .but we have in addition invented values we claim as universal."*[587] Citing the hypothetical case of having a colleague who wants his daughter to have circumcision, he concludes that Westerners cannot give up the values they have invented which they believe to be valid for all people, regardless of cultural background.

Fundamental to posing such a question are notions of personhood. Rights create a system of dynamics centred on the right-holder. Dworkin is clear that human rights are the rights we have because we are human.[588] If the question be asked from where do we get human rights, the answer must presumably lie in humanity as the source.

'The life of an ordinary person matters. The idea that the ordinary person has potential for meaning as much as a King has been a strong ethical perspective in modernity since the Reformation. People matter. There is not a hierarchy of value but an equality of value. The philosopher G. E. Moore argued that *"if a given thing possesses any kind of intrinsic value in a certain* degree, then not only must that same thing possess it under all circumstances but also, anything like it must, under all circumstances, possess it in exactly the same sense." [589]

A RESPONSE FROM EVOLUTIONARY CONCEIT

"Whatever the specialness of the human brain, there is no need to invoke spiritual forces to account for its functions being human in mind and brain appears to be the result of evolutionary process." [590]

One response to what is being proposed here is that a sense of a valuable self arises from humans having a fanciful idea that they matter. An inflated consciousness of self-importance could help humans to get through, given that we seem pre-disposed to reflect on our place in the scheme of things. We go in for religion, we go in for art, we go in for speculation, we go in for projects that try to generate meaning. Humans ponder the stars and ask questions about 'why things are?' Perhaps a sense of being significant is an understandable but misguided attempt to combat lack of meaning. In short, we are ensnared in a vanity project.

Reflecting on this has to involve some appeal to evolutionary biology. With varying degrees of success, that could attempt to theorise how apes turn into humans. Physiology and brain development would come under the spotlight for this. But evolutionary biology does not predict a world of concepts, of which any evolutionary explanation is *itself* merely one of the many concepts.

To suppose that evolutionary development could account for the basis of theories of consciousness, let alone self-consciousness is to run way ahead of the evidence. In what is known about early human history, the light of consciousness seems to come on unexpectedly.

Recent evidence points to Neanderthals being more intelligent than had been supposed. We know something about Neanderthal cooking, for example. [591]. They built wooden structures. [592] Hominins 1.4 million years ago had the ability to conceptualize a sphere in their minds and shape stones to match. [593] Early humans were clearly not intellectually primitive precursors of contemporary people.

A RESPONSE FROM HISTORY

"The frivolity of it all. We are like mischievous apes tearing up the image of God" Richard Tawney writing about the battle of the Somme[594]

Inner lives of subjects are experienced in historically contingent settings. Contemporary forms of subjectivity abound. The modern subject is a result of social transformations, violence and huge suffering. One consequence is *"the creation of hyper-individualism which intensifies attention to human rights."* [595] The relentless encroachment of scientific worldviews and objectification of reality has lead to defining subjective experience as being only in the mind or emotion. [596] But seeing subjectivity as a synonym for inner states is recent. For Aristotle, the subject was the very material out of which things were made. Self-awareness is located in perception, the material substratum of objects.[597] Reflexive experience of the perceiving self occurs with particular perceptions. *"In perceiving, we perceive that we perceive."*[598] The virtuous become aware of themselves as ethical agents through reflective mirroring; mirroring the lives of others as "other selves". [599]

Augustine's Confessions are an outstanding example of introspective awareness. His questions are very different to those of Aristotle. His account of unmediated self-reflection comes in an argument against skepticism. *"Without any illusion or fantasy, I am certain that I am and that I know that I am".*[600] The existence of the self is proven by the capacity to doubt.

Modernity has been hugely important in asserting that differences can be positive determinants in the value of everyone, not just the elite. Whatever basis is adopted for the conception of human uniqueness, its significance for the value of people is immense. A unique centre of consciousness and subjectivity generates a strong sense of value. We take it as fundamental that no one can replace another and this arises in large measure from the nexus of relationships we are involved with.[601]

Here is a lady in waiting in 18th century Britain, conscious that she is completely dependent on 'the compulsory Attendance and obligatory Dependence' that comes with her role. [602] The condescension of George 111rd and Queen Charlotte is replete with a kindness that arouses the gratitude of Frances Burney but also tightens her velvet chains. Yet it is the Keeper of the Robes who is the real tyrant, a redoubtable woman who leaves Burney vulnerable to being 'Nobody'. Yet despite a constant attempt to subjugate her and punish resistance, tattered pride remains. Frances Burney has a secret knowledge that she is entitled to consideration and respect.

RESPONSE FROM THEODICY

The main difficulty lying in the path of any argument that the cosmos provides a welcome to humankind is that of suffering. Against the fearsome litany of evils in the world, many of which are *"fundamental and incorrigible"*.[603] Indeed, Nietzsche in 'Human, All too Human' stresses the monstrosity of the social sphere and cruel totality of the human network. Everyone is a prisoner of a desire for self-preservation and can only endure because the individual considers himself more important than the rest of the world.[604] How do people cope with *"the natural cruelty of things"*?[605]

The dominant characteristic of Nietzsche' life was that of the lonely self, battling on in order to make sense of life.[606] When humanity realises that it has lost God, universal madness will break out. In his work on Nietzsche Walter Kaufmann has this to say: *"to have lost God means madness and when mankind discovers that it has lost God, universal madness will break out. . . . We have destroyed our own faith in God. There remains only the void. We are falling. Our dignity is gone. Our values are lost. Who is to say what is up and what is down? It has become colder and night is closing in"*.[607]

Human existence sits with strident, jarring notes of violence and destruction, of laws being trampled on and relationships shattered. It is a deeply disturbing sound, of greed and pride, the sound of selfishness and of people marching to war; a depressing litany of broken people and broken dreams in a broken world. It is our lust, pride and greed writ large. We were caught in a trap, enmeshed in what we do to others and what had been done to us. We live in a broken world, in a world of gaps, the wealthy from the starving, of ideals and utopias from their realisation. Deep in the heart of the world, something has been broken. The fundamental distortion was at the very centre of things. More than a piece missing, there is a warp drive taking occupants in wrong directions.

This is a load-bearing dilemma for everyone alive. 'The problem of pain' it has been styled but that conceals its crushing weight. It is far beyond the scope of this book to rehearse the various stances that have been through the centuries to the suffering that seems concomitant with the human condition. Here we can only note that philosophers and theologians of all stripes have joined intellectual hands to say that this is not inconsistent with theism. The weight of the world, so often disproportionately experienced, has not been thought to be irreconcilable with divine Personhood.

If the cosmos is impersonal, the immensity of suffering is something to be born. Either there is no Creator or the cosmos is suffused with energy only with no claim for a loving Being behind the world. Consonant with the argument put forward in this book, this provides no ground for our personhood. There is no subject to subject exchange; the universe is blind and deaf to our humanity.

Some responses have been that God is of limited power and so unable to do any more than sympathise with our predicament. Both this response and that of seeing the universe as a brute fact to be accepted fail to show how there could be any physical laws that shaped everything and made this such an unlikely place to live. The Creator is an on-looker only rather than an all-powerful Being who brought everything into existence on whom it is contingent.

The full-blown theistic response is that God has chosen to allow suffering in the system, not for inscrutable reasons to do with a providence that is veiled in complete mystery but to produce a scheme of things where good outweighs the bad. [608]Thinking in terms of systems rather than individual caprice constitutes a higher order form of explanation that is far more illuminating. Earthquakes and volcanoes are an aspect of a natural order as are weather systems rushing heat and moisture across the world. Disease is allowed in as are human endeavours to vanquish the suffering. Wars are the result of allowing humans to be territorial and aggressive: having freedom to act rather than being controlled. As Irenaeus contended, this is a divinely ordained sphere of soul-making. He asserted that the world is the best of all possible worlds because it allows humans to fully develop. People are not yet fully developed hence experiencing evil and suffering is necessary. [609]Creation has two stages: humans were first created in the image of God and will then be formed in the likeness of God. Humans are imperfect: to achieve this likeness of God, we must be refined and developed. The present world is the best of all possible worlds. John Hick identified this theodicy as an alternative to the Augustinian view of the free will of the first humans throwing the world on the wrong path at the outset. [610] Origen too responds to the problem of evil by casting the world as a schoolroom or hospital for the soul. [611]

Many more difficulties with these proposals are possible. Much more can be made by way of responses to them. It can be said, however, that they are not insuperable to the notion of an ultimate person who validates our personhood and confers a sense of value upon us.

Postscript
—*Concluding Unscientific Postscript*

We have considered the ways in which a strictly scientific explanation in terms of naturalism cannot do justice to the psychological experiences people have of feeling of worth. The cosmos ought to be against this because at best it is neutral. Our human cry for significance is not just an existential angst, it is part of us: patterned into our very being. This cannot be reduced to the mind and consciousness as a by-product of electrical and chemical processes in the brain. A sense of valuable personhood is of critical importance for our inner being to flourish.

We have probed something of the limits to scientific explanation when it comes to the spiritual core of what it means to be human—the impetus towards meaning, significance and being of worth that is a signpost to what is beyond ourselves. Building on some psychological research and concepts, we have sought to illuminate the proposition that a degree of value is a vital psycho-social need.

An impersonal universe does not respond to our subjectivity. Life is not a detective book to keep reading until we get to the end and the conclusion of the puzzle is to find you have never truly lived. It is not death we fear so much as that peril! What we dream will make us happy leaves us longing for more. Better not to have tasted. So keep struggling with the problems of life and existence for that is the journey. Many are tired of a sardonic rationalism and the props being the centre of the stage; tired of the materialism that has blighted our life and of being entertained to death. The constant stream of visual images and endless stream of sound comes our way, twenty four hours times seven. Still we are not satisfied. There has to be something less fleeting: a world where painted images do not dissolve so! We are a being that cannot come to terms with itself. Yearning to express itself but not wanting to be what it is; concealed behind a thousand ideals; harbouring innumerable contradictions in its inner being. Who is this who asks the question? Who is it, so conscious of wonder, so tortured with the lonely questions of existence? Who is this who even dares to pit himself against the vastness and claim significance? Who will explain the mystery of why we are here, who we are or why we deceive ourselves into thinking we have worth? Who will solve the riddle of the maker of tools and being of value who sighs and cries for validation? Our fragility is laid bare to ourselves.

Late modernity has witnessed nameless people looking for their faces. Lament for the Faceless is the face of ordinary people v faceless elites who control things. Reaction against 'faceless' forces, the globalists, the administrators or bureaucrats, was of a piece with 'faceless' robotics stealing people's jobs or immigrants who cover their face. Into this milieu, humankind can respond to the face of God.

Merely because experiences are neurally grounded does not negate the very real possibility that people are connecting with something beyond themselves that is objectively real. Can we prove this though? It is hard to do this from neuroscience. Certain areas of the brain have not been proven to light up with spiritual experiences despite numerous efforts to demonstrate this. The human brain uses the same circuits for many purposes.

Underlying reality is the mental nature of the universe; that a purposing Mind generates and sustains everything.

ALTERNATIVES

The presence of something in the fabric of reality that generates our personhood needs explaining.

If there is a Creator it makes sense of our existence or what has to be explained in some way. Why there was a point of definite beginning, why there is something rather than nothing, why the universe is so fine—tuned, why there is a higher law beyond ourselves determining what is right from what is wrong and why there is a conscious mind or a conscience. If all is but from impersonal chance, all dissolves into amorality! Wherever we acknowledge that there is order and gracious intelligence at the heart of things, we acknowledge the Creator. When we sense a source of our being without which we cannot exist, it is as if we are stumbling around in a house without knowing whose house it is.

What is the cause of the means by which human observers came into being; observers with the remarkable reflexive capability to observe ourselves and draw conclusions about the scheme of things? The anthropic principle is closely linked to the concept of the fine-tuning of the universe by which the exact strength of the physical forces shaping the cosmos had to lie within very narrow limits if life was to be produced.[612]

Life would have been impossible if the mass of the electron, which is roughly ten times smaller than the mass difference between the down- and the up-quark, had been larger in relation to that difference. [613] Examples of fine-tuning concern the strength of gravity, the strengths of the strong and weak nuclear forces, the mass of the Higgs boson, the total energy density of the universe in its very early stages and the relative energy density fluctuations in the very early universe.[614] Amend any of the fundamental physical properties of the universe and its very habitability hangs in the balance. For Hertog, colleague of Hawking, though he spurns the notion of string theorists that a vast landscape of multi-verses is produced through a constantly shuffling of physical laws, a three-dimensional existence was carved out in the very early universe. [615] Rejection of the anthropic principle or replacing it with other possibilities nevertheless have to demonstrate why cosmological histories generated immediately after the Big Bang should have anything to do with promoting life.

These arguments have impressed many observers though not everyone would accept this is confirmation of theistic divine ordering.[616] [617] [618]

Given this apparent life-friendliness of the universe, there are a number of possibilities that give an account of the dimension of personal consciousness by which human observers become aware of themselves and of their place in the cosmos.

One is to accept that, remarkable though all this happens to be, it is how it is and we are alive to tell the tale. The universe is a brute fact. Human observers have come to be in a state of things that encourages life; we create our own meaning., especially as we accept this situation. It is nevertheless true that the life-friendly conditions of the universe are exactly those that are consonant with what a designer might choose. Given the astronomical odds against it (literally), it is extremely unlikely that intelligent life would develop unless that was the intention. The limitations of scientific naturalism discussed in chapters above are relevant to aspects of our existence that need explaining if matter and energy are all there are.

Another strategy is to suppose that the universe is conscious such that our human awareness of ourselves is but one, localised example of this. The argument is here that of a cosmic version of the panpsychism discussed above. Even fundamental particles have a form of consciousness: it is 'degreed'. The human brain is an integrated system and is fully conscious (see above chapter six). On this account of reality, the fabric of the universe is set up for the moral values commensurate with the flourishing of conscious entities and will seek to generate about such states.

The problem is to explain why there are physical tendencies and principles that incredible fine-tuning of their constants will lead to the development of life. If these forces were set slightly differently, no such conditions exist for the particles and structures that make up the universe to be stable. It would be highly unlikely that the conditions for life would emerge.

Who or what made these laws and how did the constants come about that produced conscious observers who can speculate about their place in the cosmos, believe themselves to have moral and psychological value yet clearly have the freedom of choice that enable us to be saints or sinners?

Newton's genius was to show that a panoply of data derived from observation could be explained by recourse to a simple set of principles which could be expressed in some universal laws. A few mathematical equations could describe the workings of objects close to hand and objects much further away such as planets. The regularity of the 'laws of nature' derived in this way reflected the deep structures of the cosmos and of physical reality behind which lay the mind of God. Scientific thinking subsequently had the effect of relegating the divine to the margins. Today, an account of reality is needed that can bring together not only the physical world but our psychological and ethical experience. Any description of the fabric of reality has to accommodate all of this before laying any claim to be 'a theory of everything'.

Swinburne argues that the cumulative weight of lines of approach to God makes for coherence. He analyses the circumstances under which sentences expresses a coherent statement, possess the quality of meaningfulness and not be self-contradictory. Statements about God fulfil criteria for coherence, as does quantum theory; expressing analogical senses to words outside normal experience, such as God being personal. [619]

We are the prodigy of the planets. How we see the world must peer beyond confines of private dramas to the cosmic stage dwarfing them. It is the endless unknown that must be embraced. But how to relate the two so we are not aliens or exiles in our own home? How will significance and insignificance meet?

It maybe that we cannot tell what power lies at the heart of things. But we say there is a power that directs the motions of planets and influences our lives. What is behind that power though? Who or what made it so? If There is no personal force out there. If so the universe IS blind and deaf to the things we value most. And neither do we matter. And there is nothing there that corresponds to what's in here?

Can it be that in the most exciting period of star gazing since the world began, we do not know what nine parts of ten the universe is made? Or are we are encountering the outer fringes of the One who holds the cosmos together? And what of a crazy, infinitesimally small cosmos within matter and energy; where particles danced into existence to entangle with dancing partners though separated? Can we really maintain human significance in a universe that went on and on into the night? With what scales can we begin to weigh our little lives against an inconceivable; the significant against the insignificant?

The Creator is infinite. There can be no room for more than one infinite spirit. Look above us at the mighty universe. Then peer inside at our conscious mind. The Creator is the common ground both rationality of our minds and of the whole universe. The perfect uniformity and agreement of all its forces and parts pointed to one cause behind all things. A single pattern in the universe counted against the idea of many competing gods. One set of laws, one set of building materials. We may speak of one infinite spirit who made all things, one ultimate power behind the universe who is not the universe. We may speak of one distinct from the cosmos and who is therefore holy- and yet who gives life to all. To attempt to prove the Creator is to place God on the same level as all other things. God is neither thing nor form as if planetary object.

The steps from personal being in humankind to supra- personal being in an ultimate, divine realm need to be traced.

Step One—we have a strong psycho-social need to be valued

Step Two—the universe could have developed so as to generate no significance for its observers

Step Three - the universe could have developed so as to generate significance for its observers.

Step Four—if Step Three is invalid, we go inexorable towards an impersonal universe- no God

Step Five—hence Step Three is likely to be correct. In an impersonal, neutral universe, the human person has risen higher than its source

Or put another way:

Step One—human beings need to live in a valuing environment and feel we are people of worth

- If that is forthcoming, we thrive
- Without a sense of value (either imparted or internalised), we wither
- Sociology and psychology points in this direction
- But so too do common human experiences of central importance in contemporary life (the lack of value and powerlessness felt by millions in the West who feel the world passes them by and also intensified social comparison that bedevils the mental health of teenage girls)

Step Two—how does this come about?

- How does the universe generate animals (human participants) who not only are conscious and self-aware but have an imperative towards high worth?
- Is this mere evolutionary conceit?
- Is there something out there that corresponds to what's in here?
- Or has an impersonal universe given rise to this fundamental way we are wired up?

Step Three—

- This is not just a question of how mind is generated from matter. It is the hard problem of soft value.
- The universe is ordered. It is not a whimsical place but ordered for valuable personhood. However, the problem of suffering and providence would seem to be against this.
- Yet an ultimate Being is required to imprint valuable personhood on to matter, information and self-replicating systems
- God is the ultimate valuer, the one who confers value on humanity who are in the mind and mirror of God
- A personal God is the most satisfactory explanation of valuable personhood. We can object all we want but we only have to look within to know we need to be of value as people. On what is that based?

Endnotes

1. Einstein in Conversation with William Hermanns in Herrmanns, W. (1983) *Einstein and the Poet: in search of the Cosmic Man* Brookline Village, MA: Branden Press p132

2. Einstein, A. (1934) *The World as I see it* New York: Covici-Friede Inc

3. Einstein, A. (1914-1917) *Collected Papers of Albert Einstein Letter to Heinrich Zannger* 10th March 1914 Vol 5 p381 ed R. Schulmann Princeton, Princeton NJ: Princeton University Press

4. Einstein, A. (1934) *The World as I see it* New York: Covici-Friede Inc Essay originally published in *Forum and Century* vol 84 pp193-194

5. Einstein, A. (1956) Lettres a Maurice Solovine *quoted in* Jaki, S. (1980) *Cosmos and Creator* Edinburgh: Scottish Academic Press pp52-53

6. Einstein, A. (1956) *Lettres a Maurice Solovine* Paris: Gauthier-Villars p114-115

7. McGrath, A. (2019) *A Theory of Everything (that Matters): a short guide to Einstein, Relativity and the Future of Faith* London: Hodder and Stoughton p93

8. Holton, G. (1973) Mach, Einstein and the Search for Reality in *Thematic Origins of Scientific Thought* Cambridge, M.A.: Havard University Press p243

9. Frank, P. (1951) *Relativity, a Richer Truth* London: Jonathan Cape

10. Jaki, S. (1987) 'The Absolute beneath the Relative' in *Einstein and the Humanities Contributions in Philosophy no 32* New York: Greenwood Press ch 3

11. Heisenberg, W. (1963) *Physics and Philosophy* London: Allen & Unwin p96

12. Folsing, A. (1997) *Albert Einstein* Harmondsworth: Penguin p699

13. Bohm, D. (1951) *Quantum Theory* New York: Prentice-Hall

14. Folsing, A. (1997) *Albert Einstein* Harmondsworth: Penguin p632

15. Planck, M. (1932) Where is science going? Tr J. Murphy New York: W W Norton

16. Jammer, M. (1999) *Einstein and Religion: Physics and Theology* Princeton, N.J.: Princeton University Press p150

17. Bohm, D. (1951) *Quantum Theory* Mineola, NY: Dover Press

18. Bohm, D. (1951) *Quantum Theory* Mineola, NY: Dover Press p583, 624-625

19. Saunders, S. (2000) 'Clock-watcher' *New York Times* March 26th 2000

20. Einstein, A. (2004) *Relativity: the Special and General Theory* London: Folio Ch 9 P31

21. Pais, A. (1982) '*Subtle is the Lord*' *The science and life of Albert Einstein* Oxford: OUP

22. Jaki, S. (1987) *The Absolute beneath the Relative*' in Einstein and the Humanities Contributions in Philosophy no 32 New York: Greenwood Press ch 3 p14

23. Jose Ortega y Gasset (1967) 'El Origen deportivo del Estado' *Citius, Altius, Fortius* 9 no 1–4 p259

24. Rovelli, C. (2015) *Seven Brief Lessons on Physics* London: Allen Lane.

25. Walsh, D. (2020) *The Priority of the Person* Notre Dame, Ill.: University of Notre Dame Press p1–2

26. Walsh, D. (2020) *The Priority of the Person* Notre Dame, Ill.: University of Notre Dame Press p12

27. Ward, G. (2000) *Cities of God* (Routledge Radical Orthodoxy) London: Routledge

28. Nagel, T. (2012) *Mind and Cosmos*: Why the Materialist Neo-Darwinian Conception of Nature is Almost Certainly False New York: OUP

29. John Horgan (2016) 'World›s Smartest Physicist Thinks Science Can›t Crack Consciousness' *Scientific American* August 18, 2016

30. Wheeler, J. (1989) *Information, Physics, Quantum*,

31. Alfonso V. Ramallo (2016) *Introduction to the AdS/CFT Correspondence Physics Today* Volume 69, Issue 8 1 August 2016

32. John Horgan (2016) 'World's Smartest Physicist Thinks Science Can't Crack Consciousness' *Scientific American* August 18, 2016

33. Monod, J. (1972) *Chance and Necessity* London: Collins p20

34. Seager, W. (1991) *Metaphysics of Consciousness* London: Routledge

35. Chalmers, David (1995). "Facing up to the problem of consciousness". *Journal of Consciousness Studies*. 2 (3): 200–219

36. Tedeschi, Richard G.; Park, Crystal L.; Calhoun, Lawrence G., eds. (1998). *Posttraumatic Growth: Positive Changes in the Aftermath of Crisis*. Routledge. pp. 99, 117

37. Nagel, T. (1974). What Is It Like to Be a Bat? *The Philosophical Review*, 83(4), 435–450

38. Del Pin, S. H., Skóra, Z., Sandberg, K., Overgaard, M., & Wierzchoń, M. (2021). Comparing theories of consciousness: why it matters and how to do it. *Neuroscience of consciousness*, 2021(2),

39. Seth, A. K., & Bayne, T. (2022). Theories of consciousness. *Nature reviews. Neuroscience*, 23(7), 439–452. https://doi.org/10.1038/s41583-022-00587-4

40. Promet, L., & Bachmann, T. (2022). A comparative analysis of empirical theories of consciousness. *Psychology of Consciousness: Theory, Research, and Practice*. Advance online publication

41. Northoff, G., & Lamme, V. (2020). Neural signs and mechanisms of consciousness: Is there a potential convergence of theories of consciousness in sight?. *Neuroscience and biobehavioural reviews*, 118, 568–587.

42. Dennett, D. (1993) *Consciousness Explained* London: Penguin Science

43. James, W. [1904] 1976. "Does 'Consciousness' Exist? " In *Essays in Radical Empiricism. Vol. 3, Works of William James, 3–19*. Cambridge, Mass.: Harvard University Press

44. Deacon, T, (2003) *Incomplete Nature: How Mind Emerged from Matter* New York: Norton p23

45. Milll, J.S. (1843) *System of Logic London: Longmans, Green, Reader and Dyer Book 111, ch6 s1*

46. Morowitz, H. (2004) The Emergence of Everything: how the world became complex Oxford: OUP

47. Bennett, M. (2023) *A brief history of Intelligence* London: William Collins

48. Melissa Heikkilä (2023) 'Why it'll be hard to tell if AI ever becomes conscious' *MIT Review* October 17th 2023

49. Musser, G. (2023) *Putting Ourselves Back in the Equation: why physicists are studying human consciousness and Ai to unravel the mysteries of the universe* London: OneWorld

50. O'Craven, K.M. & Kanwisher, N. (2000) 'Mental imagery of faces and places activates corresponding stimulus-specific brain regions' *Journal of Cognitive* Neuroscience 12. 1013–23. See also Greene, J. D. et al (2001) 'An fMRI investigation of emotional entanglement in moral judgment *Science* 293, 2105–8

51. McGilchrist, I. (2019) *The Master and His Emissary: The Divided Brain and the Making of the Western World* Princeton,N.J.: Yale University Press; 2nd edition

52. https://www.apa.org/monitor/2013/11/right-brained Anderson, J.A. et al (2013) An Evaluation of the Left-Brain vs. Right-Brain Hypothesis with Resting State Functional Connectivity Magnetic Resonance Imaging August 14, 2013

53. LeDoux, J. (2003) The emotional brain, fear and the amygdala *Cell Mol Neurobiology* 2003 Oct;23(4–5):727–3

54. Blakeslee, S. (1996) Dr. Joseph Ledoux: Using Rats to Trace Routes of Fear *New York Times* November 5, 1996

55. Wexler, B. (2007) *Brain and Culture.*: Neurology, ideology and social change. Cambridge: MIT Press

56. Tallis, R. (2011) *Aping Mankind: Neuromania, Darwinits and the misrepresentation of humanity*. London: Acumen

57. Cozolino, L.J. (2010). *The neuroscience of psychotherapy: Healing the social brain*, New York: W.W. Norton

58. Siegel, D.J. (2010) *The mindful therapist: A clinician's guide to mindsight and neural integration*. W. W. Norton & Company. Kindle Edition.

59. Clinton, Tim; Sibcy, Gary (2012) Christian counselling, interpersonal neurobiology, and the future. *Journal of Psychology and Theology 40* (2), 141–145, 2012.

60. Beauregard, M. (2007). Mind does really matter: Evidence from neuroimaging studies of emotion self-regulation, psychotherapy, and placebo effect. *Progress in Neurobiology*, 81, 218–236

61. Wheeler, J. A. (1975) *The Nature of Scientific Discovery* Ed. O Gringerich Washington: Smithsonian Press pp261–96

62. John Wheeler, interview with Ken Ford. "John Wheeler-Wheeler's drawing of the Big U: Concept of Observer Participancy" video posted to You Tube https://www.youtube.com/watch?v=ttestU-obkw accessed March 2023

63. Kumar, M. (2009) *Quantum: Einstein, Bohr and the Great Debate about the nature of reality*. London: Icon books p246

64. Tegmark, M. (2015) 'Consciousness as a state of matter' Chaos, Solitons and Fractals 76 pp238–270

65. Lockwood, M. (1989) *Mind, Brain and the Quantum* Basil Blackwell p236

66. Kim, J. (1998). *Mind in a Physical World: An Essay in the Mind-Body Problem and Mental Causation*. Cambridge, Mass.: MIT Press and Bradford Books

67. Lockwood, M. (1989) *Mind, Brain and the Quantum* Basil Blackwell p13–14

68. Armstrong, D. M. (1993) *A Materialist Theory of the Mind*. 2d ed. London: Routledge.

69. Marshall, I. M. (1989) Consciousness and Bose-Einstein condensates *New Ideas in Psychology* Volume 7, Issue 1, 1989, Pages 73–83

70. Lockwood, M. (1989) *Mind, Brain and the Quantum* Basil Blackwell p228

71. Penrose, R. (2004) *The Road to Reality*. London: Jonathan Cape

72. Hofstadter, D. (2007) *I am a strange loop* New York: Basic Books p415

73. De Witt, B. & Graham, N. (2015) *The many worlds interpretation of quantum mechanics* Princeton: Princeton University Press

74. Russell, B. (1921) *The Analysis of Mind*. London: George Allan & Unwin

75. www.bbc.co.uk/radio4/pm June 27th 2013

76. As reported in the London Daily Mail, August 25th 2007

77. James, W. (1890) *The Principles of Psychology*. Boston

78. Donaldson, S. (2004) *Hooking Up: Protective Pairing for Punks*. Article written to advise male survivors of prisoner rape. From Scheper-Hughes, N. & Bourgois, P. eds (2004) Violence in war and peace. Blackwell Publishing. Malden. MA p353

79. Leibmann, M. Ed (1994) *Art Therapy with Offenders*. London: Jessica Kingsley Publishers

80. Swann, W. Jr. (1999) *Resilient Identities: Self, relationships, and the construction of social reality*. Basic books: New York

81. Moore, J. (1995) Person- Central Psychotherapy. From Walker, M. (ed) *Peta: a Feminist's Problem with Men*. Buckingham: Open University p15

82. www.bbc.co.uk/radio4 Today Programme 21st April 2010

83. Author's client notes- name withheld and used with permission

84. Swann, W. Jr. (1999) *Resilient Identities: Self, relationships, and the construction of social reality*. Basic books: New York

85. Philipps, A. (2010) *On Balance*. London: Hamish Hamilton

86. Gilbert, P. (2009) *The Compassionate Mind*. London: Constable.

87. Cooley, C.H. (1902) *Human Nature and the Social Order*. New York: Scribner

88. Feyneyhough, C. (2008) *The Baby in the Mirror*: A child's world from birth to three. London: Granta Books

89. Reddy, V. (2008) *How Infants Know Minds*. Cambridge, MA.: Harvard University Press

90. Bowlby, J. (1969) *Attachment and Loss vol 1* New York: Basic Books

91. Ainsworth, M. (1967) *Infancy in Uganda: Infant care and the growth of love* Baltimore: John Hopkins University Press p429

92. Dawson, G. (1994) Development of emotional expression and emotion regulation in infancy in G. Dawson & K.W. Fischer eds *Human Behaviour and the developing brain* New York: Gulliford p346-379

93. Trad, P.V. (1986) *Infant Depression* New York: Springer-Verlag

94. Rosenblum, L.A. (1987) Influences of environmental demand on maternal behaviour and infant development in N.A. Krasnegor et al eds *Perinatal development: a psychobiological perspective* Orlando, Fl: Academic Press p377-395

95. Damasion, A.R. (1994) *Descartes' Error* New York: Grosset/Putnam

96. Van der Kolk, B. & Fisler, R.E. (1994) Childhood Abuse and neglect and loss of self-regulation *Bulletin of the Menninger Clinic* 58, 145-168

97. Trinh, M. (1992) *The Framer Framed*. London: Routledge

98. Author's client notes- name withheld and used with permission. See also Spence, J. (1988) *Putting Myself in the Picture*. London: Real Comet Press

99. Author's client notes- name withheld and used with permission.

100. Author's client notes- name withheld and used with permission

101. Hegel, G.W.F. (1971) *The Philosophy of Mind*. Oxford: Clarendon Press

102. Hegel, G.W.F. (1979) *The Phenomenology of Spirit*. Oxford: OUP

103. Sartre ibid p231

104. Derrida, J. (2008) *Psyche: Inventions of the other*. P. Kamuf and E. Rottenberg ed. Stanford University Press

105. Author's Client Notes- used with permission.

106. Foucault. M. 1979) *Discipline and Punish*. Harmondsworth:Penguin

107. Honneth, A. (2007) *Reification: A Recognition-Theoretical View*. Oxford: Oxford University Press

108. Taylor, C (1992), *Multiculturalism and the Politics of Recognition*, Princeton, Princeton University Press p24 & 50

109. Taylor, C (1992), *Multiculturalism and the Politics of Recognition*, Princeton, Princeton University Press p38

110. Arendt, H. (1958) *The Human Condition*. Chicago: University of Chicago Press p184

111. Markell, P. (2003) *Bound by Recognition*. Princeton: Princeton University Press

112. Taylor, C. (2007) *A Secular Age*. Cambridge, M.A.:Belknap Press of HUP p213

113. BBC2 Documentary. The Indian Ocean. 22nd April 2012

114. Honneth, A. (1995) *The Struggle for Recognition: The Moral Grammar of Social Conflicts*. Cambridge: Polity

115. Honneth, A. (2003) *Redistribution or Recognition?: A Political-Philosophical Exchange*, co-authored with Nancy Fraser. London: Verso

116. Honneth, A. (2007) *Reification: A Recognition-Theoretical View*. Oxford: Oxford University Press

117. Lankov, A. (2013) *The Real North Korea: Life and Politics in the Failed Stalinist Utopia*. Oxford; OUP

118. Vaughan, A.T (1995) "The Origins Debate: Slavery and Racism in Seventeenth Century Virginia" from *Roots of American Racism: Essays on the Colonial Experience*. New York. Oxford University Press p171

119. 'Sarah's Bubble'- www.timetochange.org.uk March 2010

120. Smith, M.M. (2006) *How Race is Made: Slavery, Segregation, and the Senses*. Chapel Hill, NC: University of North Carolina Press,

121. Gaita, R. (2000) *A Common Humanity: Thinking About Love, Truth and Justice*. London: Routledge. pxxi

122. Sartre, J.P. (1958) *Being and Nothingness*. London: Methuen p47

123. Sartre, J.P. (1958) *Being and Nothingness*. London: Methuen p221

124. Sartre, J.P. (1958) *Being and Nothingness*. London: Methuen p47

125. Sartre, J.P. (1958) *Being and Nothingness*. London: Methuen p93

126. Tallis, R. (2009) *The Kingdom of Infinite Space: A fantastical journey round your head*. Yale University Press

127. Sartre, J.P. (1958) *Being and Nothingness*. London: Methuen p231

128. Bartsch, S. (2007) *The Mirror of the Self: Sexuality and the gaze in the early Roman Empire*. Chicago: University of Chicago Press.

129. Elliot, C. (2003) *Better than Well: American medicine meets the American dream*.

130. Orbach, S. (2009) *Bodies*. London: Profile Books

131. Robert Stolorow & George Atwood (1992). 'Three realms of the unconscious'. In Mitchell, S. A. ed (1999) *Relational Psychoanalysis- The emergence of a tradition* London: Routledge

132. Cozolino, L. J. (2012) *The Neuroscience of Human relationships: attachment and the developing social brain*. New York: Norton

133. Cozolino, L.J. (2017) *The Neuroscience of Psychotherapy* New York: Norton p370

134. Steed. C. D (2019) *The significance of high value in human behaviour* London: Routledge

135. https://quotepark.com/topics/bitter/?q=1848043&page=17 accessed July 2021

136. Russell, B. (1918) *Mysticism and Logic and other essays* London: Edward Arnold

137. Whitton, E. (2003) *Humanistic Approach to Psychotherapy*. London: Whurr Publishers. p39. See also Thorne, B. (2001) *Therapeutic and Spiritual Dimensions*. London: Whurr Publishers.

138. Ward, K. (1992) *In defence of the soul* Oxford: One world p11

139. Steed. C. D (2019) *The significance of high value in human behaviour* London: Routledge

140. Steed, C. D. (2018) *A question of inequality and why it matters* London: Tauris

141. Miller, A. *Death of a Salesman*. Harmondsworth: Penguin Plays 2000

142. Author's client notes- name withheld and used with permission

143. Bill Rawlings. "A life without work" – BBC2 Documentary 29th October 2010.

144. Author's client notes- name withheld and used with permission

145. Tajfel, H., & Turner, J. C. (1979). An integrative theory of intergroup conflict. In W. G. Austin & S. Worchel (Eds.), *The social psychology of intergroup relations* (pp. 33–47). Monterey, CA: Brooks/Cole

146. Gay, P. (2006) *Freud: A life for our Time*. London: Max p390

147. Maslow, A. (1977) A Theory of Meta-motivation: The Biological Rooting of the Value Life. In Chiang, H-M. & Maslow. A. Eds. *The Healthy Personality*. New York: D.Van Nostrund Co. p28

148. Wilkinson, R. & Pickett, K. (2009) *The Spirit Level: why more equal societies almost always do better* –Harmondsworth: Penguin Books Ltd

149. Steed, C. D. (2018) *A Question of Inequality and why it matters*. London: I B Tauris

150. Author's client notes- name withheld and used with permission.

151. Mearns, D. & Thorne, B. (2000) *Person-Centred Therapy Today: new frontiers in theory and practice*. Sage

152. Author's client notes- name withheld and used with permission

153. Author's client notes- name withheld and used with permission

154. Author's client notes- name withheld and used with permission

155. Author's client notes- name withheld and used with permission

156. Time Magazine- March 2nd 2009

157. Briggs, A., Halvorson, H. & Steane, A. (2018) *It Keeps me Seeking* Oxford: OUP 108

158. Sierra Club Language Equity Guide invoking 'A Progressive's Style Guide' https://s3.amazonaws.com/s3.sumofus.org/images/SUMOFUS_PROGRESSIVE-STYLE-GUIDE.pdf accessed March 2023

159. Marmot, M. ed (2005) Social Determinants of Health Oxford: ⊠ Oxford University Press

160. Steed, C. D. (2018) *A question of inequality and why it matters* London: Tauris

161. Strayer, R. (2022). Teaching religion in world history. World History Bulletin, 38, p. 67

162. The Times May 3, 1978, page 16 - An ideal way to clear the mind- re-published in Levin, B. (1979) *Taking Sides* London: ⊠Jonathan Cape Ltd p.123

163. Schopenhauer (1909) *The World As Will And Idea* tr R. B. Haldane & J. Kemp Vol. III London Kegan Paul, Trench, Trübner & Co. p 573

164. McCabe, I. (2015) Carl Jung and Alcoholics Anonymous: The Twelve Steps as a Spiritual Journey of Individuation London: Routledge

165. Frankl, V. (2004) *Man's Search for Meaning* London: Rider p62

166. Frankl, V (1973), *The Doctor and the Soul*, Harmondsworth, Penguin Books, p27

167. Frankl, V. (2004) *Man's Search for Meaning* London: Rider p60

168. Frankl, V. (2004) *Man's Search for Meaning* London: Rider p75

169. Graber, K. (1991) *Ghosts in the Bedroom: A Guide for Partners of Incest Survivors*. Deerfield Beach, Florida: Health Communications, Inc. p34

170. https://ellisjones.com.au/the-importance-of-identity/ accessed June 2022

171. Miller, A. *Death of a Salesman*. Harmondsworth: Penguin Plays 2000

172. Heinrich Päs, (2023) Rethinking reality: Is the entire universe a single quantum object? *New Scientist* 5/7/23

173. Teilhard de Chardin, P. (1959) *The Phenomenon of Man* tr B.Wall New York: Harper and Brothers

174. Descartes, R. (1996) Meditations on First Principles in *Meditations on First Philosophy with selections from the Objections and Replies* ed & tr J. Cottingham p59 Cambridge: Cambridge University Press

175. Valberg, J.J. (2007) *Dream, death and the self*. Princeton,N.J.: PUP

176. Scruton, R. (2012) *The Face of God* New York: Continuum Books p33

177. The discussion of personhood comes from James Ussher's 1648 systematic theology (*A Body of Divinity: The Sum and Substance of the Christian Religion*)

178. In a Profile, BBC Radio 4 October 20th 2019

179. In an interview, BBC Radio 4 September 24th 2019. www.bbc.co.uk/radio4/thetodayprogramme

180. Taylor, C (1992), *Multiculturalism and the Politics of Recognition*, Princeton, Princeton University Press p38

181. Fukuyama, F. (2018) *Identity: The Demand for Dignity and the Politics of Resentment* New York: Farrar, Straus & Giroux

182. De Waal, F. (2021) *Different: gender through the eyes of a primatologist* New York: Norton

183. Cooke, L. (2021) *Bitch: a revolutionary guide to sex, evolution and the female animal* New York: Basic Books

184. 'Advocating for Transgender and non-binary youths' American Psychological Association July/August 2022. *Monitor on Psychology*

185. Heinrich, J. et al (2010) The weirdest people in the world? *Behavioural and Brain Sciences* vol 33, no 2–3. See also Arnett, J. (2008) The neglected 95%: Why American psychology needs to become less American. *American Psychologist* 63(7):602–14

186. 'Dismantling racism'. American Psychological Association April/May 2021. *Monitor on Psychology*

187. Oppenheimer, H. (1983) *The Hope of Happiness*. London. SCM Press

188. Van Inwagen, Peter, *Being: A Study in Ontology* (Oxford, 2022; online edn, Oxford Academic, 15 Dec.

189. *Philosophia Prima sive Ontologia* (1730)

190. Heidegger, M. (2010) Basic Writings: Martin Heidegger London: Routledge Classics

191. Jean-Paul Sartre (2021) *Being and Nothingness*. New York: Simon and Schuster p57-58

192. O'Rorty, A. (1976) Introduction: *The Identities of Persons* Berkeley, CA: University of California Press p9

193. David Leech Anderson of the Mind Project https://mind.ilstu.edu/curriculum/what_is_a_person/what_is_a_person.html

194. Daniel Schiff, (2002) *Abortion in Judaism* Cambridge University Press p. 4

195. Haldane, John; Lee, Patrick (2003). "Aquinas on Human Ensoulment, Abortion and the Value of Life". Philosophy. 78 (2): 255-278.

196. Aquinas, *Commentary on III Sentences* 3:5:2.

197. Neaves W (2017). "The status of the human embryo in various religions". Development. 144 (14): 2541-2543

198. Aquinas *Summa Theologiae* I:75:4

199. Norman M. Ford (1989) When Did I Begin? Conception of the Human Individual in History, Philosophy and Science (Cambridge & New York, Cambridge University Press

200. Torchia, J. O.P (2007) *Exploring Personhood: An Introduction to the Philosophy of Human Nature* Washington.D.C.: Rowman & Littlefield Publishers

201. Pecere, P. (2020) Soul, Mind and Brain from Descartes to Cognitive Science: A Critical History Springer

202. Nimbalkar, N, (2011) John Locke on Personal Identity *Mens Sana Monogr.* Jan-Dec; 9(1): 268-275.

203. Locke, J. (1975) *An essay concerning human understanding* Book II ch XXVII 26

204. Locke, J. (1975) *An essay concerning human understanding* Book II ch XXVII.11 'Of Ideas of Identity and Diversity' Oxford: Clarendon Press

205. Butler, 'Of personal Identity' Dissertations 1

206. Montaigne Essays II.17-18

207. Rorty, A. O. (2007) 'The Vanishing Subject' from Kleinman, A. et al *Subjectivity* Berkeley: University of California Press ch 1 p41

208. Kant, I. (1949) *Critique of Pure Reason* tr Lewis White Beck Chicago: University of Chicago Press sec 2 IV 428 p86-87

209. Torchia, J. (2008) *Exploring Personhood: an introduction to the Philosophy of Human Nature New York: Rowman and Littlefield p222

210. Hanfling, O. (1999) 'Machines as Persons' in Human Beings as Persons *Royal Institute of Philosophy Supplement 29* Cambridge: Cambridge University Press

211. Kierkegaard, S (1980) *The Sickness Unto Death*, Howard V. and Edna H. Hong (ed. and trans.) (s Writings 19), Princeton, NJ: Princeton University Press

212. Schore, A. (2003) *Affect Dysregulation and Disorders of the Self* New York: WW Norton p37

213. Van der Kolk, B. & Fisler, R.E. (1994) Childhood Abuse and neglect and loss of self-regulation *Bulletin of the Menninger Clinic* 58, 145–168

214. Main, M. & Solomon, J. (1986) Discovery of an insecure-disorganised/disoriented attachment pattern in T.B. Brazleton & M.W. Yogman (eds) *Affective development in Infancy* Norwood, N.J.: Ablex

215. Solomon, J. & George, C. (1999) *Attachment Disorganisation* New York: Guilford Press

216. Nijhuis JG 2003 Foetal behaviour. The brain and behaviour in different stages of human life. *Neurobiol Aging* 24: S41–S46

217. The Emergence of Human Consciousness: From Foetal to Neonatal Life. Hugo Lagercrantz and Jean-Pierre Changeux in *Paediatric Research*, Vol. 65, No. 3, pages 255–260; March 2009.

218. Lagercrantz H, Hanson M, Evrard P, Rodeck C 2002 The Newborn Brain. Cambridge University Press, Cambridge, p 538

219. Merker B. Consciousness without a cerebral cortex: A challenge for neuroscience and medicine. *Behavioural and Brain Sciences*. 2007;30(1):63–81 Cambridge University Press

220. Johnson MH 2005 Subcortical face processing. *Nat Rev Neurosci* 6: 766–774

221. Cooley, C.H. (1902) *Human Nature and the Social Order*. New York: Scribner

222. Buber, M. (1924) *I and thou* RG Smith (ed) London: Continuum

223. Buber, M. (1924) *I and thou 100th (anniversary reprint)* tr RG Smith New York: Simon and Schuster

224. Scruton, R. (2012) *The Face of God* New York: Continuum Books p34

225. McFayden, A. (1990) *The Call to Personhood* Cambridge: Cambridge University Press p22

226. Gomez, L. (1997) *An Introduction to Object Relations* London: Free Association Books

227. Brown, W. et al (1998) *Whatever happened to the soul? Scientific and theological Portraits of human nature* Minneapolis, MN: Fortress Press

228. Seybold, K. (2007) *Explorations in Neuroscience, Psychology and Religion*. Burlington, Vt: Ashgate p99

229. Siegel, D. & Schore, A. & Cozolino, L. (2021). *Interpersonal Neurobiology and Clinical Practice*. New York: W. W. Norton and Company

230. Hardy, A. (1966) *The Divine flame : an essay towards a natural history of religion* London: Collins

231. James, W. (1982) *The Varieties of Religious Experience: a study in human nature* London: Penguin p2

232. Hay, D. & Nye, R. (1998) *The spirit of the child* London: HarperCollins

233. Solms, M & Turnbull, O. (2018) The Brain and the Inner World: An Introduction to the Neuroscience of Subjective Experience London: Routledge

234. Wolford, G., Miller, M.B. & Gazzinga, M. (2000) 'The left hemisphere's role in hypothesis formation.' *The Journal of Neuroscience* 20, RC 64-7

235. Freud, S. (1900) *The Interpretation of Dreams*. Motto on the Title page.

236. Laing, R. D. (2010) *The Divided Self: An Existential Study in Sanity and Madness* London: Penguin.

237. Macmillan, M. (2000) *An odd kind of fame: Stories of Phineas Gage* Cambridge, MA.: MIT Press

238. Damasio, A. (1999) *The feeling of what happens: Body and Emotion in the making of consciousness* New York: Harcourt

239. Harris J (1985) *The value of life*. Routledge, Abingdon

240. Griffin J (2009) *On human rights*. Oxford University Press, Oxford

241. Jaworska A (2010) Caring and full moral standing redux. In: Feder Kittay E, Carlson L (eds) *Cognitive disability and its challenge to moral philosophy*. Wiley Blackwell, Oxford

242. Fineman M (2008) The vulnerable subject: anchoring equality in the human condition. Yale J Law Feminism 20:1-71

243. Finnis J (1995) The fragile case for euthanasia: a reply to John Harris. In: Keown J (ed) Euthanasia examined. Cambridge University Press, Cambridge

244. Chan S, Harris J (2016) Human animals and non-human animals. In: Beauchamp T, Frey R (eds) The Oxford handbook of animal ethics. Oxford University Press, Oxford

245. Stephens, W. ed (2006) *The Person: readings in Human Nature* Upper Saddle River, NJ: Pearson Prentice Hall

246. Baumeister, R.F. (2015) 'Emergence of personhood: lessons from self and identity' in Jeeves, M. ed (2015) *The Emergence of Personhood: a quantum leap* Grand Rapids, MI: W. B Eeerdmans p69

247. Baumeister, R.F. (2005) *The Cultural Animal: Human Nature, meaning and social life* New York: OUP

248. Tattershall, I. (2015) 'Human Evolution' in Jeeves, M. ed *The Emergence of Personhood: a quantum leap* Grand Rapids, MI: W. B Eeerdmans Ch 3 p47

249. Wojtyla, K. (1995) *Love and Responsibility*. Tr. H.T. Willetts. New York: Farrar, Strauss and Giroux.

250. Wojtyla, K. (1979) *The Acting Person*. Tr A. Potocki. Dordrecht, the Netherlands:D. Reidel

251. John Paul 11 (1994) 'Address to the International Theological Commission.' December 5th 1983. In *Human Rights in the Teaching of the Church: From John XX111rd to John Paul 11nd*. Vatican City: Libreria Editrice Vaticana . 40

252. Williams, T. (2005) *Who is my Neighbour? Personalism and the Foundations of Human Rights.* Washington, D.C.: The Catholic University of America Press. p119

253. Smith, D (1999), *Bauman, Prophet of Postmodernity,* Cambridge, Polity Press p187

254. 'Personalism' Stanford Encyclopedia of Philosophy *First published Thu Nov 12, 2009; substantive revision Wed Apr 27, 2022* https://plato.stanford.edu/entries/personalism/

255. Evans, C. S. (1979) *Preserving the Person* Downers Grove. Ill: IVP p11

256. Walsh, D. (2020) *The Priority of the Person* Notre Dame, Ill.: University of Notre Dame Press pix

257. Guidice, G. (2017) *The Dawn of the Post-Naturalness Era CERN-TH-2017-205* https://arxiv.org/pdf/1710.07663.pdf accessed March 2023

258. Quoted at Brainy Quote www.brainyquote.com

259. Crick, F. (1994) *The Astonishing Hypothesis* New York: Touchstone p3

260. Leahy, T.H. (1992) 'The mythical revolutions of American psychology' *American Psychologist* 47, 308–18

261. Ritchie, J. (2008). *Understanding naturalism.* Stocksfield: Acumen

262. Galileo Galilei (1957) 'The Assayer' (1623) in *Discovering and Opinions of Galileo* ed Stilman Drake New York: Anchor

263. Goff, P. (2019) *Galileo's Error: Foundations for a new science of consciousness* London: Rider

264. Goff, P. (2017) *Consciousness and Fundamental Reality* New York: Oxford University Press

265. Dembski, W. A. (1998). Introduction: Mere creation. In W. A. Dembski (Ed.), *Mere creation: Science, faith and Intelligent Design.* Downers Grove, IL: InterVarsity Press.

266. Halvorson, H. (2014). Why methodological naturalism? In K. J. Clark (Ed.) *The Blackwell companion to naturalism.* Oxford: Blackwell

267. Todd, S. C. (1999). A view from Kansas on that evolution debate. *Nature, 401,* 423

268. Monton, B. (2009). *Seeking God in science: An atheist defends Intelligent Design.* Toronto, ON: Broadview

269. Ayer, A. J. (2001) *Language, Truth and Logic* London: Penguin Classics; New Edition

270. McGrath, A. E. (2002). *A scientific theology: Reality* (Vol. 2). Edinburgh: T & T Clark

271. Niiniluoto, I. (2002). *Critical scientific realism.* Oxford: Oxford University Press

272. Provine, W. (1988) 'Progress in evolution and Meaning in Life' in *Evolutionary Progress* ed Matthew Nitecki Chicago: Chicago University Press p64–70

273. Frank, A (2023) Scientists Found Ripples in Space and Time. *The Atlantic* June 29th 2023

274. 'Muon Magnetism could hint at a breakdown of physics standard model' https://www.sciencenews.org/article/muon-physics-standard-model-particles

275. Einstein, A., Podolsky, B. & Rosen, N. *Phys. Rev.* 47, 777 (1935)

276. *Nature* 577, 461–462 (2020)

277. Paley, W. (2008) *Natural Theology: Or Evidence of the Existence and Attributes of the Deity, Collected from the Appearances of Nature* (Oxford World's Classics) Oxford: OUP

278. Dawkins, R. (2006) *The Blind Watchmaker* London: Penguin Books

279. Williams, R. N., & Robinson, D. N. (Eds.). (2014). *Scientism: The new orthodoxy.* New York, NY: Bloomsbury Academic

280. Atkins, P. (1994) *Creation revisited* Harmondsworth: Penguin p115

281. Kant, I. (1998) *Critique of Pure Reason*, translated by Paul Guyer and Allen W. Wood, Cambridge: Cambridge University Press

282. Book 1, part iii, section 6 of *A Treatise of Human Nature* by David Hume, published in 1739

283. Russell, B. (1959) *The problems of philosophy* New York: OUP p63

284. Newton, Isaac (1730–1979) *Opticks* 4th ed. New York: Dover Publications

285. Popper, K. (1965) *Conjectures and Refutations* New York: Harper p34

286. Popper, K. (1965) *Conjectures and Refutations* New York: Harper p37

287. Duhem, P. (1906–1991) *The Aim and Structure of Physical Theory.* Princeton: Princeton University Press

288. Pierce, C.S. (2000) referred to in *The End of Certainty and the Beginning of Faith: Religion and Science for the 21st century* Macon, G.A.: Smyth and Helwys

289. Peacocke, A. (2001) *Paths from Science towards God* Oxford: Oneworld p27

290. Peacocke, A. (2001) *Paths from Science towards God* Oxford: Oneworld p28

291. Godfrey-Smith, P. (2022) *Theory and Reality* ⊠ Chicago: University of Chicago Pressp29

292. Medawar, P.B. (1969) *Induction and Intuition in Scientific Thought* London: Routledge

293. Popper K.R. (1959) *The Logic of Scientific Discovery.* New York: Basic Books

294. Kuhn T.S. (1996) The Structure of Scientific Revolution, 3rd ed. Chicago: U. of Chicago Press

295. Bayes, T. (1763) 'Essay towards solving a problem in the Doctrine of Chances' Philosophy Trans R Society London 53 370–418

296. 1st July 2023

297. Mackie, J. L. (1982) "A Critique of Cosmological Arguments", from *The Miracle of Theism: Arguments for and against the Existence of God* New York: Oxford University Press

298. Davies, P. (2003) 'Introduction: towards an emergentist worldview' in *From Complexity to Life: On Emergence of Life and Meaning* ed Niels Henrick Gregersen Oxford: OUP p14

299. Bradley, F.H. (1914) *Essays on Truth and Reality*, Oxford: Clarendon Press.

300. Royce, J. (1892) 1892, *The Spirit of Modern Philosophy: An Essay in the Form of Lectures*, Boston: Houghton Mifflin Company quoting Falckenberg, R. (1886), *Geschichte der neueren philosophie von Nikolaus von Kues bis zur gegenwart*, Leipzig: Veit; p476

301. Hoffman, Donald D. (2008). "Conscious Realism and the Mind–Body Problem". *Mind and Matter*. 6 (1): 87–12

302. Chalmers, David J. (2020). "Idealism and the Mind–Body Problem" (PDF). In Seager, William (ed.). *The Routledge Handbook of Panpsychism*. Routledge

303. Whitehead, A.N. (1938) Science and the Modern World 'Science and the Modern World' from *Modes of Thought* New York: Capricorn Books p156

304. Whitehead, A.N. (1978) *Process and Reality* ed David Ray Griffin and Donald W. Sherburne New York: Free Press 105–106

305. Whitehead, A.N. (1926) *Religion in the Making: Lowell Lectures* Cambridge: CUP

306. Hartshorne,C. (1991) 'A reply to my critics' in The Philosophy of Charles Hartshorne ed Lewis Edwin Hahn Library of Living Philosophers vol 20 La Salle Il: Open Court

307. Nagel, T. (1979) 'Panpsychism' in *Mortal Questions* Cambridge: Cambridge University Press p181

308. Coleman, S. (2014) 'The Real Combination Problem: Panpsychism, Micro-subjects and Emergence' *Erkenntnis* 79 p22

309. Chalmers, D. (1996) The Conscious Mind in Search of a Fundamental Theory Oxford: OUP p126

310. Strawson, G. (2008) *Real Materialism and Other Essays* Oxford: OUP p20 & 39

311. Goff, P. (2019) *Galileo's Error: Foundations for a new science of consciousness* London: Rider

312. Hossenfelder, S. (2022) *Existential Physics* London: Atlanta Books p186

313. Nagel, T. (2012) *Mind and Cosmos: Why the Materialist Neo-Darwinian Conception of Nature is Almost Certainly False* Oxford: Oxford University Press p3

314. Parfitt, D. (1998) 'The Puzzle of Reality' in *Metaphysics: the big questions* ed P V Inwagen & D. W. Zimmerman Oxford: Blackwell ch49 p418

315. Barrow, J.D. & Tipler, F.J. (1986) *The Anthropic Cosmological Principle* intro John. A. Wheeler Oxford: OUP pvii

316. Barrow, J.D. & Tipler, F.J. (1986) *The Anthropic Cosmological Principle* Oxford: OUP 12

317. Carter, B. (1974) Confrontation of cosmological theories with observation ed M.S. Longair Redel: Dordrecht p291

318. Pantin, C.F.A. (1965) *Biology and personality* ed I.T. Ramsey Oxford: Blackwell pp103–4

319. Wheeler, J. A. (1975) The Nature of Scientific Discovery ed O Gringerich Washington: Smithsonian Press pp261–96

320. Jammer, M. (1974) *The philosophy of quantum mechanics* Nork: Wiley pp24–33

321. Sutter, P. (2021) What is multiverse theory? https://www.livescience.com/multiverse accessed April 2023

322. Toynbee, A. (1987) A Study of History Oxford: OUP

323. Keynes, J. M. (2016) The General Theory of Employment, Interest, and Money London: Houghton Mifflin Harcourt

324. American Journal of Sociology Volume 109, Number 1 July 2003

325. Albright, J. et al (2017) *Bourdieu's Field Theory and the Social Sciences* Basingstoke: Palgrave Macmillan

326. Walby, S. (2009) Globalization and Inequalities: Complexity and Contested Modernities London: Sage

327. Latner, J. (1973) The Gestalt Therapy Book: A Holistic Guide to the Theory, Principles and Techniques of Gestalt Therapy Developed by Frederick S. Perls and Others Gestalt Journal Press http://www.gestaltpress.com/about-us/

328. Lewin, K. (1976) Field theory in social science;: Selected theoretical papers Chicago: University of Chicago Press

329. Lucretius *On the Nature of the Universe*. See also Malin, S. (2001) *Nature Loves to Hide: Quantum Physics and the Nature of Reality* Oxford: OUP p13

330. Briggs, A., Halvorson, H. & Steane, A. (2018) *It Keeps me Seeking* Oxford: OUP p87

331. Hawking, S. (1988) *A brief history of time* p174

332. Hawking, S. (1988) *A brief history of time* p174

333. Midgley, M. (2002) Pluralism: The Many Maps Model https://philosophynow.org/issues/35/Pluralism_The_Many_Maps_Model

334. Vopson, M. (2022) Experimental protocol for testing the mass–energy–information equivalence principle, *AIP Advances* (2022). DOI: 10.1063/5.0087175 New experiment could confirm the fifth state of matter in the universe https://phys.org/news/2022-03-state-universe.html

335. *Bell, J. S. (1987) Speakable and Unspeakable in Quantum Mechanics. Cambridge University Press. See also Whitaker, A. (2016). John Stewart Bell and Twentieth Century Physics: Vision and Integrity. Oxford University Press*

336. Briggs, A., Halvorson, H. & Steane, A. (2018) *It Keeps me Seeking* Oxford: OUP 90

337. Van Raamsdonk, M. (2010) Building up spacetime with quantum entanglement *General Relativity and Gravitation* 42 pp2223–2329

338. Jacksland, R. (2020) Entanglement as the world-making relation: distance from entanglement *Synthese* 198 pp9661

339. Quoted in Hovis, R.C. & Kraugh, H. (1993 P.A.M Dirac and the beauty of physics *Scientific American* 268 May

340. Bohr, N., 1999. *Complementarity Beyond Physics* (1928–1962). Vol. 10 of Niels Bohr Collected Works, ed. D. Favrholdt; gen. ed. F. Aaserud. Amsterdam: Elsevier.

341. Saunders, S. (2000) 'Clock-watcher' *New York Times* March 26th 2000

342. Einstein, A. (2004) *Relativity: the Special and General Theory* London: Folio Ch 9 P31

343. Pais, A. (1982) 'Subtle is the Lord' *The science and life of Albert Einstein* Oxford: OUP

344. Herbert, N. (1993) *Elemental Mind: Human Consciousness and the New Physics* New York: Penguin. p 160

345. Nima Arkani-Hamed, Jaroslav Trnka (2013) The Amplituhedron Cornell University arXiv:1312.2007 [hep-th] https://arxiv.org/abs/1312.2007 accessed August 2023

346. Anil Ananthaswamy (2022) Is Our Universe a Hologram? Physicists Debate Famous Idea on Its 25th Anniversary *Scientific American* https://www.scientificamerican.com/article/is-our-universe-a-hologram-physicists-debate-famous-idea-on-its-25th-anniversary/

347. Ward, K. (1996) *God, chance and necessity* Oxford: One world p28

348. Hick, J. (1999) *The Fifth Dimension* London: One World

349. Wolchover, N. (2017) Why Is M-Theory the Leading Candidate for Theory of Everything? Quanta Dec 18th 2017

350. Bhaksar, R. (2008) A Realist Theory of Science London: Verso

351. Bhaksar, R. (1979) *The Possibility of Naturalism* London: Routledge

352. Bhaksar, R. (1986) *Scientific Realism and Human emancipation* London: Routledge

353. Bhaksar, R. (1989) *Reclaiming Reality* London: Routledge

354. Bhaksar, R. (2000) *From East to West* London: Routledge

355. Bhaksar, R. (2002) *Reflections on Meta-reality* London: Routledge

356. Davies, P. (1988) *The cosmic blueprint* New York: Simon and Schuster p142

357. Hossenfelder, S. (2018) *Lost in Math: How Beauty leads Physics Astray* New York: Basic Civitas Book

358. Penrose, R. (1994) *Shadows of the Mind* London: Vintage p417

359. Ward, K. (1998) *In defence of the soul* Oxford: OneWorld p43

360. *The Complete Works of Aristotle* ed Jonathan Barnes Princeton: Princeton University Press 1984

361. Rorty, R. (1991) *Objectivity, Relativism and Truth, Philosophical Papers 1.* Cambridge: CUP p60

362. Andrei Buckareff (ed.), Yujin Nagasawa (ed.) (2016) *Alternative Concepts of God: Essays on the Metaphysics of the Divine* Oxford: Oxford University Press

363. Drees, W.B. (2016) *The Divine as Ground of Existence and of Transcendental Values: An Exploration* Oxford Scholarship Online, https://academic.oup.com/book/11702/chapter-abstract/160668057?redirectedFrom=fulltext accessed July 2023

364. Bohm, D. (1980) *Wholeness and the Implicate Order* London: Routledge p3

365. Bohm, D. (1980) *Wholeness and the Implicate Order* London: Routledge p25

366. Davies, P. (1996) 'The Synthetic Path' in Brockman, J. (ed) *The Third* Culture New York: Simon & Schuster Touchstone p308

367. Polkinghorne, J. (1998) *Belief in God in an Age of Science* New Haven and London: Yale University Press p9

368. Baggott, J. (2011) *The Quantum Story* Oxford, Oxford University Press p62

369. Nahm, M. et al (2012) Terminal lucidity: A review and a case collection Archives of Gerontology and Geriatrics Volume 55, Issue 1, July–August 2012, Pages 138–142

370. Kinard, J. (2023) Why Dying People Often Experience a Burst of Lucidity *Scientific American* June 12, 2023

371. Gang Xu, Temenuzhka Mihaylova, Duan Li, Fangyun Tian, Peter M. Farrehi, Jack M. Parent, George A. Mashour, Michael M. Wang, Jimo Borjigin. Surge of neurophysiological coupling and connectivity of gamma oscillations in the dying human brain. *Proceedings of the National Academy of Sciences*, 2023; 120 (19)

372. Calvin, J. (1979) *Institutes of the Christian Religion* Book 1.1 Grand Rapids, MI.: Eeerdmans

373. Bergson, H. (1914) Presidential Address *Proceedings of the Society for Psychical Research* 27 157-75

374. Huxley, A. (1954) *The Door of Perception* New York: Harper Row

375. James, W. (2016) *Human Immortality: Two Supposed Objections to the Doctrine* Leopold Classic Library

376. Beauregard, M and O'Leary, D. (2009) *The Spiritual Brain: A Neuroscientist's Case for the Existence of the Soul.* New York: HarperOne

377. At Mind Matters News: A neuroscience theory that actually helps explain the brain Michael Egnor August 30th 2021 ref Epstein, R. (2021) Brain as Transducer: What if the brain is not a self-contained information processor? What if it is simply a transducer? *Discover Magazine* https://www.discovermagazine.com/mind/your-brain-is-not-a-computer-it-is-a-transducer August 2021

378. Wildman, Wesley J., ' Ground- of-Being Theologies', in Philip Clayton (ed.), *The Oxford Handbook of Religion and Science* (2008; online edn, Oxford Academic, 2 Sept. 2009)

379. Pannenberg, W. (2001) *Metaphysics and the Idea of God.* Grand Rapids, MI.: Eerdmans P45

380. Hegel, GWF. (1970) Hegel's Philosophy of Nature: being Part Two of the Encyclopaedia of the Philosophical Sciences tr A.V. Miller Oxford: Clarendon

381. Illingworth, J.R. (1898) *Divine Immanence* London: Macmillan p6

382. Illingworth, J.R. (1898) *Divine Immanence* London: Macmillan p15

383. Psalm 19v1

384. Russell, B. (1903) *A free man's worship* Volume 12 of *The Collected Papers of Bertrand Russell*, entitled *Contemplation and Action, 1902–14* (London, 1985; now published by Routledge)

385. Folsing, A. (1997) *Albert Einstein* Harmondsworth: Penguin

386. *Mind, Language and Reality. Philosophical Papers, vol. 2.* Cambridge: Cambridge University Press, 1975. 2003 paperback

387. Putnam, H. et al (2017) Philosophy in an Age of Science: Physics, Mathematics and Skepticism Cambridge: HUP

388. Spencer, N. (2023) *Magisteria: the entangled histories of science and religion* London: Oneworld

389. Reference for example, Bashford, A. (2023) *An intimate history of evolution: the story of the Huxley family* London: Allen Lane

390. Inwagen, P. V. & Zimmerman, D.W. (1998) *Metaphysics: the big questions* Oxford: Blackwell

391. Galloway, G. (1914) *The Philosophy of Religion* Edinburgh: T & T Clark p468

392. Galloway, G. (1914) *The Philosophy of Religion* Edinburgh: T & T Clark p498

393. Galloway, G. (1914) *The Philosophy of Religion* Edinburgh: T & T Clark p504

394. Hartshorne, C. (1948) *The Divine Relativity*, New Haven: Yale University Press

395. Hartshorne, C. (1972) *Whitehead's Philosophy*, Lincoln: University of Nebraska Press

396. Capra, F. (1982) *The Turning Point* London: Flamingo p279

397. Capra, F. (1982) *The Turning Point* London: Flamingo p331

398. Capra, F. (1975) *The Tao of Physics*. London: Flamingo

399. Prigogine, I. (1980) *From Being to Becoming* San Francisco: Freedman

400. Zong San Mou, (1980) *The Characteristics of Chinese Philosophy* Taipei: Student Book Co., Ltd

401. Zi Chen Zhao (趙紫宸), 'Christianity and Chinese Culture' in Xiao Yang Zhao (ed.), Zhao Zichen Juan (Zhao Zichen's Articles) (Beijing: China Renmin University Press, 2015; original work in Truth and Life 2 (9–10) (1927).

402. Yaqing Qin (2018) *A Relational Theory of World Politics* Ch 6 - Meta-relationship and the *Zhongyong* Dialectics Published online by Cambridge University Press

403. Laozi, Daodejing, Chapter 5

404. Capra, F. (1975) *The Tao of Physics*. London: Flamingo p213

405. Vic Mansfield An Exploration of the Parallels between Modern Physics and Eastern Mysticism". Physics Today Templeton Press. Retrieved December 14, 2014

406. Bernstein, J. (1982). *Science Observed*. New York: Basic Books

407. Sunday Times News Review Tasioulas, J. & Shadbolt, N. '6 ways to contain AI' May 7th 2023

408. Steed, C.D. (2018) *We Count: we matter*. London: Routledge p62

409. Rubin, I.I. (1975) *Essays on Marx's theory of Value* London: Black Rose Books p25

410. Marx, K. (1975) *Economic and Philosophical Manuscripts: Early Writings* London: Penguin p325

411. Hilton, S. (2015) *More Human* London: W.H. Allen

412. John 4v24

413. Illingworth, J. R. (1898) *Divine Immanence* London: Methuen p11

414. Illingworth, J. R. (1898) *Divine Immanence* London: Methuen p14

415. Seneca. *Naturales quaestiones* Williams, G.D. (2012). *The Cosmic Viewpoint: A Study of Seneca's 'Natural Questions'.* Oxford University Press.

416. Basil of Caeserea Hexameron iii.10

417. Pannenberg, W. (1990) *Metaphysics and the Idea of God* Grand Rapids, MI.: Eerdmans p34

418. Rahner, K. (1994) *Spirit in the World* London: Continuum

419. Kant, I. (1929) *Inaugural Dissertation and Early Writings on Space* tr John Handyside Chicago: Open Court Pub Co p45

420. Caird, E. (1889) *The Critical Philosophy of Immanuel Kant* New York: Macmillan vol 1 p210.

421. Caird, E. (1889) *The Critical Philosophy of Immanuel Kant* New York: Macmillan vol 1 p211

422. Kant, I. (1955) *Critique of Pure Reason* Tr F. Max Muller New York: Doubleday Anchor Books B.167 f

423. The Monologion. (2002) COMPLETE PHILOSOPHICAL AND THEOLOGICAL TREATISES of ANSELM of CANTERBURY Translated JASPER HOPKINS and HERBERT RICHARDSON The Arthur J. Banning Press Minneapolis p7.

424. The Monologion. (2002) COMPLETE PHILOSOPHICAL AND THEOLOGICAL TREATISES of ANSELM of CANTERBURY Translated JASPER HOPKINS and HERBERT RICHARDSON The Arthur J. Banning Press Minneapolis 1, p. 11.

425. Tapp, C. (2014) The Uniqueness of God in Anselm's Monologion *Logical Analysis and History of Philosophy* 17(1):72–9

426. The Monologion. (2002) COMPLETE PHILOSOPHICAL AND THEOLOGICAL TREATISES of ANSELM of CANTERBURY Translated JASPER HOPKINS and HERBERT RICHARDSON The Arthur J. Banning Press Minneapolis

427. Such as Augustine's Confessions or Paul saying that what he fails to will what he should (Romans 7).

428. The Monologion. (2002) COMPLETE PHILOSOPHICAL AND THEOLOGICAL TREATISES of ANSELM of CANTERBURY Translated JASPER HOPKINS and HERBERT RICHARDSON The Arthur J. Banning Press Minneapolis

429. Augustine, On the Trinity, 1.1, tr. A. W. Haddan in Basic Writings of Augustine, 2 vols., ed. Whitney J. Oates

(New York: Random House, 1948), 2: 667.

430. Augustine, On the Trinity, 1.1, tr. A. W. Haddan in Basic Writings of Augustine, 2 vols., ed. Whitney J. Oates (New York: Random House, 1948), 2: 773.

431. Steed, C. D. (2021) *The Red Stain of Cain* London: Europe Books

432. Zizioulas, J. (1975) 'On Human Capacity and Incapacity: A Theological Exploration of Personhood *Scottish Journal of Theology.* 419–20

433. Barth, K. (1956) *Church Dogmatics 1.1.353* tr Geoffrey Bromiley Edinburgh: T & T Clark

434. Barth, K. (1956) *Church Dogmatics 3.2.219* tr Geoffrey Bromiley Edinburgh: T & T Clark

435. Torrance, A. (1996) *Persons in Communion* Edinburgh: T & T Clark p214

436. Barth, K. (1956) *Church Dogmatics 1.1.348* tr Geoffrey Bromiley Edinburgh: T & T Clark

437. Torrance, A. (1996) *Persons in Communion* Edinburgh: T & T Clark p214

438. Ridderbos, H. (1975) *Paul: an outline of his theology* Grand Rapids, MI.: W B Eeerdmans

439. Gorman, M. (2016) Apostle of the Crucified Lord: A Theological Introduction to Paul and His Letters Grand Rapids, MI.: W B Eeerdmans

440. Macaskill, G. (2019) Living in Union with Christ: Paul's Gospel and Christian Moral Identity Ada, MI.: Baker Academic

441. Hart, D. B. (2022) *You are Gods: nature and supernature* Notre Dame, In: University of Notre Dame Press p10

442. Swinburne, R. (2004) *The Existence of God* Oxford: Clarendon Press

443. Aquinas, T. (1937) *De Veritate*, English translation by Meyrick H. Carré Bristol: University of Bristol

444. Long, S. (2011) *Analogia entis: on the analogy of being, metaphysics, and the act of faith* Notre Dame, Indiana: University of Notre Dame Press p3

445. McInerny, R. (1996) *Aquinas and Analogy*, Washington, D.C.: The Catholic University of America Press.

446. Sokolowski, R. (1995) The God of Faith and Reason: Foundations of Christian Theology ⊠ Washington: Catholic University America Press

447. Phelan, G. (1941) *Saint Thomas and Analogy* The Aquinas Lecture Marquette University Press: Milwaukee p25

448. Long, S. (2011) *Analogia entis: on the analogy of being, metaphysics, and the act of faith* Notre Dame, Indiana: University of Notre Dame Press p21

449. Aristotle (1979) *Categories* tr and notes J. Akrill Oxford: Clarendon Press

450. Thomas Aquinas (1980) Scriptum Super Sententiis Avebury Press: internet archive

451. Long, S. (2011) *Analogia entis: on the analogy of being, metaphysics, and the act of faith* Notre Dame, Indiana: University of Notre Dame Press p31

452. Long, S. (2011) *Analogia entis: on the analogy of being, metaphysics, and the act of faith* Notre Dame, Indiana: University of Notre Dame Press p34

453. Gilson, E. (1956) *The Christian Philosophy of St Thomas Aquinas* tr L.K. Shook New York: Random House

454. Aquinas, T. (1937) *De Veritate*, English translation by Meyrick H. Carré Bristol: University of Bristol q23, article 7, ad9

455. Leff, G. (1965) *Medieval Thought from St Augustine to Ockham* Baltimore: Penguin p15

456. Aquinas (1911) Summa Theologiae pt 1a, qu 59, art 1 London: Burns and Oates

457. Russell, B. (1957) *'Why I am not a Christian' and other essays* London: George Allen Unwin ch1 p8

458. Stump, E. (2002) *Aquinas* London: Routledge ref Summa Theologia pt 1a,qu.6,art 3

459. Cottingham, J. (2005) *The Spiritual Dimension: religion, philosophy and human value* Cambridge: CUP p48

460. Aquinas, *Summa Theologica* 1a q.93 a.4

461. Aquinas, *Summa Theologica* 1a q.93 a.6

462. McLaren, W. (1912) *Our Growing Creed: The Evangelical Faith as Developed and re-affirmed by current thought.* Edinburgh: T. & T. Clark.p114

463. Wiesel, *Dialogues 1,* "One Generation After" from Roth, J.K. & Berenbaum, M. eds (1989), *Holocaust. Religious and Philosophical Implications.* NY, Paragon House pxiii

464. Buber, M. (1937) *I and Thou.* Trans Walter Kaufman. New York: Simon & Schuster

465. Author's client notes- name withheld and used with permission

466. Cozolino, L. (2016) *Why Therapy Works* New York: W. W Norton p128

467. Jones, J. (1984) *The Redemption of Matter: Towards the Rapprochement of Science.* Lanham,Md.: University Press of America

468. M. A. Nielsen and I. L. Chuang, (2000) "Quantum Computation and Quantum Information"; Cambridge University Press

469. Tononi, G., Boly, M., Massimini, M. *et al.* Integrated information theory: from consciousness to its physical substrate. *Nat Rev Neurosci* 17, 450–461 (2016)

470. Sober,E. (2008) 'Evolution without metaphysics'. In J. Kvanig ed. *Oxford Studies in Philosophy of Religion* vol 3 Oxford: OUP

471. Carr, B.J., Rees, M.J.: The anthropic principle and the structure of the physical world. Nature 278, 605 (1979)

472. *Luce, Arthur (1968). Berkeley's Immaterialism. A Commentary on His "A Treatise Concerning the Principles of Human Knowledge".* New York: Russell and Russell

473. *Berkeley, George; Turbayne, Colin Murray (1957). A Treatise Concerning the Principles of Human Knowledge. Forgotten Books*

474. *Turbayne, Colin Murray, ed. (1970). Berkeley: Principles of Human Knowledge, Text and Critical Essays. Indianapolis: Bobbs-Merrill s3*

475. *Engle, Gale; Taylor, Gabriele, eds. (1968).* Berkeley's Principles of Human Knowledge: Critical Studies. *Belmont, Cal.: Wadsworth*

476. Levinas, E. (2003) *Humanism of the Other* tr Nidra Poller Chicago: University of Illinois Press p44

477. Grice, H.P. (1957) 'Meaning'. *The Philosophical Review* 66 377–88

478. Cichetti, D. & Tucker, D. (1994) Development and self-regulatory structures of the mind *Development and Psychopathology* 6 p544

479. Schore, A. (2003) *Affect Dysregulation and Disorders of the Self* New York: WW Norton p8

480. Smith, C. (2011) *What Is a Person?: Rethinking Humanity, Social Life, and the Moral Good from the Person Up* Chicago: ⊠ University of Chicago Press

481. Wheeler, J. A. (1975) *The Nature of Scientific Discovery* Ed. O Gringerich Washington: Smithsonian Press pp261–96

482. John Wheeler, interview with Ken Ford. "John Wheeler-Wheeler's drawing of the Big U: Concept of Observer Participancy" video posted to You Tube https://www.youtube.com/watch?v=ttestU-obkw accessed March 2023

483. Kumar, M. (2009) *Quantum: Einstein, Bohr and the Great Debate about the nature of reality*. London: Icon books p246

484. Eric Cavalcanti, (2020)The Conversation 'A new quantum paradox throws the foundations of observed reality into question' August 24, 2020 Nature Physics https://phys.org/news/2020-08-quantum-paradox-foundations-reality.html accessed March 2024

485. Eccles, J. (1989) *Evolution of the Brain: creation of the self* London: Routledge p241

486. Wallace, B. A. (2000) *The Taboo of Subjectivity: towards a new science of consciousness* Oxford: OUP p139

487. Bandura, A. (2001) 'Social Cognitive Theory: an agentic perspective' *Annual Review of Psychology* 52: 1–26

488. Schore, A. (2003) *Affect Dysregulation and Disorders of the Self* New York: WW Norton p133

489. Bowlby, J. (1969) *Attachment and Loss* vol 1 p 242 New York: Basic Books

490. Schore, A. (1997) The early organisation of the nonlinear right brain and the development of a predisposition to psychiatric disorders *Development and Psychopathology* 9 p595–631 New York: Cambridge: University Press

491. Krystal, H. (1997) De-somatisation and the consequences of infantile psychic trauma *Psychoanalytic Inquiry* 17 126–150

492. De Bellis, M.D. et al (1999) Developmental traumatology Part 11: brain development *Biological Psychiatry* 45 p1281

493. Mackes, N.K. Golm, D. et al (2020) Early childhood deprivation is associated with alterations in adult brain structure despite subsequent environmental enrichment *Proceedings of National Academy of Sciences - PNAS* January 7, 2020 117 (1) 641–649

494. Nelson, C.A. et al (2014) *Romania's Abandoned Children: Deprivation, Brain Development, and the Struggle for Recovery* Cambridge, M.A.: Harvard University Press

495. Verny, T. (2002) *Tomorrow's Baby* New York: Simon & Schuster p201

496. John-Baptiste, A. (2024) *Ashley John-Baptiste: The Untold Story of His Journey from Foster Care.* ⊠ Independently published

497. Leidenhag, J. (2021) *Minding Creation:theological panpsychism and the doctrine of creation* London: T & T Clark

498. Sell, A. (1995) *Philosophical Idealism and Christian Belief* Cardiff: University of Wales Press

499. Newton Optics Query 28

500. Genesis 16v13 NRSV

501. Anderson, R. (1982) *On Being Human* Pasadena: Fuller Seminary Press pp.210-11

502. Hoekema, A. (1986) *Created in God's Image* Grand Rapids: Eerdmans pp. 216-17

503. Bonhoeffer, D. (1959) *Creation and Fall* London: SCM Press p29

504. Brueggeman, W. (1982) *Genesis* Atlanta, Ga.: John Knox Press p32

505. Blocher, H. (1984) *In the beginning* Leicester: IVP p85

506. Calvin Institutes 11.ii.1

507. McDowell, C. (2015) *The Image of God in the Garden of Eden* Winona Lake: Eisenbrauns p118

508. Westerman, C. (1984) *Genesis 1-11: A commentary* Minneapolis: Fortress Press p146

509. Garr, W. R. (2003) *In his own image and likeness: Humanity, Divinity and Monotheism* Leiden: Brill

510. McLean, S. (1981) *Humanity in the Thought of Karl Barth* Edinburgh: T. & T. Clark p. 46

511. Barth, K. (1958) Church Dogmatics: the doctrine of creation Vol 3 part 1. p196

512. Barth, K. (1958) Church Dogmatics: the doctrine of creation Vol 3 part 2 p323

513. Cortez, M. (2008) Body, Soul, and (Holy) Spirit: Karl Barth's Theological Framework for Understanding

Human Ontology *International Journal of Systematic Theology Volume 10* Number 3 July 2008 p331

514. Price, D. (2002) *Karl Barth's Anthropology in Light of Modern Thought* Grand Rapids: Eerdmans p. 247

515. Cortez, M. (2008) Body, Soul, and (Holy) Spirit: Karl Barth's Theological Framework for Understanding

Human Ontology *International Journal of Systematic Theology Volume 10* Number 3 July 2008 p333

516. Luther Sermons on Genesis

517. Berkouwer, G. C. (1962) *Man: The Image of God* Grand Rapids: Eerdmans pp. 93-4;

518. Calvin Institutes Bk 1 Ch XV p3

519. Hodge, C. (1872) *Systematic Theology* Vol 11 Edinburgh: Nelson p97

520. Plantinga, A. (2011) *Where the conflict really lies* Oxford: OUP p11

521. Simpson, G. G. (1967) *The meaning of evolution* New Haven: Yale University Press pp 344-345

522. John 1v14 and 32 New International Version

523. 1 John 1v1-3 New International Version

524. *From Adversus Haereses (Against Heresies)*, 4. 34. 5-7

525. Smith, James K.A. (2016) *You Are What You Love: The Spiritual Power of Habit.* Grand Rapids: Brazos Press p22-3.

526. Underhill, Evelyn (1912*) Mysticism: A Study in the Nature and Development of Man's Spiritual Consciousness.* London: Methuen

527. 1 Corinthians 13v12-13

528. Pinker, S. (1997) *How the Mind Works* New York: W. W, Norton p558

529. Changeux, J-P. (1985*) Neuronal Man: the biology of Mind* tr Laurence Gary New York: OUP p282

530. Nouwen, H. (1994) *The Wounded Healer*. London: Darton, Longman & Todd p7

531. Scruton, R. (2012) *The Face of God* New York: Continuum p2

532. Schopenhauer (1909) *The World As Will And Idea* tr R. B. Haldane & J. Kemp Vol. III London Kegan Paul, Trench, Trübner & Co. p 573

533. McCabe, I. (2015) *Carl Jung and Alcoholics Anonymous: The Twelve Steps as a Spiritual Journey of Individuation* London: Routledge

534. Yalom, I. (1980) *Existential Psychotherapy* New York: Basic Books p5

535. Quoted in Troyat, H. (1971) *Leo Tolstoy* London p523

536. Tillich, P. (1952) *The Courage to Be*. New Haven and London: Yale University Press p66

537. Ernesto Spinelli (2005) *The Interpreted World* (2nd ed: London: Sage pp. 59-60

538. Carlsen, M.B. (1988) *Meaning-making: therapeutic processes in adult development.* New York: Norton

539. Heidegger, M. (1962) *Being and Time* tr J Macquarrie and E Robinson New York: Harper and Row

540. Caputo, J. (2018) *Hermeneutics: facts and interpretation in the age of Information* London: Penguin p31

541. Munslow, A. & Harlan, D. Eds (2006) Re-thinking History. *The Journal of Theory and Practice*. Vol 10. Routledge

542. Bennis, Warren G.; Thomas, Robert J. (2002). *Geeks and Geezers: How Era, Values, and Defining Moments Shape Leaders - How Tough Times Shape Good Leaders*. Harvard Business School Press

543. Badaracco Jr., Joseph L. (2016*). Defining Moments When Managers Must Choose Between Right and Right*. Harvard Business Review Press

544. Caputo, J. (2018) *Hermeneutics: facts and interpretation in the age of Information* London: Penguin

545. *Kolb, Bryan (2013). Brain Plasticity and Behaviour.* Psychology Press

546. Hornby, N. (2006) *A Long Way Down*. London: Penguin p23

547. Freud, S. (1957). On narcissism: An introduction. In *The Standard Edition of the Complete Psychological Works of Sigmund Freud, Volume XIV (1914–1916): On the History of the Psycho-Analytic Movement, Papers on Metapsychology and Other Works* (pp. 67–102) London: Hogarth Press

548. Schwartz, J., & Begley, S. (2002). *The mind and the brain: Neuroplasticity and the power of mental force*. New York: Regan Books/Harper-Collins Publications

549. Marrone, M. (2014) *Attachment and Interaction: From Bowlby to Current Clinical Theory and Practice* London: Jessica Kingsley Publishers

550. Wexler, Bruce E. (2008*). Brain and Culture Neurobiology, Ideology, and Social Change.* MIT Press.

551. Advert from Emmaus – a charity for the homeless. Cambridge.

552. Author's client notes- name withheld and used with permission.

553. Author's client notes- name withheld and used with permission

554. Zeldin, T. (1998) *An Intimate History of Humanity*. London: Vintage Books p142

555. Pritchard, D. Ed (2012) *War, Democracy and Culture in Classical Athens*. Cambridge, CUP

556. Hegel, G.W.F. (1991) *Elements of the Philosophy of Right*. Ed A.W. Wood. Cambridge: Cambridge University Press

557. Peters, R.S. & Benn, S.I. (1959) *Social Principles of the Democratic State* . George Allen and Unwin. Ch 5

558. Adler, M. (1978) *Aristotle for Everybody*. New York: Bantam p114

559. Diogenes Laertius, *Life of Diogenes the Cynic*

560. Nussbaum, M (1993) *Non-relative Values; An Aristotelian Approach*, in Nussbaum & Sen, A eds, *The Quality of Life*, Oxford, Clarendon Press p52

561. Baker, P. ed. (2008) *The Putney Debates: The Levellers*. London: Verso

562. Hutchinson, J. (1996) *Champions of Charity: War and the Rise of the Red Cross*. Boulder & Oxford: Westview

563. Honour, H. (1978) *The New Golden Land: European Images of America*. London: Allen Lane p58

564. Hall, C. (1991) 'Missionary Positions' in Grossenberg, L. and Nelson, C. (eds) *Cultural Studies Now and in the Future*. London: Routledge.

565. Prince, Mary (2004). *The History of Mary Prince: A West Indian Slave Narrative*. Mineola, NY: Dover. p. 20

566. Memphis Daily Commercial May 17th 1892, quoted in Wells, I. B. (1892) *Southern Horrors* from Scheper-Hughes, N. & Bourgois, P. eds. *Violence in War and Peace*. Malden, MA. Blackwell Publishing p127

567. Evers, C. (1971) *Evers*. New York

568. Litwack, L. (2004) *Hellhounds*. From Scheper-Hughes, N. & Bourgois, P. eds. *Violence in War and Peace. Malden, MA*. Blackwell Publishing p125

569. The Times, *Africa's Killing Fields,* March 29th 2006

570. Quoted at the time on BBC radio 4, source unknown. C.f. Holzgrefe, J.L. & Keohane, R.O. (eds) (2003) *Humanitarian Intervention*, Cambridge, Cambridge University Press

571. Chrysostom, Eight Orations, 6

572. Belsey, Ca. (2007) *Why Shakespeare?* Palgrave

573. Gross, K. (2006) *Shylock is Shakespeare*. Chicago: University of Chicago Press

574. Bloxham. D. (2009) *The Final Solution: A Genocide*. Oxford: OUP

575. Dean, M. (2008) *Robbing the Jews: The Confiscation of Jewish Property in the Holocaust*. Cambridge:CUP

576. Levi, P. *"If this is a Man"*

577. Kung, H. (1991) *Global Responsibility: In Search of a New World Ethic*. London. SCM Press p26–27

578. Kung, H. (1991) *Global Responsibility: In Search of a New World Ethic*. London. SCM Press p31

579. Nussbaum, M. (2013) *Creating Capabilities* Cambridge, M.A.: HUP

580. Parekh B (2000) *Rethinking Multiculturalism*, Basingstoke: Macmillan p124.

581. Habermas, J. (1986) Postmetaphysical Thought.

582. The Times, November 18th 2005

583. Kung, H. (1990). *Global Responsibility: In Search of a New World Ethic*. London. SCM Press p90

584. Kung, ibid p92

585. Munro, R (1997), *Ideas of Difference: stability, social spaces & the labour of division*, Oxford, Blackwell Publishers p18

586. Saleci, R (1997) *Hate Speech and Human Rights* in Dean ibid p81

587. Castoriadis, C (1991), *Philosophy, Politics, Autonomy: Essays in Political Philosophy*, Oxford, Oxford University Press p37–38

588. Dworkin, R. (1977) *Taking Rights Seriously*. Cambridge: Harvard University Press

589. Moore, G. E. (1922) 'The Conception of Intrinsic Value'. In *Philosophical Studies*. London: Routledge & Kegan Paul pp253–78

590. Edelman, G.M. & Tononi, G. (2000) *A universe of Consciousness: How matter becomes imagination* New York: Basic Books p6

591. *University of Trento, "Neanderthal cuisine: Excavations reveal Neanderthals were as intelligent as Homo sapiens," Phys.org, October 13, 2023*

592. *Casey Luskin, "Evidence of Woodworking Extends High Human Intelligence Far Back into the Mid-Pleistocene, "Evolution News and Science Today, September 20, 2023.*

593. *Phi Jacobs, "Were these stone balls made by ancient human relatives trying to perfect the sphere?" Science, September 5, 2023*

594. Tawney, R.H. (1953) commenting on his experiences at the battle of the Somme, from, *The Attack and Other Papers*, London, George Allen and Unwin

595. Kleinman, K. et al (2007) *Subjectivity: ethnographic investigations* Berkeley: University of California Press p4

596. Daston, L. & Galison, P. (1992) 'The image of Objectivity' *Representations* 40:81–128

597. Aristotle Metaphysics 1028 35

598. Aristotle Nichmachean Ethics 1170 28

599. Aristotle Nichmachean Ethics 1170 b6

600. Augustine City of God XI 27

601. White, V. (1996) *Paying Attention to People*. London. SPCK

602. Burney, F. (2012) *The Court Journals and Letters of Frances Burney*. Vol One ed P. Sabor; Vol Two ed S. Cooke. Oxford: Clarendon Press.

603. Nietzsche, F. (1986) *Human, All too Human* R.J. Hollingdale. Cambridge: CUP 8.45

604. Safranski, R. (2002) *Nietzsche: a philosophical biography*. Granta: London p168

605. Nietzsche, F. (1999) *Birth of Tragedy* tr Ronald Spiers Cambridge: CUP 1,1119 18

606. Cate, C. (2003) *Friedrich Nietzsche: a biography* London: Pimlico Press

607. Kaufmann, W (1974), *Nietzsche, Philosopher, Psychology, AntiChrist*, 4th ed, Princeton, NJ, Princeton University Press p97

608. Svendsen, Lars Fr. H. (2010). *A Philosophy of Evil*. Dalkey Archive Press. p. 51

609. Irenaeus, Against Heresies (Book IV, Chapter 37).

610. Hick, John *(1966). Evil and the God of Love*. London: Macmillan

611. Scott, Mark S.M. (July 2010). "Suffering and Soul-Making: Rethinking John Hick's Theodicy". *The Journal of Religion*. 90 (3): 313-334

612. Wood, G. (2006). The Fine-Tuning Argument: "Design Inference" Version. *Religious Studies*, 42(4), 467–471

613. Hogan, C.J. (2007) Quarks, electrons, and atoms in closely related universes. In: Carr, B. (ed.) Universe of Multiverse?, pp. 221–230. Cambridge University Press, Cambridge

614. Rees, M. (2000) *Just Six Numbers: The Deep Forces That Shape the Universe*. Basic Books, New York

615. Hertog, T. (2023) *On the Origin of Time* London: Torva

616. Lewis, G.J., Barnes, L.A. (2016) *Fortunate Universe: Life in a Finely Tuned Cosmos*. Cambridge University Press, Cambridge

617. Barnes, L.A. (2012) The fine-tuning of the universe for intelligent life. *Publ. Astron. Soc. Aust*. 29, 529

618. Susskind, L. (2005) *The Cosmic Landscape: String Theory and the Illusion of Intelligent Design*. Back Bay Books, New York

619. Swinburne, R. (1977) *The Coherence of Theism* Oxford: OUP page70

Index

Abduction, 95
Ainsworth, Mary, 33
Amplituhedron, 118
Analogy of Being, xiv, 164–65
Anselm, 158
Anthropic principle, 101–3, 173
Aquinas, Thomas, 67, 68, 93, 150, 151, 166–67, 183
Arendt, Hannah, 36
Aristotle, xxiii, 65, 66, 84, 125, 153, 156, 166, 196, 203
Artificial intelligence, xi, 17
Atkins, Peter, 91
Attachments, 33, 179, 194
Augustine of Hippo, 67, 161, 186, 203, 205
Ayer, A J, 83

Bandura, Albert, 177
Barth, Karl, 162, 183
Basil of Caesaria, 154
Bauman, Z, 75
Bayes, Thomas, 96
Beauregard, Mario, 137
Bergson, Henri, 136
Bhaskar, Roy, 122
Bio-centrism, 100
Bishop Berkeley, 98, 104, 174–75
Bohm, David, 5, 129
Bohr, Niels, 3, 115
Bonhoeffer, Dietrich, 183
Bourdieu, Pierre, 106
Bowlby, J, 33, 194
Brain, 20–21, 79
Buber, Martin, 70, 146, 170

Buddhism, 84
Butler, Bishop, 68
John-Baptiste, Ashley, 179
Brueggeman, Walter, 183

Calvin, John, 136, 184
Capra, Fritjof, 152
Cardinal Cajetan, 166
Carter, Brandon, 103
Chalmers, David, 13, 99
Chrysostom, John, 199
Coleman, Sam, 99
Complementarity, 115
Confucianism, 151–2
Conscious Observer, xvi, 109
Consciousness, xi, 9, 13, 59, 82, 84, 97, 98, 100, 109
Cooley, Charles, 32, 70
Copenhagen model, 18, 25, 26, 104, 115, 177
Correspondence, xviii
Cozolino, Loius, 40, 170
Crick, Francis, 81
Critical Realism, 122
Culliford, Larry, xx

Daoism, x, xxii, 84, 151, 180
Dark energy, dark matter, 86
Darwin, Charles, 89, 103
Davies, Paul, 122
Dawkins, Richard, 89
De Waal, Frans, 63
Decoherence, 115
Democritus, 125
Dennet, Daniel, x, 16
Derrida, Jacques, 35

Descartes, 13, 20, 39, 59, 68, 98, 137
Devaluation, 49
Dicke, Robert, 101
Dignity, 45, 46
Dimensions, 119
Diogenes, 196
Dirac, Paul, 5, 85, 122

Einstein, Albert, ix, xv, xxii, 1–9, 85, 86, 107, 115
Emergence, 16, 97, 122
Equality, 200
Evaristo, Bernadino, 60
Everett, Hugh, 27
Existential Physics, 100
experiment, 3, 19
Faraday, Michael, 106
Field theory, 105
Frankl, Victor, 53
Fraser, Nancy, 37
Freud, Sigmund, 48, 73, 194
Fröhlich, Jurg, 26
Fukuyama, Francis, 62

Gaze, 33
Greber/Gebser, J. xvi
Gaita, Raimond, 38
Goethe, 54
Gage, Phineas, 73
Guidice, Gian, 77
Galileo, 81–2
Gravitational waves, 86
Goff, Philip, 99
Gestalt theories, 106

Hagar, 181
Hardy, Alistair, 72
Hartshorne, Charles, 98, 150
Habermas, Jurgen, 200
Hawking, Stephen, ix, 5, 111–2
Hebb, D, 22
Hegel, GFW, 34, 36, 39, 138, 172, 196
Heidegger, Martin, 65, 192
Heisenberg, Werner, 3, 25, 85
Heraclitus, 123
Higgs boson, 107
Hofstadter, 'Godel, Escher, Bach', 27
Holograph, 18, 19, 121, 177
Honneth, Alex, 34, 37

Hossenfelder, Sabine, 100, 123
Hubble Space Telescope, 105
Human dignity, 201
Hume, David, 93, 156
Husserl, Edmund, 65, 75
Huxley, Aldous, 136

Identity, 57, 60
Immanence, 141
Induction, 93, 95
Inferiority, 47
Information, 123, 173
Interpersonal neurobiology (IPNB), 23
Irenaeus, 186, 205
James, William, xx, 30, 98, 136

Jung, C J., 53

Kant, Immanuel, xiii, 2, 5, 25, 60, 69, 82, 92–93, 156–58, 172, 197
Kaluza, Theodor, 121
Kierkegaard, Soren, 69
Kaluza, Theodor, 121
Keynes, John Maynard, 105
Kierkegaard, Soren, 69
Klein, Oscar, 121

Laing, R. D., 73
Large Hadron Collider, xxi, 92, 128
Leibniz, Gottfried, 26
Levi, Primo, 199
Levinas, Emmanuel, 175
Locke, John, 68, 175
Lewin, Kurt, 106
Lockwood, Michael, 26
Lucretius, 106
Luther, Martin, 184

Maslow, Abraham, 48
Maternal Gaze, xiv, 70, 175
Matter, the nature of, 2, 83, 85, 117, 139
McGrath, Alistair, 2
Mercury, Freddy, 43
Metaphysical idealism, 97
Metaphysics, 2
Methodological naturalism, x, xv, 81, 83

Mill, John Stuart, 16
Miller, Arthur, 46, 57
Minkowski, Herman, 6, 116
Monism, 5, 132
Montaigne, 68
Multiverse, 104
Musser, George, 19
Maxwell, James, 106
Maldacena, Juan, 121
Monologion, 158, 160
Meanings, 192

Nagel, T., xi, 7, 99, 101
Narcissism, 194
Naturalism, x, xv, 7, 81, 90, 92
Neuroscience, 13, 194
Newberg, Andrew, xx
Newton, Isaac, 89, 94, 106, 180
Nietzsche, Friedrich, 204
Nussbaum, Martha, 200

Observer, x, xiv, 25, 28, 55
Oppenheimer, Helen, 64
Ortega, Jose, 6
Orwell, George, 34

Paley, William, 89
Panpsychism, x, 98–100
Papineau, David, xiv
Parallel universes, 87
Parfitt, Derek, 102
Parmenides, 123
Participation, 156, 163
Paul (of Tarsus) Apostle, 185, 187
Peacock, Arthur, 95
Penrose, Roger, 123
Perls, Frtiz, 106
Personalism, 75, 101
Personhood, xi, xii, xvi, 7, 5, 60, 66, 70, 73, 80, 89, 125, 128, 133, 139, 161
Philips, Adam, 31
Plantinga, Alvin, xiii
Plato, 21, 66, 84, 121, 153, 172
Pope John Paul, 11nd, 75
Popper Karl, 86, 94
Positivism, 83
Prigogine, lya, 151
Process theology, 150

Quantum entanglement, 4, 25, 88, 113, 116
Quantum physics, ix, 4, 8, 25, 96, 114

Royce, Josiah, 98
Rahner, Karl, 156
Reality, nature of, x, xvi, xix, 12, 84, 118
Relativity, ix, 5
Robinson, Mary, xiv
Rovelli, Carlo, 6
Russell, Bertrand, 43, 94

Said, Edward, 37
Sartre, J, P., 34, 38, 39, 65
Schopenhauer, Arthur, 53, 70
Schore, Allan, 22
Schrodinger, Erwin, 19, 116, 132
Science, limits to, 8, 80, 81
Scruton, Roger, 60
Seneca, 39
Seth & Bayne theories, 14
Shakespeare, William, 39
Siegal, Dan, 72
Significance, 45
Slavery, 197
Solovine, Maurice, 2
Strawson, Galen, 99
Subjectivity of consciousness, 14–15
Systems theory, 106
String theory, 106, 121
Spiritual realm, 118
Stratification of reality, 122.
Seneca, 154
Swinburne, Richard, 164
Simpson, George Gaylord, 184
Siddartha Gautama, the Buddha, 191
Subjectivity, x

Tajfel's social identity, 48
Tawney, Richard, 201
Taylor, Charles, 35, 36, 60
Teilhard de Chardin, 58
Terminal lucidity, 135
Tertullian, 162
Theory of Everything, ix, xi, 123
Tillich, Paul, 192
Topography, 119
Toynbee, Arnold, 105

Transducer, 134, 137

Upanishads, 84
Ussher, Archbishop, 60

Valberg, JJ, 60
Validation, 20, 34, 47, 92, 109
Value, 7, 46, 113
Virgil, 73
Von Neumann, John, 26
Vopson, Melvin, 112

Wifi as metaphor, xiv, 133–34
Witten, Edward, 120
Ward, Graham, 7
Wilson, Edward, xv

Waldeman, Mark, xx
Winslett, Kate, 51
Webb James, telescope, xxi, 94, 105
Walsh, David, 6
Witten, Ed, 8
Wheeler, John, 8, 25, 103
Wilson, Bill (AA), 53
Wolff, Christian, 65
Wilson, Edward, 79
Whitehead, A.N., 98, 150
Walby, Sylvia, 106
Winnicott, Douglas, 194

Zizioulas, John, 162,

www.ingramcontent.com/pod-product-compliance
Lightning Source LLC
Chambersburg PA
CBHW060558230426
43670CB00011B/1869